MAKING SENSE

A STUDENT'S GUIDE TO RESEARCH AND WRITING

SOCIAL SCIENCES

THIRD EDITION

MARGOT NORTHEY / LORNE TEPPERMAN

OXFORD
UNIVERSITY PRESS

OXFORD
UNIVERSITY PRESS

70 Wynford Drive, Don Mills, Ontario M3C 1J9
www.oupcanada.com

Oxford University Press is a department of the University of Oxford.
It furthers the University's objective of excellence in research, scholarship,
and education by publishing worldwide in

Oxford New York

Auckland Cape Town Dar es Salaam Hong Kong Karachi
Kuala Lumpur Madrid Melbourne Mexico City Nairobi
New Delhi Shanghai Taipei Toronto

With offices in

Argentina Austria Brazil Chile Czech Republic France Greece
Guatemala Hungary Italy Japan Poland Portugal Singapore
South Korea Switzerland Thailand Turkey Ukraine Vietnam

Oxford is a trade mark of Oxford University Press
in the UK and in certain other countries

Published in Canada
by Oxford University Press

Library and Archives Canada Cataloguing in Publication

Northey, Margot, 1940–
Making sense : a student's guide to research and writing : social sciences /
Margot Northey and Lorne Tepperman.—3rd ed.

Previously published under title: Making sense in the social sciences : a
student's guide to research, writing and style.

Includes bibliographical references and index.
ISBN-13: 978-0-19-542590-1
ISBN-10: 0-19-542590-1

1. Social sciences—Authorship. 2. Report writing. 3. English
language—Rhetoric. I. Northey, Margot, 1940– . Making sense in
the social sciences. II. Tepperman, Lorne, 1943– III. Title.

H61.8.N67 2006   808'.0663   C2006-903520-2

Cover Image: Corbis/First Light
Cover Design: Gillian Tsintziras and Brett Miller

3 4 – 10 09 08
This book is printed on permanent (acid-free) paper ♾.
Printed in Canada

TABLE OF CONTENTS

Good writing does not come naturally. Usually, it requires hard work, following the old formula of 10 per cent inspiration and 90 per cent perspiration.

Writing in university or college is not fundamentally different from writing elsewhere. Yet each piece of writing has its own special purposes, and these determine its particular substance, shape, and tone. *Making Sense in the Social Sciences* examines both the general precepts for effective writing and the special requirements of social science research. It also points out some common errors in student composition and suggests how to avoid or correct them. Written mostly as a set of guidelines rather than strict rules—since few rules are inviolable—this book should help you escape the common pitfalls of student writing and develop confidence through an understanding of basic principles and a mastery of sound techniques.

We intend this book to teach students how to write good term papers, examinations, and research reports for social science courses. Writing well in the social sciences demands not only a good writing style, but also a good understanding of research design, theory, measurement, argument, and communication. All these qualities must be present in order for you to get your ideas across clearly and persuasively.

Much of what appears in the following chapters is written as though you were conducting and describing a research project of your own. Nevertheless, the same principles apply, with equal force, to understanding, describing, and criticizing the work of any other social scientist, amateur or professional.

The discussion that follows has two related goals. One is to show you how to conduct and present your own research: research that makes sense to a reader who may not already be persuaded of your views. The other goal is to show you how to make sense of the work of other researchers, so that you can use and evaluate their findings in essays, book reviews, and examination answers.

Making sense in the social sciences is similar, in many ways, to making sense in the physical sciences and humanities. However, some problems described here are more marked in the social sciences, which use more varied research methods, than the physical sciences and humanities. Some problems are unique to particular disciplines of social science, but others are not. We discuss only the common ones here, using examples from all the social sciences.

In writing the third edition of *Making Sense in the Social Sciences*, we relied on reactions to the first two editions and suggestions for change and improvement. We have made some major changes in response to these suggestions. For example, we have added new material on qualitative and quantitative methods of research, on ethics, and on researching online. We have also made some smaller changes, updating many of the examples and bibliographic references of the previous edition, for instance. These improvements, we believe, have helped us better reflect the current state of this changing academic field.

In addition, we have included many references to a social science literature that has continued to change briskly over the sixteen years since we wrote the first edition. Most particularly what has changed is the reduced emphasis on quantitative research and reasoning. We have noted the diminishing importance of the distinction between quantitative and qualitative methodologies; the non-universal nature of all methodologies, each having its particular area of competence and pertinence; and the value of multi-method analysis in obtaining stable results and opening up communications between subdisciplines (for more on these issues, see Meter, 1994).

Today, there is no single model of analysis in social science, but rather a set of more or less closely related approaches for exploring data and the links between macro and micro levels of reality. We discuss some methodological developments of the last ten years and contrast them with older methods. We have provided illustrative examples of how different types of analysis contribute to social science knowledge in several areas, including sociology, anthropology, demography, criminology, education, women's studies, and political science. However, in the midst of variety, we find a few simple themes that are repeated throughout the book: especially, the connectedness of research methods and the connectedness of the social sciences.

In his fascinating book *Once Upon a Number* (1998), the great popularizer of mathematics John Allen Paulos points out some differences and similarities between stories and statistics. Statistics, typically, address generalities: the characteristics of large populations and large trends, for example. These generalities are so large that we can scarcely hope to picture individuals who personify them. Largely for this reason, statistics often leave people cold; yet they capture the "truth" about a population because they are usually based on an unbiased sampling of that population.

By contrast, the best stories are particular, not general: they sketch particular people caught in particular dramas at a particular time and place. Yet, despite their particularity, stories often capture our interest in a way that statistics do not. Stories also tell "truths" about the human condition. In the end, every population is just the sum of the unique stories that make it up. Clearly, statistics and stories are just two sides of the same coin, the forest and the trees respectively. Both are true, but each speaks to a different part of our need to know the truth.

And, just as statistics have a mathematical logic, so too do stories. Stories have logical structures in the same sense that sonatas and symphonies do. Good authors (and composers) know these standard forms and genres of exposition. Their skilful manipulation is largely what makes people respond to them emotionally. It is unclear whether these forms are, in some sense, essential and universal: whether, for example, every successful love story will necessarily have the same structure, wherever and whenever it is written; or whether they merely reflect particular features of a time, culture, or civilization. In either event, successful stories are no more random than the social statistics describing a crime rate or a population of families. There is order in good writing just as there is in society itself.

Forgive the abstraction, but these points have to be made for two reasons. First, this book is both about good writing and about the analysis of society—the goal of all social science. We hope to show you that these two goals are related and compatible. They fit well in one book, and you can learn about both at the same time. Second, this edition of the book emphasizes—as the first edition did not—the essential compatibility of statistical analysis and story-telling, of quantitative and qualitative analysis, of "scientific" and "interpretive" approaches to reality. More than ever, social scientists in every discipline recognize the need to bring these approaches together in their research enterprises. Students need to be made aware that this important change is taking place; our book makes a small contribution to this change in thinking.

The value of what is presented here is not limited to writing good term papers, exams, and research projects. More sensible communication in the social sciences is useful outside school as well: in education, government, business, even in analyzing the events of everyday life. We hope you will use the principles learned from this book long after you have stopped writing papers that only a professor will read. Dip into the book or read it through, then e-mail us (via lorne.tepperman@utoronto.ca) to tell us what you think.

ACKNOWLEDGEMENTS

It's always interesting to revisit a place or topic with new friends. In revising MAKING SENSE IN SOCIAL SCIENCE for a third edition, I was privileged to work with two people who hadn't been involved with earlier editions. The first was my marvelous undergraduate assistant, Weeda Mehran. Weeda drafted chunks of material on several new and expanded topics for this edition: specifically, material on community-based research, feminist research, ethical issues in research, qualitative methods, and how to review the literature. Thank you, Weeda, for your instincts, insights, and friendly exposition. It's been great working with you. Second, I have enjoyed working with Eric Sinkins, the Oxford University Press editor who advised about changes the book needed and made sure they were done properly. Your low-key helpfulness was just the ticket, so thank you, Eric.

The book is dedicated to all of the undergraduates who struggle daily to understand how social science is different from common sense and armchair speculation on the one hand, and jargon-filled data juggling on the other. We hope this book will make sense of it for them.

We would like to acknowledge the use of the following diagrams: "The Research Cycle," from Peter Li, "Methods of sociology research" in *The Social World: An Introduction to Sociology*, by Lorne Tepperman and Jack Richardson. "Predictors of Life Satisfaction and Firm Performance," from Catherine M. Daily and Janet P. Near, "CEO satisfaction and firm performance in family firms: Divergence between theory and practice" in *Social Indicators Research*. "A Model of Relationships between Demographic, Social, and Economic Change in a Pre-industrial Society," from E.A. Wrigley, *Population and History*. "Early-Universal Marriage and Polygyny among Women in Traditional Economy and a Stationary Population: A Schematic Framework," from Helen Chojnacka, "Early marriage and polygyny: Feature characteristics of nuptiality in Africa" in *Genus*, "The Qualitative and Quantitative Paradigms Compared," from Charles S. Reichardt and Thomas D. Cook, "Beyond Qualitative versus Quantitative Methods," in *Qualitative and Quantitative Methods in Evaluation Research*, edited by T.D. Cook and C.S. Reichardt. A portion of Chapter 1 was adapted from *Macro/Micro: A Brief Introduction to Sociology*, by Lorne Tepperman and Michael Rosenberg (Scarborough: Prentice-Hall Canada, 1995), reprinted with permission by Pearson Education Canada.

Symbols for common errors

NOTE: If any of the following markings appear on one of your essays or reports, consult Chapter 8 or 9 or Glossary II for help.

agr	agreement of subject and verb
amb	ambiguity
awk	awkwardness
cap	capitalization
cs	comma splice
dang	dangling modifier (*or* dm)
D	diction
gr	grammar or usage
mod	misplaced modifier
¶	new paragraph
//	parallelism
ref	pronoun reference
p	punctuation
quot	quotation marks
rep	repetition
RO	run-on sentence
frag	sentence fragment
ss	sentence structure
sp	spelling
sp inf	split infinitive
sub	subordination
T	tense
trans.	transition
⌒	transpose (change order of letters or words)
wdy	wordy
ww	wrong word

CHAPTER 1

WRITING AND THINKING

Research is a game, with players, rules, goals. Note, however, that it is a game played largely in people's heads. It is a game of thinking and then writing down our thoughts. Winning is accomplished by producing superior thoughts and writing them down in a persuasive manner, which requires planning and training. Nowhere is this more obvious than in the writing of essays, tests, research papers, and books, where writing and thinking are everything.

You are not likely to produce clear, persuasive writing unless you have first done some clear thinking, and thinking cannot be hurried. It follows that the most important step you can take is to leave yourself enough time to think. Psychologists have shown that you can't always solve a difficult problem by simply putting your mind to it—by "determined reasoning." Sometimes when you're stuck it's best to take a break, sleep on it, and let the unconscious or creative part of your brain take over for a while. Often relaxation will help you produce a new approach or solution. Keep the research in your unconscious and keep your eyes open for new ideas. Just remember that leaving time for creative reflection isn't the same as sitting around listening to music until inspiration strikes out of the blue.

STARTING STRATEGIES

Writing is about making choices: choices about the ideas you want to present and how you want to present them. Practice makes the decisions easier to come by, but no matter how fluent you become, with each piece of writing you still have to choose.

You can narrow the field of choice from the start if you realize that you are *not* writing for anybody, anywhere, without any particular reason. With any writing you do, it's always sound strategy to ask yourself three basic questions:

- What is the purpose of this piece of writing?
- Who is it that I am writing for?
- What does the reader expect?

Your first reaction may be, "Well, I'm writing an essay for my instructor to satisfy a course requirement," but obviously this won't help. To be useful, your answers have to be precise. Thus, a better answer might be, "I want to study *X* using research method *Y* to prove *Z* for course *A*." Here are some suggestions for finding precise answers to questions about your purpose and your reader.

THINK ABOUT YOUR PURPOSE

Your purpose may be any one or more of several possibilities:

- to show that you understand certain terms or theories;
- to show that you can do independent research;
- to apply a specific theory to new material;
- to provide information;
- to show your knowledge of a topic or text;
- to demonstrate your ability to evaluate secondary sources;
- to show that you can think critically or creatively.

An assignment designed to see if you have read and understood specific material calls for a different approach from one that is meant to test your critical thinking or research skills. If you don't figure out the exact purpose of your assignment, you may find yourself working at cross-purposes and wasting time.

THINK ABOUT YOUR READER

Thinking about the reader does *not* mean playing up to the instructor. To convince a particular person that your own views are sound, you have to consider his or her way of thinking. If you are writing a paper on Israeli communes for a sociology professor, your analysis will be different than if you are writing for an economics or history professor. You will have to decide which terms you should explain and what background information you should supply. In the same way, if your reader does not support the idea of a common currency between Canada and the United States, and you intend to propose that Canadians use American money, you should anticipate any arguments that your reader may raise so you can address them in advance.

If you do not know who will be reading your paper—your professor, your tutorial leader, or a marker—just imagine someone intelligent, knowledgeable, and interested, who is skeptical enough to question your ideas but flexible enough to adopt them if your evidence is convincing.

THINK ABOUT THE TONE

When writing to friends, you probably use a casual tone, but academic writing is more formal. Just how formal you need to be will depend on the assignment and instruction you have been given. If your anthropology professor asks you to express yourself freely and personally in a journal, you may be able to use an informal style. Essays and reports, however, require a formal tone. Here are some signs of writing that may be too informal for academic work.

USE OF SLANG

Although the occasional slang word or phrase may be useful for special effect, frequent use of slang is not acceptable in academic writing. Slang expressions are usually regional and short-lived: they may mean different things to different groups at different times. (Just think of how widely the meanings of *hot* and *cool* can vary, depending on the circumstances.)

FREQUENT USE OF CONTRACTIONS

Generally speaking, contractions such as *can't* and *isn't* are not suitable for academic writing, although they may be fine for letters or other informal kinds of writing—for example, this handbook. This is not to say that you should avoid using contractions altogether: even the most serious academic writing can sound too stilted or unnatural without any contractions at all. Just be sure that when you use contractions in a college or university essay you use them *sparingly*, since excessive use of contractions makes formal writing sound chatty and informal.

Finding a suitable tone for academic writing can be a challenge. The problem with trying to avoid excessive informality is that you may be tempted to become excessively formal. If your writing sounds stiff or pompous, you may be using too many high-flown phrases, long words, or passive constructions (see Chapter 7). When in doubt, remember that a more formal style will always be acceptable.

BUDGETING TIME

THINK ABOUT THE LENGTH AND VALUE

Before you start writing, you will also need to think about the assignment in relation to the time you have to spend on it. If both the topic and the length are prescribed, it should be easy for you to assess the level of detail needed and the amount of research you will need to do. If only the length is prescribed, that limit will help you decide how broad or how narrow a topic you should choose (see Chapter 8 for more on this). You should also think about how important the assignment is in relation to the rest of your work for the course. A piece of work worth 10 per cent of your final grade will not demand as much attention as one worth 30 per cent.

HOW LONG WILL IT TAKE? THE RULE OF THIRDS

Any question can be answered in the time you have available, whether that's three minutes, three hours, or three months. There is no such thing as a question that *must* take a week, or a month, or a year. In other words, any essay, book report, or exam answer can be written in the time you have available.

Other things being equal, however, an intelligent answer that took three hours to complete will be better than an intelligent answer that took only three minutes. If you have only three minutes to answer, do the best you can in the time available and you will be respected for the result. However, if you have three hours to answer, by all means use that three hours to its fullest. Your instructor will be expecting more from a three-hour answer than from a three-minute answer.

Many students who struggle with their writing do so not because they have too little time to complete an assignment, but because they do not make the most effective use of their time. For example, research by Levy and Ransdell (1995) shows that students tend to overestimate the time and effort they devote to reviewing their work; as a result, they often spend too little of their time revising. This research also finds that what most distinguishes writers of the highest- and lowest-quality documents is the amount of time they devote to revising: writers who revise the most get the highest grades.

If you have trouble budgeting your time for an assignment, one strategy you can consider is the "rule of equal thirds," suggested by Sanford Kaye in an excellent book called *Writing Under Pressure*. He recommends that whatever it is you're writing—an essay, book report, or exam answer—you should always spend about one-third of your time thinking, reading, and preparing to answer; another third of your time writing the first draft; and the final third of your time cleaning up and revising. So, for example, if you have three months to write an essay, spend one month thinking about the problem, collecting information at the library, and collecting whatever other data you may need. Spend your second month writing a first draft of the essay, and spend your final month rereading, reorganizing, and revising your essay, and checking it for errors and typos. Let's consider each of these steps in a little more detail.

THE FIRST THIRD

You should spend the first third of your available time applying everything you know about methods of research to the topic of your assignment. This is the time for background reading, designing your research, measuring your variables, and collecting and analyzing your data.

Before you can start writing this essay, you need to find out what you don't know. You also have to develop strategies for limiting what you need to know. If, for example, you decide you want to write something on modern family life, you will find hundreds of books and thousands of articles on that topic at the library. You cannot read all of that material; you need a strategy to narrow down the question you are going to answer, and a way to decide which things you have to read and which things you can ignore. (We discuss ways of limiting your essay topic in Chapter 8.)

THE SECOND THIRD

Once you have narrowed your question and read and thought about your topic, you are ready to start writing your three-month essay. Force yourself to obey the "equal thirds" rule: if you look at your calendar and it tells you that today is the first day of month number two, lay down your books and start writing. Eventually, when you have a lot of experience writing, you will know how and when to relax this rule, but at the beginning, try to follow it mechanically.

Some people insist on making a detailed plan of their essay before they start to write, but an outline might not help you if you are one of the many people— all the way from beginning writers up to professionals—whose greatest problem is anxiety about starting to fill up the blank page in front of them. If you are one of these people, we suggest you *not* worry about making a detailed outline before you start to write. After all, you have thought and read about your problem for a month: it's time to start writing. In the second third of your time available, sit down and start filling up pages. But when you do, follow certain rules that will make the writing much easier and more systematic.

What distinguishes a good three-hour answer from a good three-minute answer is *not* whether the answer is "right": it's how clearly you present your argument and how thoroughly you explore your reasons for giving the answer you do. Developing strong arguments is the most important thing you are going to do during this second third of your assignment. In fact, learning to make good arguments is what post-secondary education is all about. A well-developed written argument should contain the following:

- a beginning: what is the question to be answered? what does it mean? what do I have to show? what is my tentative answer to the question?
- a middle: many "because" clauses arguing on one side of the question; many "because" clauses arguing on the other side.

- an ending: what is the final answer to the question? what are the implications of the answer, if any, for theory, for social policy, and for everyday life?

As a rough estimate, in a 10-page, 2500-word essay, no more than two pages (or 500 words) should be spent on the beginning and no more than two pages should be spent on the ending. The remaining part—six pages or more—should be spent on the middle part, in which you develop your arguments with *"because" clauses*.

"Because" clauses are central to good prose writing and should make up at least two-thirds of anything you write. "Because" clauses give your reasons for answering the question in one way, rather than another. They are the means through which you present your evidence—data collected to support your argument.

At the same time, you are going to offer many opposing "because" clauses, which present the opinions and arguments of others. You must review opposing positions and discuss them fairly and thoroughly in your essay, otherwise your work will appear one-sided. After reviewing all of these opposing "because" clauses, you will have a chance to rebut the opposing views to show why you do not find them persuasive—why they do not lead you to support their position, instead of the one you declared at the outset of the essay.

There is no one model you must follow for presenting your argument and challenging opposing views. Usually we prefer to present the opposing argument first, show why we think it is unsound, and then give the argument that supports our position. Our supposed 10-page essay might look like this:

Beginning (one to two pages)
(1) What is the question, and what is our tentative answer to that question?

Middle (six to eight pages)
(2) Arguments against our answer (one to two pages)
(3) Arguments against those arguments (one to two pages)
(4) Arguments for our answer (two to four pages)

End (one to two pages)
(5) What is our final answer? (This includes refinements, adjustments, and implications.)

You should proportion your time to this use of space. Remember, the central portion of your essay—in which you present your "because" clauses and opposing "because" clauses—should receive at least 60 per cent of your writing time (as well as space). This rule applies whether it's 60 per cent of one week, one month, or one year.

As you go along giving your "because" clauses, you may find that there is reading you should have done, data you should have collected, or data you should have analyzed. Go ahead and make these final adjustments to your database, but remember: this stage of work—the middle third of your time—is mainly a writing stage. If you find you are spending a lot of time doing extra reading or data collection, you have organized your time poorly. Most of that work should have been done in the first third of your time.

THE THIRD THIRD

Some people may wonder why we have allotted as much as a third of our writing time to the cleaning-up stage. It is because this is an important stage, and many students rush through it, or skip over it altogether. As a result, they turn in essays that are messy, full of grammatical and spelling errors, and lacking a careful reference section. These same essays, once they are read for content, tend to have glaring holes in the logic and large gaps in the evidence presented.

All of this can make an instructor or a grader think that the student wrote the entire essay in a single evening when, in some cases, the student may just have failed to do a proper clean-up on the essay, having devoted all of his or her time to reading, then writing a first draft. You should never hand in the first draft of an essay. Once you have written the first draft of your essay, there are several things you can do that will help you review and improve your work:

- Submit your essay to the "laugh test." Imagine reading your essay out loud to your parents, your friends, or even a public audience. If the thought of this makes you cringe in horror or feel terrible embarrassment, it may be because what you have written does not truly express thoughts you are willing to take responsibility for. Think of your essay as a conversation with the grader and rewrite it so no part of it is embarrassing, no matter who might read it. After rewriting your essay, the thoughts you express should not be embarrassing.
- Read the revised essay out loud to your family or friends, or give it to a friend and ask him or her to read it carefully and criticize it honestly. Nobody likes criticism, but when you are handing in something for criticism by a stranger—as you are doing with this essay—you may prefer to get criticism from a friend first. You may receive a more accurate assessment of your work if the person you ask to read your essay is not a classmate: if someone who is not familiar with the material you

are studying can follow your reasoning and find your argument convincing, you can be certain that you have written a clear and persuasive essay. Just make sure that your friendly reader understands that you want honest criticism and not just reassurances intended to boost your confidence.

- Once you have reviewed your work and received criticism from a family member or friend, you can begin to revise your essay. Rewrite the passages in question, adding new information or clearer explanations so that an average reader will be able to follow and accept your argument. When you are writing something, you cannot control who is going to read the piece, or what ideas they bring to the reading. Even though you may be writing your essay for a professor with a background in the area, you should develop your terms and ideas clearly.

Remember, writers are *always* at the mercy of their readers, and you must prepare for the worst. It's always safer to add clarification to something that might be ambiguous than to assume that the person reading your paper will understand what you are trying to explain. What's more, it's best to try to anticipate what readers might say and what questions they might have: this way, you can deal with their possible criticisms before they have a chance to make them.

So submit your work to the laugh test; undergo friendly criticism; and rewrite and rethink as much as you have time for in that final third of your time. Then take care of cosmetic details by looking for typos, spelling mistakes, and grammar problems. If you are using a word processor, it's a good idea to run your essay through a spell checker to catch spelling mistakes you might have missed while proofreading. Never rely solely on a spell checker though, since it will find only misspelled words and not words that are spelled correctly but used incorrectly (such as *they're* for *their* or *it's* for *its*).

THE ESSAY YOU ARE GOING TO WRITE

Suppose the essay you are going to write is worth 20 per cent of your final mark in the course. If so, you should spend about 20 per cent of your time in this course writing it. If you are spending about eight or nine hours a week on *each* of your courses, you should spend about 220 hours on a full-year course, and therefore, about 44 hours on an essay for that course. Let's make this 45 hours, to keep the calculations simple. (Cut these numbers in half if you are taking a half-year course.)

When you write your essay, keep a log of the hours you are spending and force yourself to follow the time budget you have established. If you are following the model we have presented above, your schedule should look like this:

First third: 15 hours. Think, read, make notes, prepare to answer.

Second third: 15 hours. Write the first draft of your essay. This comprises the following:

>The beginning. State the question and rough answer your essay will give: 2.5 hours.

>The middle. Write the "because" clauses of your essay: a total of 10 hours, comprising

>>2.5 hours to state the case against your argument;

>>2.5 hours to rebut the case against your argument;

>>5.0 hours to support your own case.

>The ending. Refine and change your opening position. State the implications of your conclusion: 2.5 hours.

Third third: 15 hours. Do the laugh test. Clean up and revise your essay. Add new evidence, where needed. Fix spelling and typing errors. Make accurate footnotes and references.

WRITING AN EXAM ANSWER

When you are answering an exam question, things are different, but not much. You can prepare, write, and revise, and you can still follow the equal thirds rule when you do this.

Suppose you are writing an essay test in which you have to answer two half-hour questions. Once you have read through the test paper and have decided which question you are going to answer first, this is what you should do next:

- Prepare. Spend ten minutes just thinking about the question and making notes to yourself on the back of your exam booklet or on scratch paper. Make sure you understand the question, and make sure you have decided on an answer by the end of the first ten-minute period.
- Write. Spend ten minutes writing an answer: about one or two minutes to open the discussion; six to eight minutes for "because" clauses; another one or two minutes for closing statements.
- Clean-up. Spend ten minutes reading your answer to check for errors, things you have left out, spelling mistakes, and so on. Make the appropriate corrections.

You will find that leaving two or three blank lines between each written line makes it easier to clean up your answer. The extra space will allow you to add details or make corrections neatly if you have to. If you have studied and prepared well, argued your "becauses" convincingly, and cleaned up neatly, you should impress your reader and get a good grade.

IS THIS APPROACH TOO MECHANICAL?

Writing anything to a formula like the "rule of equal thirds" is stilted and mechanical. This is not how Chaucer wrote *The Canterbury Tales*, for example, or even how Stephen King wrote *Carrie*. Good authors know the "formulas" of writing so well that they can depart from them creatively, and in time you, too, will be able to do this.

However, much of what you do as a student is learn "the forms"—the craft and the rules of writing within your particular discipline. These rules both constrain and empower you; like traffic rules, they keep you moving ahead and make wasteful detours and dangerous accidents less likely. Learn the rules we offer in this book, follow them, and when you are ready, relax the rules and set your own course. Meanwhile, let the rules guide your early efforts at making sense.

CHAPTER 2

DESIGNING A PROJECT

Once you have thought about your reader and the purpose of your work and how you plan to budget your time, the next step is to think about design. In this chapter, we introduce another set of rules about writing. These rules, which build on the rules discussed in the last chapter, apply to particular kinds of arguments you are making. The rules offered in the last chapter still apply, but here we show you how to shade or nuance those rules to make your case more effectively.

Good design is fundamental to good research. By "good design" we mean planning a project in advance to produce results that are persuasive. Good design is just as important to a social scientist as to an architect or engineer: without it, the project you're building will not stand up for long. A badly designed research project cannot produce a well-argued, sensible report or exam answer because its results will not answer the question you are trying to address. Knowing the question you are trying to answer and the types of data and analysis that would best answer it is the essence of good design.

As noted in the Preface, the principles of good research design are valuable not only in conducting and reporting good research, but also in interpreting and criticizing the work of others. We have sometimes written the suggestions that follow as though you, the student, were designing your own project, but they can also be used to understand, describe, and criticize research that someone else has done. In this way, they can help improve your ability to make sense in a book report, as well as in an essay or exam answer.

This chapter examines four main types of research design and points out the dangers of mixing them, or of ignoring design concerns outright. Much of our discussion in this chapter is based on survey research, which provides the simplest model of what research design and analysis are aiming at in social science. However, the points made here apply just as well to library research or field observation. Some of the material may, at first, seem difficult because it is unfamiliar and uses an unfamiliar vocabulary; for this reason, we have provided a glossary of important social science terms at the end of the book.

STARTING POINTS

CHOOSE A GOOD PROBLEM

The first step toward doing any good work is choosing a problem that is worth working on. The topic you choose should be of some theoretical or practical importance, and yet small enough to be studied in a skilful way in the time available. Overreaching yourself—starting more than you can finish well or spending too much effort answering a question that is, when looked at objectively, not worth answering—will not produce worthwhile results. Above all, the topic you choose should be one that is of interest to you, the writer, since you will be investing much time and energy to complete the task. You will find it easier to dedicate yourself to a subject that interests you than to one that does not, and you will do a better job as a result.

KNOW THE TYPE OF DESIGN YOU ARE USING

Different designs have typical patterns, and if you deviate from the appropriate pattern for the design you have chosen, there is a strong chance that you will not answer the question that is, or should be, of central interest. For example, if your goal is to understand the *causes* of alcoholism, describing the *effects* of alcoholism should take a secondary place. (It is sometimes difficult to distinguish between causes and effects; however, we will say more about this in discussing systemic design.) So, knowing the design to use is closely tied up with clearly understanding the question you are trying to answer.

TYPES OF DESIGNS

There are many ways to describe and classify research designs. Courses on theory and research methods will introduce you to other useful classifications, but in the meantime, the methods discussed below will help you make sense of your own research goals and those of others.

For our present purposes, the four main types of research design are *relational*, *predictive*, *explanatory*, and *systemic*. We define these four types by how many dependent and independent variables each is examining. Before continuing, therefore, we must define these different types of variables.

TYPES OF VARIABLES

A *variable* is a characteristic or condition that can differ from one person, group, or situation to another. (We call the people being described *units of analysis*.) So, for example, we might select twenty political science majors (our units of analysis) at a given university and from each collect such information as gender, grade-point average, socio-economic background, and level of participation in campus politics. These characteristics are variables in the sense that they can vary among the people we are studying.

An *independent variable* is a causal or explanatory variable: a condition or characteristic that we presume to be the cause of change in a dependent variable. A *dependent variable* is a characteristic or condition that is altered or affected by changes in another variable: we assume that it is the effect of an independent or causal variable. Here, level of participation in campus politics is the dependent variable we are hoping to explain through reference to three independent variables: gender, grades, and socio-economic background. Using the information we have collected, we could examine whether variations in gender, grade-point average, or socio-economic background influence campus political participation: that is, whether males engaged more than females, students with higher grade-point averages more than students with lower grades, or students from wealthier backgrounds more than students from poorer backgrounds.

A third type of variable is the intervening variable. An *intervening variable* is, as its name suggests, one that intervenes between the independent and dependent variable. It is the means by which an independent variable affects the dependent variable. For a variable to be considered intervening, it must be influenced by the independent variable and must influence the dependent variable. Thus, it must be both an effect of the first cause and a cause of the later effect.

A fourth type, the *conditioning variable*, controls whether the independent variable will have a strong or weak, positive or negative effect on the dependent variable. Unlike the intervening variable, the conditioning variable is not an effect of the independent variable, nor is it a cause of the dependent variable. The conditioning variable may suppress, magnify, or otherwise distort the relationship between an independent and dependent variable. Said another way, it sets the conditions under which causes will influence effects.

To see how these variables fit together, consider some research on the relationship between domestic equality and marital satisfaction. The results of research in this area are confusing. Some research says that marital satisfaction (the dependent variable) increases when spouses share responsibility for household duties equally (the independent variable); other research finds it makes little difference. We resolve the confusion when we introduce a third variable, attitudes toward gender equality, as a conditioning variable. Among wives with traditional ideas about marriage and gender relations, an unequal division of domestic labour does not affect marital satisfaction. Among wives with modern ideas about marriage and gender relations, an unequal division of domestic labour decreases marital satisfaction.

In short, independent variables are *causes*; dependent variables, *effects*. The numbers of presumed causes and effects define the type of research design to be followed. Since any piece of research can examine one or many causes and one or many effects, four types of design are logically possible. We depict them in Figure 2.1.

We will consider these types of design in order, going from the simplest (the relational) to the most complex (the systemic).

FIGURE 2.1 TYPES OF RESEARCH DESIGN

		Number of "causes," or independent variables	
		One	Two or More
Number of "effects," or dependent variables	ONE	Relational Study	Explanatory Study
	TWO OR MORE	Predictive Study	Systemic Study

RELATIONAL STUDIES

Relational studies examine one cause and one effect, and the conditions under which the relationship between them is strong or weak, positive or negative. In a *strong relationship*, a large change in one variable produces a large change in the other; in a *weak relationship*, a large change in one variable produces only a small change in the other. In a *positive relationship*, two variables increase and decrease together; in a *negative relationship*, one variable increases as the other decreases.

The purpose of a relational study is to examine the conditioning variables that decrease or increase the effect of the independent variable. For example, take the case of suicide rates, a classic social science concern. Researchers have long known that suicide rates differ according to gender and marital status: one gender seems more suicide-prone than the other; and one marital status, more suicide-producing than another. Taken individually, these independent variables do not produce strong effects; taken together, however, they do. Some researchers have shown that the suicide rate is highest for married females and single males, and much lower for single females and married males. Thus, the relationship between suicide rate and gender is mediated by marital status. Marital status is the conditioning variable here. Marriage suppresses the probability of suicide in males and increases it in females. To discover why, we must study the nature of marriage.

This investigation, which identifies and explores the context within which an independent variable has the effect it does, is a standard example of a relational study. Nevertheless, within this group there are various subtypes. One of the most important is the deviant-case analysis.

DEVIANT-CASE ANALYSIS

The deviant-case analysis is a research design that studies a single case that fails to conform to an expected pattern. In the deviant case, a cause that usually produces a particular effect produces a different effect (or no effect at all). By failing to support a given hypothesis, the deviant case forces us to revise and enrich the original hypothesis. The purpose of the researcher, as in the suicide study above, is to discover what variable is changing the usual effect of the independent variable.

We start a deviant-case analysis by conceding that there are exceptions to the theory we are testing.

The first study. Political scientist Robert Michels wanted to discover whether groups with democratic ideals could put these ideals into practice, and if not, why. Also, he wanted to understand why oligarchy was so common in both large and small organizations. He chose to study the German Socialist party, a group known for its ideological commitment to democratic participation. It stood to reason that if this group could not maintain a democracy, none could. He found that, in fact, it could not. Michels then studied the oligarchic tendencies in the party, using a combination of observations, interviews, documents, and historical analysis. He concluded that even in groups committed to democracy, the goal may be impossible to reach.

The deviant-case analysis. Half a century later, the sociologist S.M. Lipset (1956) re-assessed Michels' study by examining a typesetters' union that had indeed succeeded, where many others had failed, in remaining democratic. His goal was to understand why and how organizations might deviate from the general tendency to lapse into oligarchy. He found that various factors, including leadership practices and group traditions, increased the likelihood that a group committed to democracy might indeed accomplish that goal. Thus, he found the conditions under which a group might violate or deviate from Michel's general principle or law of oligarchy.

With deviant-case analysis, we enrich our theories and find new variables. We must now study them more systematically with experimental, quasi-experimental, or correlational methods. With single-case analysis we have only explored, not explained, oligarchy in a general sense.

PREDICTIVE STUDIES

There are two main types of predictive study, with one main characteristic in common. In our terminology, predictive studies examine one cause and two or more effects. Much pure research and most applied research is predictive in this sense. The two main types and many subtypes of predictive study differ in one main way: in whether the independent (causal) variable under consideration is identified by a theory, as in pure research, or by a policy (for example, organization mandate, resources, or feasibility), as in applied research.

PREDICTIVE STUDIES WITH CAUSES DEFINED BY THEORY

The theoretical, or pure-research, group includes speculative studies, experiments, and quasi-experiments.

SPECULATIVE STUDIES

Speculative studies imagine the effects of an independent variable on many dependent variables. Since they are imaginative, we sometimes call them *thought experiments*. They are carried out by applying some loose theory or intuition to a combination of imagined and real data. We could put Plato's *Republic*, Thomas More's *Utopia*, or Michael Young's *Rise of the Meritocracy* in this category. Such studies might try to answer questions like the following: How would Canadian society change if no one ever died? What would have happened in the Second World War if the atom bomb had not been invented? How would people use their time if no one had to work? Would people still have children the old-fashioned way if they could clone "genetically perfect" children?

These varied speculations have some common features: they all examine one independent variable and attempt to predict, or speculate about, its many likely effects; they can be informed by observable data, but they cannot be tested; and they all require that the researcher understand, theoretically, the connections between independent and dependent variables in the real world.

Good speculation must consider what is already known. For example, we can at least partly predict the likely effects of people living forever, given the already observable effects of a longer life expectancy. The effects of people not having to work at all can be at least partly predicted by the observable effects of increased leisure on modern lifestyles. No one knows whether the condition speculated about will continue what is already happening, or whether, after a certain critical point, relationships between the independent and dependent variables will change in dramatic, unforeseeable ways.

This kind of thought experiment has led to the production of what is sometimes called "alternative histories," in which scholars ponder what might have happened if the Nazis had won the Second World War, or if the Catholic Church had prevented the rise of Protestantism, or if the Spanish Armada had defeated Queen Elizabeth's British fleet and colonized England.

EXPERIMENTS

Experiments study the observable effects of actual interventions to test the predictions made by a carefully reasoned theory. Often researchers try to anticipate the direction and approximate size of the outcomes. They may predict whether a named intervention will increase the dependent variable by 10 per cent or cut it in half. Doing this research requires laboratory work (to reduce outside influence); controlled data collection (including random or unbiased sampling of the people to be studied, and precise measurement); and quantitative data and analysis. Real experiments differ from thought experiments both in the precision with which researchers perform them and in the possibility of verifying predictions.

Many consider the classical experiment the ideal means of testing a relationship between dependent and independent variables. Though experimentation is not possible in most of the social sciences, familiarity with the experimental approach will give the reader a better sense of what researchers are hoping to achieve by other means.

In a typical experiment, there are two groups, or *conditions*: the *experimental condition*, in which subjects are manipulated in some way that researchers predict will have a certain effect on their behaviour; and the *control condition*, in which subjects are *not* manipulated in this way. To see how much the experimental manipulation changes behaviour, we need a *baseline*—a measure of the behaviour before the experimental manipulation takes place. This is the purpose of the control group, which is identical to the experimental group in all the important respects except that it does not receive the experimental manipulation. If the experimental group changes more than the control group, we can then credit that change to the experimental manipulation.

Consider the following example. An experimenter wants to test the theory that drunken behaviour is not the result of a drug or alcohol acting on body chemistry, but a result of people's expectations about the effects of drugs and alcohol and a wish to take advantage of the deviance that intoxication legitimates.

The hypothesis is that people who think they have consumed a depressant substance will act more drunkenly than people who think they have consumed a stimulant drug (who, we hypothesize, will behave in a more than usually sober manner). We expect people who know nothing about the expected effects of the substance they have consumed (i.e., the control group) to behave more soberly than the first group and less soberly than the second.

Three groups of undergraduates, randomly sampled from a psychology class, agree to take part. We test individual subjects on a simulated automobile driving task for five minutes each to establish their baseline driving skill. Then each is given a placebo, a chemically inert substance—here, a capsule filled with sugar. We give each participant false information about the expected effects of the capsule he or she has taken: some are led to believe they will feel energized, others that they will feel drunk; subjects in the control group are given no hint of what effect they should expect the substance to have. After a 20-minute interval, each participant is directed to drive the simulated automobile for another five minutes.

We measure the change in driving skills for each subject, and calculate an average change score for each of the three groups. The finding? Subjects in the group that believed they had received a depressant felt drunk, and those in the group that believed they had taken a stimulant did not. However, there was no significant difference observed in their driving skills. The depressant group did not drive worse, nor did the stimulant group drive better, than the control group after taking the capsules. The experimenter therefore rejects the hypothesis as invalid.

Random sampling is important in this case, and in other types of research, because it increases the likelihood that the results we get are unbiased and can therefore be generalized to the population at large. The use of a control group is important because it provides a baseline against which to compare the experimental group. We cannot assume that people's attitudes or behaviours remain constant over time unless purposely modified by the experimenter. In the current example, if everyone's driving gets worse (or better) over the course of the experiment, we need to compare the change in the experimental group with the change in the control group to be certain that the change in the experimental group is not the result of the experimenter's manipulation.

QUASI-EXPERIMENTS

Like experiments, quasi-experiments study the observable effects of actual interventions. Typically, we carry out quasi-experiments in situations where true experiments cannot be done because we cannot control the selection of subjects or the conditions in which they will be studied. This is not to say that quasi-experiments are sloppy or merely speculative: they often involve precise data collection and can be useful in analyzing how behaviours change over time. Yet they are not true experiments.

To allow for the influence of outside factors, quasi-experiments may also use control groups for comparison. Consider this example, which may strike the reader close to home. It seems obvious that the level of student funding at colleges and universities affects how long it will take students to complete their course of studies, or even whether they will complete their course of study at all. In universities or programs where more fellowships and scholarships are available, or where tuition is low or free, more students enter their desired programs of study and leave them with degrees in a reasonable period of time.

Noting this fact, an imaginary provincial government decides to run a small quasi-experiment. In one university, tuition will be free, and every full-time student will receive $10,000 towards living expenses. In another university, tuition will be free, but no living expenses will be provided. In a third university, the old conditions, whereby students pay tuition and receive no living expenses, continue to prevail. We let the system run for four years and then measure the proportion of students in each university who have completed their four-year degree program. If our hypothesis about student funding is correct, University A, with no tuition costs and full funding, will have graduated a greater proportion of its students than University C, with regular tuition costs and no funding; University B will fall in between.

The problem with this study is that the researchers would not be able to select the experimental or control groups randomly, or prevent other changes in these communities that might also contribute to an observed difference. For example, if the students at University A came from significantly wealthier families than the students at University C, the resulting differences would be smaller than if students in these two universities came from equally wealthy families. (The differences would be greatest if we applied the experimental condition—free tuition and full funding—to the poorest student body in the province and observed whether that brought their completion rate up to par with the richest student body in the province.)

In short, without systematic matching or controls, the quasi-experiment yields a weaker conclusion than the experiment. However, that conclusion is nonetheless more secure than that provided by research without the before-and-after measurement, the control group, and the rigorous collection and analysis of observable data.

PREDICTIVE STUDIES WITH CAUSES DEFINED BY POLICY

The group of policy, or applied-research, studies includes social-impact assessments, demonstration projects, and evaluation studies.

SOCIAL-IMPACT ASSESSMENTS

Social-impact assessments predict the likely effects of a policy intervention, using a combination of thought experiment, expert opinion, and surveyed public opinion. They are not testing a hypothesis: they are trying to predict how people would react to these interventions and, given their likely extent and seriousness, what course of action should be pursued: this one, or another (similarly analyzed), or none at all.

Researchers have conducted social-impact assessments in many oil-producing regions of the world (including Alberta, Newfoundland, and Scotland) to predict the probable impact of oil extraction on the surrounding area. Such assessments have paid attention to likely effects on the environment, local economy, community organization, and way of life. Such predictions are influential in deciding where and how quickly to develop the oil industry.

More recently, research has been done to evaluate the effect of gambling casinos on local communities in which they are situated. On the one hand, these casinos increase tourism and spending, so they increase local revenues. On the other hand, they also increase social problems (problem gambling, for example), which force a community to spend more of its revenue on social and health services. As a result, some argue there should be no further opening of casinos until social-impact assessments are conducted on the communities in which these casinos will be built.

As an exercise, you might ask yourself what kinds of data researchers might use to carry out this speculative, future-oriented research.

DEMONSTRATION PROJECTS

Demonstration projects resemble quasi-experiments, but they are motivated by concerns about a policy that has already been adopted, as opposed to one under consideration. They study the effects of actual interventions in a natural field setting. Here too, political and organizational feasibility determines the choice of intervention. Deciding whether to continue and increase the scope of intervention is based on observed, not expected, impacts.

For example, suppose that a government ministry decides to keep fewer inmates in prisons. The ministry believes that a halfway house may help released prisoners adjust to life outside the prison environment better than if they are suddenly released into the community. So, an experimental halfway house is set up and a sample of inmates is released into it. The behaviour of inmates is observed for, say, 24 months following release, and compared with the behaviour of similar inmates released directly into the community. Levels of adjustment to life outside prison—for example, rates of re-arrest and unemployment, or levels of psychological well-being and social integration—are measured for the two groups and compared. If the group released into the halfway house does much better, the ministry may decide to extend this arrangement to larger numbers of released inmates. The demonstration project may also call attention to parts of the original plan that need fixing before it is adopted more widely.

Ideally, inmates will be randomly selected to enter the halfway house (the experimental condition) and take part in the control group. Practical considerations may make a strict experimental design impossible, but the aim here is to learn from trial and error, not (as in the social-impact assessment) from speculation.

EVALUATION STUDIES

Evaluation studies examine demonstration projects and other programs to decide whether they have had the predicted effects, and if not, why not. There are two main types of evaluation study: *process evaluation*, which often uses qualitative data (to be discussed in Chapter 5), determines whether or not the new arrangement—for example, the halfway house—has worked as it was supposed to; *outcome evaluation* determines whether the new arrangement has produced the desired result (in this case, better-than-usual adjustment).

All three types of study in the applied-research group—social-impact assessment, demonstration project, and evaluation study—are predictive in the sense that they focus on the effects of a real or anticipated intervention. Remember that, using our terminology, every predictive study is characterized by one and only one independent variable—here, the intervention—and many dependent variables, or outcomes. Whether we can reasonably risk the intended intervention in the real world largely guides the choice between a social-impact assessment and a demonstration project. Only a demonstration project can be evaluated, since only it produces real, not anticipated, results.

EXPLANATORY STUDIES

Explanatory studies aim to explain why something happens or has happened. There is a dependent variable (or effect) that is to be explained by two or more independent variables (or causes). Most student papers, and many professional research projects, are of this type.

We might use an explanatory study to examine divorce. Whether we study it on a macro-social level—that is, trying to explain what social conditions produce high divorce rates—or on a micro-social level—that is, trying to explain under what kinds of family conditions couples break up—we find ourselves having to deal with many variables. Often there are economic circumstances that provide opportunities for divorce (for example, both spouses have an income) or stresses that increase the chance of divorce (for example, both spouses are tired from overwork and hate coming home to more demands). There are cultural variables that influence people's openness to the idea of divorce: they include religious beliefs about divorce, beliefs about what a "good marriage" or "marital satisfaction" is, and beliefs about the social acceptability of divorce. There are also legal aspects: whether divorces are easy or hard to get, cheap or costly, fast and clean or messy and dragged out. Thus, we cannot explain the occurrence or rate of divorce without taking all of these variables into account.

Trying to explain a dependent variable with only one independent variable will produce unsatisfactory results, no matter how promising the independent variable selected. This is because most social effects are produced by a combination of causes. Furthermore, working with only one independent variable provides no basis for judging how *relatively* important that cause is in explaining the effect under study. You should therefore plan to include two or more promising independent variables in your explanation.

The social sciences differ in their adherence to this rule. Psychology and economics, for example, are much more likely to examine the effects of one independent variable at a time. The rule applies much more to the remaining social science disciplines, although it is often flouted by amateur social scientists—people who write social science books for the mass audience. For example, books claiming to show that violent television programs cause juvenile violence, or that liberal values destroy family life often make the mistake of examining only one independent variable in an effort to explain one dependent variable.

APPLIED EXPLANATORY STUDIES

Explanatory design is also used in applied research, which is action- or policy-oriented. Three examples are the needs assessment, the market survey (or political poll), and the Royal Commission. The first two are used by a large variety of organizations, the third only by government, yet they share common features: all three designs are used to study one effect of interest by examining and weighing many (potential) causes to see which of these causes has the greatest bearing on the effect.

NEEDS ASSESSMENTS

Needs assessments are explanatory studies that begin with a thorough description of some social problem (for example, alcoholism) or social group (for example, alcoholics), and aim to find out how widespread and how harmful the problem is. A needs assessment is often used by a government organization (as a smaller, less formal alternative to a Royal Commission) or other service-providing, usually non-profit organization. We call such a study a needs assessment because it is an attempt to assess whether a policy or program is needed to reduce the problem.

After describing the problem, the needs assessment typically theorizes about its causes. Ultimately, it recommends whether the organization that has commissioned the study *should* take action, given its findings about the extent of the problem, its likely causes, and the organizational resources for influencing these causes. Such a study usually precedes other types of research—namely, the demonstration project and the social-impact assessment—that focus on possible interventions.

MARKET SURVEYS AND POLITICAL POLLS

Market surveys and political polls are applied explanatory studies concerned with selling something to someone, be it a refrigerator to a homeowner, or a political candidate to a voter. In each instance, the researcher is concerned with finding out the level of support for the product, the characteristics of respondents who are the strongest supporters or worst detractors, and the reasons for support and non-support.

The goal of such research is to change marketing strategy to produce more effective sales. This is done by (1) advertising the product more directly to those kinds of people who, according to the study, are its greatest supporters; (2) changing the product, in fact or in appearance, to make it more appealing to its detractors; or (3) changing the sales pitch to make it capitalize more effectively on the secret fears and wishes of consumers—their *real* reasons for support and non-support.

ROYAL COMMISSIONS

Governments in Canada, the United Kingdom, and other Commonwealth countries commonly call Royal Commissions to study a social problem and find out what people think is causing it. (Governments in other countries conduct similar government inquiries under other names.) The Report of a Royal Commission differs from the smaller needs assessment in that it is used to examine broad issues of major concern to the public, and in that it pays attention to both expert opinion and public sentiment about the problem and its possible solution. In a sense, it is a politicized needs assessment, aimed as much at enhancing the government's image as at solving the problem. Important Royal Commissions in Canada have included the MacDonald Commission on the future of the Canadian economy, the Badgley Commission on the extent and causes of sexual child abuse, the LeDain Commission on the non-medical use of drugs, the Kent Commission on monopoly ownership in the mass media, the Royal Commission on the status of women, and the Royal Commission on Aboriginal peoples. Each produced a great deal of descriptive research, theorized about the cause of present problems, and suggested legislation to deal with them.

SYSTEMIC STUDIES

Systemic studies try to explain two or more effects by two or more causes. Such studies are common in all the social sciences. The subject under study typically comprises many people and many parts: it may be a group, an organization, a community, or a society. The ultimate goal of this research is to understand how a system of interlinked parts and persons works: how the parts affect one another, often in indirect, reciprocal, and self-modifying ways.

Explaining the causes of the Second World War would require a systemic study, for not only did the war have many causes, but what we think of as the war—its outbreak, course, and conclusion—also had many effects (economic, diplomatic, military, and social), all influencing one another and jointly keeping the war alive. Even more obviously, it would be impossible to explain the continuing violence that has broken out in the last twenty years—in the former Yugoslavia, Rwanda, Congo, Afghanistan, Iraq, Angola, and Sudan, to name only a few—without a systemic design that took into account historical patterns of ethnic conflict, religious conflict, regional conflict, economic conflict, and political conflict, as well as external influences (e.g., the role of the United States, the United Nations, China, the European Union, and various multinational corporations).

A systemic design is necessary when you have started on an explanatory design and found too many interlinked causes and effects for a neat solution. Try shifting to a systemic design, and then focus your attention on how these linkages maintain one another. (Some might even argue that a systemic design is always appropriate if you are explaining how or why something happens, since you are always interested in knowing the reciprocal links among all the variables.)

A good example of where systemic design may be useful is in the study of family conflict and family secrecy. We need to understand families as systems of roles, in which each person and each role keeps the others in check. Every family has problems, and every family has special ways of recognizing, containing, or dealing with its problems. Families often work hard to keep these problems hidden from outsiders to present the appearance of calm conformity to the outside world. If they succeed, no one but the family members themselves will know about the hidden secrets, conflicts, and strains. Still, that does not mean they do not affect the family.

Family secrets are so common and so persistent that we must allow for the possibility that they contribute to the way the family functions, and to the survival and well-being of family members. For example, secrets help the family develop without feeling its identity is shamed or threatened. Also, they preserve intimacy that is related to love, closeness, and emotional commitment. Secrets shared among family members also strengthen internal cohesion and solidarity. Finally, keeping secrets protects the family from outsiders.

However, keeping secrets may also have negative effects on the family and its individual members. Also, keeping secrets fosters a tolerance for deception and lying in close relationships. People who keep secrets may develop an inability either to take responsibility for their own actions or to force others to take responsibility for theirs. Most important, power imbalances increase when one person knows more than, or something harmful about, another. The result may be threats or blackmail. At the least, anxiety about the unwanted disclosure of the secret is likely to harm family relations. We can conclude that families are better off solving their problems than hiding them.

This example shows that a study that starts as a simple analysis of a small family problem—for example, persistent truancy from school or medical absences from work—may end up exploring the linkages among all these variables that repeatedly support and intensify one another's effects. We may end up learning a lot about the relationships between unemployment, drinking, spousal abuse, and child truancy, for example. Examining an issue such as why abused spouses and children do not reveal their secrets to teachers, employers, friends, or the police is too complicated a matter for an explanatory study, and much better suited to a systemic design.

CLOSING COMMENTS

To summarize, an explanatory study focuses our attention on one dependent variable. It measures and compares the influence of many causes on one effect. A predictive study, on the other hand, focuses attention on one independent variable, and examines or speculates on its many effects. The relational study is like neither of these: it focuses attention on conditioning variables that change the effect of one independent variable on a dependent variable. Finally, the systemic study focuses attention on the interdependence of all causes and effects. It is therefore concerned with analyzing an entire system of independent, dependent, intervening, and conditioning variables.

It should now be clear why, as a beginning researcher, you are wise to avoid mixing research designs. After all, different designs answer different questions, focusing attention on different variables or relations between variables and drawing attention away from the rest. (There is one exception to this general rule: sometimes mixing relational and explanatory designs is permissible. We shall say more about the usefulness of this strategy in the next chapter.)

Given too little time to do everything well, you should first attend to the central question in your paper: the dependent variable (in an explanatory study), the independent variable (in a predictive study), the most important conditioning variable(s) (in a relational study), and the relations among all variables (in a systemic study). Remember that it is always best to err on the side of saying too much about your central concern and too little about the rest.

Mixing designs can be effective if the researcher is aware of doing so; in this event, we should bring each design to a satisfactory completion. However, the average student researcher has limited time and money, and limited expertise in every design; therefore, we call for modest goals. Do what you can do well. Choose one task—one design—and take it to completion. There is no need to apologize for what you have not done if what you *have* done is excellent.

chApter 3

THEORIZING ABOUT A PROJECT

BASIC IDEAS IN THEORY-MAKING

This chapter will introduce some basic ideas in theory-making: namely, the ideas of explanation, paradigm, theory, and prediction. You will be warned to keep aware of your main and secondary questions always, and to explore their connection to both larger and smaller issues of theoretical importance. We finish with a discussion of seven theoretical problems to avoid.

EXPLANATIONS

Most essays and journal articles in social science contain explanations. An explanation is a clear and thorough account of the problem or situation we are studying. As we saw in Chapter 1, the process of explaining has at least two parts: developing a theory to help the researcher think about relationships between the dependent and independent variables, and collecting data to test the correctness (validity) of that explanation.

There are at least six kinds of explanation in social science:

- *causal explanation* identifies the immediate cause of a particular event (for example, how European diseases helped conquer the Native peoples of North America);
- *probabilistic explanation* identifies the causal effect on a series of events (for example, how workplace stress increases the risk of heart attacks in workers in some industries);
- *meaningful and purposive explanation* identifies the causal effect of actors' motives, aims, and goals (for example, how beliefs about blondes contribute to blondes being more popular with men than brunettes);
- *functional explanation* identifies the systemic effect (or outcome) of one event as the cause of another (for example, why the need for social cohesion is likely to promote capital punishment, war, or scapegoating);

- *evolutionary explanation* identifies the survival instinct as the cause of the event (for example, why young women tend to marry older men);
- *deductive explanation* provides an account that can be deduced from established general laws. Here, explanation is an account of a *particular* event or relationship that is deducible from *general* principles of social life acting in *particular* circumstances.

Consider this example of a deductive explanation of why women do more housework than men in most North American households:

General principle:
People try to improve their well-being.

Particular circumstance:
In our society in 2007, most men earn more per hour than women.

Deductions:

- Men will lose more potential pay than women by doing unpaid housework.
- Housework by men will reduce family income.
- Income loss will reduce family well-being.
- Therefore, women should do more housework than men.

This is an observation about domestic inequality explained by general principles. This explanation also points to theoretically interesting anomalies (or deviant cases): for example, why, in some families,

- husbands do *less* housework although their wives earn more income than they; or
- husbands do *more* housework although their wives earn less income than they.

A study of deviant cases produces more variables for our explanation. To explain the first deviant case, where husbands do less housework than expected, we need to understand *patriarchy*: a cultural belief in the legitimacy of gender inequality and male dominance underlying all circumstances, however irrational. To explain the second deviant case, where husbands do more housework than expected, we need to understand *companionate marriage*: a cultural belief in equality and task-sharing between husbands and wives. Now, the explanation runs as follows:

General principle:
People act to improve their well-being.

Particular circumstance:
In our society in 2007,

- most men earn more per hour than women;
- some couples value a companionate marriage;
- some couples value traditional gender roles.

Deductions:
Domestic work will reflect the ways couples choose to improve their well-being:

- In couples that seek to improve their financial well-being, husbands will do less housework than wives only if they earn more than their wives.
- In couples that seek to improve their marital satisfaction, husbands will do the same amount of housework as their wives, regardless of what each earns.
- In couples that seek to adhere to traditional gender roles, husbands will do less housework than their wives, regardless of what each earns.

We continue this way to study anomalies and deviant cases until we understand all the principles that yield all the types of household work arrangements we have observed. Every explanation is thus a series of "because" clauses repeatedly answering the question *why*. Thus,

- *Why* do women do more housework than men?
  Because families forgo more income if men do the housework.
- *Why* do families forgo more income if men do the housework?
  Because our society values the traditional work of women—housekeeping and parenting—at near to zero. And,
  Because we pay women in the labour force less than men for work of equal value.
- *Why* does our society value women's work—whether domestic or paid—less than men's work?
  Because in a society dominated by men, the work of women was traditionally done for free. The culture taught that women were more generous and nurturing than men.

- *Why* were women believed to be more generous and nurturing than men? *Because* that cultural belief supported male dominance.

Thus, every explanation can lead to *infinite regress* in time. Each effect has many causes; each cause has many effects. Therefore, every explanation must be a heavily edited story—a model, rather than a true snapshot, since all explanations require simplification. However, explanations also require notions of causation. Here are the general qualities of a good explanation, no matter what is being explained:

- logical consistency: In a good explanation, the "because" clauses make sense.
- parsimony: A good explanation makes the fewest untestable assumptions.
- agreement with the evidence: In a good explanation, the logical deductions can be tested with empirical evidence, and the evidence confirms them.
- predictive power: A good explanation predicts what we can expect to find when we study other cases.
- falsifiability: A good explanation could be proven wrong by contrary evidence, if researchers were to find such evidence.
- persuasiveness: A good explanation is more believable than any other explanation.

What makes an account or explanation persuasive varies historically and culturally. Some explanations are hard for a society to accept; others are easy. For example, at certain stages of western European (and North American) history, even well-informed people were ready to accept witchcraft as an explanation for many natural events; today, few are willing to do so. Yet even within the framework of Western science, some explanations are easier than others to accept. Most scientists accept evolutionism and the big bang theory; few are ready yet to accept extrasensory perception, UFOs, and telekinesis. Explanations of natural events that rely on these factors are unlikely to persuade. Still, it is sometimes hard to convince people of the truth of something, even when it is obviously true, while convincing people of the truth of something, even when it is obviously false, is sometimes easy.

What follows is an examination of the ways to ensure that your explanation will make sense. Many points made below will apply just as readily to the predictive, systemic, and relational designs discussed in the last chapter. Bear in mind also that these points will be just as useful in evaluating and criticizing the explanations other people provide as in building your own.

PARADIGMS

In every social science there are different *paradigms*—ways of thinking about the same question. They are founded on various basic assumptions about how the world works, and they lead to different conclusions about important questions to ask and appropriate data to collect.

For example, two competing paradigms in sociology and anthropology are the structural-functionalist paradigm and the conflict paradigm. The functionalist interprets criminal behaviour as evidence of inadequate upbringing, psychopathology, or membership in a deviant subgroup. The conflict theorist, by contrast, interprets such behaviour as evidence of alienation, economic need, or protest against the ruling interests of society.

Each way of interpreting criminality leads a researcher to ask different questions, collect different kinds of data, and reach different conclusions. Nothing prevents you from collecting data that address *both* paradigms simultaneously—in fact, some philosophers even believe that the advancement of scientific knowledge continues by this adversarial process—but social scientists often work in one paradigm at a time.

KNOW HOW YOUR QUESTION RELATES TO YOUR PARADIGM

If your explanation relies more on one paradigm than another, be sure of the assumptions you are making and the larger questions that your approach suggests. Collect data that will clearly connect your research to other research within the same paradigm.

For example, suppose you are arguing that there is no drug problem in Canadian society today—that concerns of a nationwide drug problem are the product of some group that is promoting the idea because it is in their interest to do so. Such an argument would fall into the category of a conflict theory of law and deviant behaviour. To be consistent, you should also hold the following views, which are also central to conflict theory:

- that people hold unequal wealth and power in Canadian society;
- that they act to preserve or increase their wealth and power; and
- that widespread social beliefs, especially those that are spread by the mass media, are aimed at preserving the position of the wealthy and powerful.

The criticism of this position is that not every belief is promoted by the wealthy and powerful. Though the wealthy and powerful act in their own interests, as do other people, not every act or belief contributes to their well-being. The belief in a drug problem, for example, may not do so; the researcher must show that it does.

Once you are aware of the general and particular criticisms of your position, make sure you address them. Even if you cannot collect all the information needed to challenge them, at least show that you are aware of such criticisms and suggest further research that would adequately deal with them.

REMEMBER YOU ARE LOOKING FOR TRUTH

As important as it is to settle your work within a paradigm, you should not get carried away. Your real purpose is to answer a question, not to prove that some paradigm is better or worse than another. A paradigm will prove its usefulness by helping you answer the question at hand.

You may find that more than one paradigm contributes to your understanding of a particular problem. Many perspectives and, perhaps, many disciplines may contribute to a good answer. If so, admit that fact, even if it means using a paradigm you had not previously accepted. Theories are to be used by researchers, not researchers by theories. Denying, for partisan reasons, the weaknesses in your own paradigm and the strengths in another is bad research practice, mere intellectual one-upmanship. Findings and interpretations produced in this way will not hold up for long and will do little to advance social science.

THEORIES

THE RESEARCH CYCLE

The process of creating and testing a good theory follows a research cycle, such as the one depicted in Figure 3.1. You begin with a *theory*: a set of logically related statements about some phenomenon of interest. From this theory you logically *deduce* hypotheses. To deduce something is to infer it on purely logical grounds from a set of earlier conclusions or assumptions. For example, if February in Toronto is always cold and damp, and people are eager to avoid getting pneumonia, it follows by deduction that a high proportion of Torontonians will likely be wearing overcoats and galoshes next February 18. (This also yields a piece of practical advice: if you're travelling to Toronto for a Valentine's Day party, bring warm clothing.)

However, this deduction about Toronto and Torontonians in February is merely a hypothesis. *Hypotheses*, sometimes called *propositions*, are statements about presumed relationships between two or more variables. They give rise to specific predictions that no one knows to be true, but that can be proved true

FIGURE 3.1 THE RESEARCH CYCLE

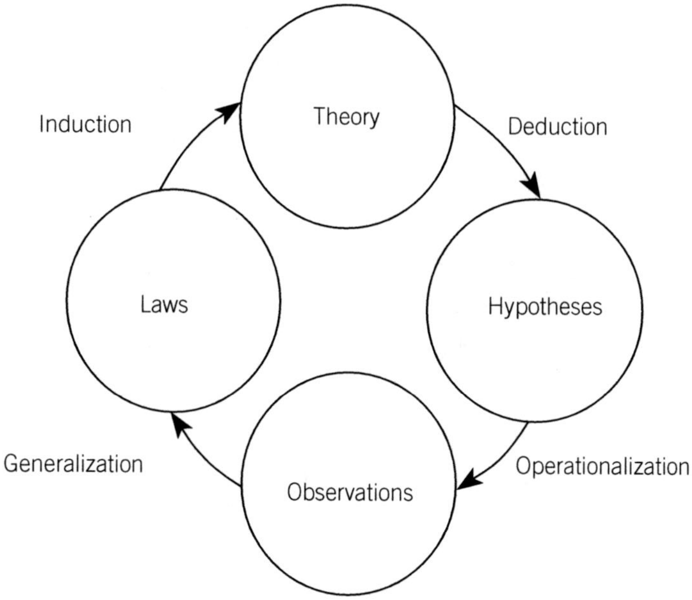

SOURCE: Li (1986). © 1986. Reprinted by permission of McGraw-Hill Ryerson Limited.

or false, valid or invalid, by the collection and analysis of data. Next February 18, you may find most Torontonians dressed in bathing suits. This is unlikely, but possible: we need evidence to test our original hypothesis.

To take a different and more plausible example, consider whether mothers with demanding professional careers (as lawyers or doctors, for instance) are more likely to experience guilt and anxiety than mothers with routine, 9–5 jobs (as retail clerks, for example). You start with the premise—suggested by your theory—that people are likely to experience guilt and anxiety if they are failing to meet their obligations or the expectations others have of them.

You may then premise that even today, working mothers are expected to meet the responsibilities traditionally associated with women, which include raising their children and taking care of housework. From this you may deduce that mothers with demanding, 24/7 professional careers will have less time to spend at home than mothers with routine, 9–5 jobs and, as a result, will be much more likely to fail to meet their domestic obligations. This being so, they are much more likely to experience guilt and anxiety in their lives.

Next comes the process of *operationalizing* the concepts in your hypothesis so you can test it for truth or falsity. An operational definition is a practical or working definition of a concept, attached to specific measures of the concept. Operationalization creates empirical measures of the key concepts (we will discuss measurement at length in the next two chapters). The measurement procedures produce *observations* that either support the hypothesis or prove it wrong. Thus, for example, we should be able to agree on the meaning of the term "social class," define that meaning, specify ways to measure it, and be able to show that the measurements behave similarly in different societies (on this, see Evans and Mills, 1999). Even so seemingly simple an idea as "education"— often used in this book, perhaps the most often used variable in social science research, and among the most effective predictors across a wide variety of models—hides a mass of conceptual and measurement issues that need careful consideration (Smith, 1995).

Assume, however, that we have managed to operationalize the key variables to carry out observations. From these specific observations come *generalizations*: conclusions about the general significance of the observations for the hypothesis as originally stated.

The last stage of the cycle is *induction*, the process of fitting the generalized results (or laws) together with the theory as originally stated. Where these two fail to fit together, they call for a reformulation of the theory. Then the cycle begins again, with another study and new hypotheses.

To follow up on a previous example that dealt with working mothers, the empirical (i.e., observed or measured) data may reveal any of the following:

    (a) that mothers with demanding careers are indeed much more likely to feel guilt and anxiety than mothers with routine, 9–5 jobs;

    (b) that they are only somewhat more likely to feel guilt or anxiety; or

    (c) that they are less likely to feel guilt and anxiety than mothers with routine, 9–5 jobs.

If result (a) is achieved, the hypothesis is considered to have been supported or confirmed, so, the theory that produced the hypothesis is also considered confirmed. If result (b) or (c) is achieved, the hypothesis is not considered confirmed, and neither is the theory that gave rise to it. However, result (b), being in the direction predicted (though not of the right size), gives greater confidence in the general correctness of the theory than does (c). Result (b) would probably lead the researcher to look for reasons observed guilt and anxiety proved less than predicted (for example, reasons having to do with sampling or measurement, which will be discussed later). Result (c) would less certainly lead the researcher to examine such factors, and might instead lead him or her to rethink the theory.

It is important to stress that we never prove a theory finally and decisively correct in this way (or any other!). We speak of a theory being proved true or false only as a shorthand to say that, for the time being, it is more valid or true than any other theory about the same phenomenon. A better theory or a better test may prove it invalid tomorrow.

GETTING TO KNOW YOUR OWN THEORY

THE USE OF FLOW CHARTS

Reaching a clear understanding of what you are arguing is more difficult than you might think, but following some easy steps will help. Start by listing all your variables. Then lay them out in a diagram connecting the variables influencing one another by labelled arrows, with a plus sign (+) showing a positive relationship between two variables and a minus sign (–) showing a negative one. (Remember that in a positive relationship, the connected variables increase and decrease together, while in a negative relationship, one variable increases as the other decreases.) Some pairs of variables may not be connected at all.

Diagramming an explanation forces you to deal consciously with what you think is going on: What are the key variables? What are the important relationships and non-relationships? What parts of the overall theory can be analyzed separately from the others? And, therefore, how must you analyze the data to test your theory?

A typical explanatory diagram (or *flow chart*) displays the dependent variable on the right-hand side and the independent variables on the left. Thus, the order of supposed causation flows from left to right, through intervening variables that come into effect after (or occasionally at the same time as) the independent variables. We depict one version of such a flow chart, called a path model, in Figure 3.2.

This flow chart, from a recent study of CEOs by Daily and Near (2000), clearly depicts the hypothesized or assumed relationships between the independent variables of interest—various measures of satisfaction and well-being—and the dependent variable, firm performance. This is a study to discover whether, when other factors are equal or held constant, happier bosses build more profitable businesses. It proposes that firm performance varies with the satisfaction and well-being of the firm's boss on and off the job.

Interestingly, the analysis of questionnaire data from 221 owners/managers of family-owned and -controlled automobile dealerships finds that every predicted relationship but one is significant in the predicted direction. For example, all the measures of satisfaction and well-being are correlated with one another. The one exception is the relationship between satisfaction and firm performance: the data

FIGURE 3.2 PREDICTORS OF LIFE SATISFACTION AND FIRM PERFORMANCE

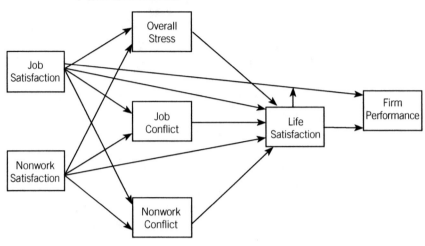

SOURCE: Daily and Near (2001). Reprinted with kind permission of Springer Science and Business Media.

show no significant connection between these two variables. There is no evidence, then, that happier bosses build more profitable businesses.

The same left-to-right convention cannot be used in depicting a systemic model, in which many independent and dependent variables affect one another simultaneously, and even feed back on one another repeatedly. Figure 3.3, which aims at explaining why pre-industrial populations keep returning to a particular size, is an example of a systemic model. Try tracing the argument it charts.

The positive and preventive checks noted by the demographer Thomas Malthus are both in evidence here. As population size increases, the size of an average landholding decreases, mortality rises, and the population size falls back to its earlier level. This is the positive check on population growth. Also, as population size increases, the supply of labour increases; real income per head decreases; people marry later (or not at all), community fertility or childbearing declines; and the population size falls back to its earlier level. This is the preventive check, preventive in the sense that it prevents a rise in the death rate.

Consider, finally, an even more complex systemic chart [Figure 3.4] showing all of the factors that go into explaining the survival of *polygyny*—the now rare arrangement in which one man is married to multiple women at the same time. As the chart shows, any explanation of this practice must take into account such economic factors as the scarcity of labour; traditional cultural practices that bear on social status, mating, and sexuality; and demographic factors such as

FIGURE 3.3 A MODEL OF RELATIONSHIPS BETWEEN
DEMOGRAPHIC, SOCIAL, AND ECONOMIC CHANGE
IN A PRE-INDUSTRIAL SOCIETY

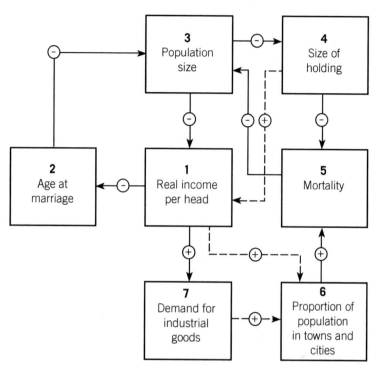

SOURCE: Wrigley (1969). Reprinted by permission of the publisher.

high mortality (owing to poor health) and high fertility (owing to strong pro-natalist attitudes).

Nothing displays more clearly than this chart why it would be almost impossible to legislate an end to the practice of polygyny without also changing the social, economic, cultural, and demographic factors that support the practice. Specifically, the author (Chojnacka, 2000:194) predicts and observes a decrease in polygyny as a result of

(a) increasing rates of population growth, which lead to enlarged supply of labour;

(b) the increasing role of capital in agriculture—even in the form of initially primitive tools and machinery—leading to higher labour productivity; and

(c) increasing productivity of labour, also because of out-migration of redundant labour from agriculture to urban areas.

FIGURE 3.4   EARLY-UNIVERSAL MARRIAGE AND POLYGYNY
AMONG WOMEN IN A TRADITIONAL ECONOMY AND
A STATIONARY POPULATION

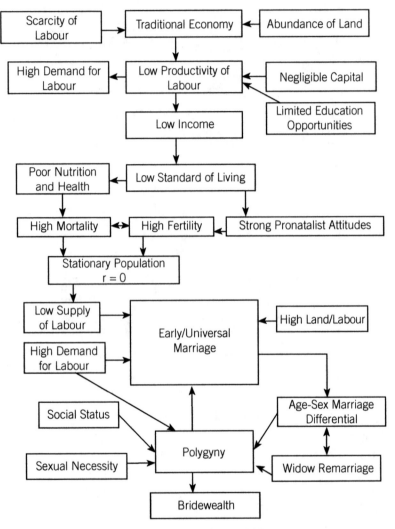

SOURCE: Chojnacka (2000). Reprinted by permission of the publisher.

GET A FRIEND TO HELP YOU THEORIZE

Knowing your own theory is, as we have seen, not so easy. That is why you sometimes need a disinterested person to help you remember why you are doing this project and what you expect to learn from it.

Find a friend or relative with five minutes to spare, preferably someone without social science training. Then try to explain what you are arguing and why.

If you can make the main pieces of your argument fit together for this audience, you probably know what you're doing. If you have trouble making sense to your listener—or to yourself—try again, with the same or, even better, another audience. Repeated failures to make sense in this setting suggest that your argument is not sound or that you are not comfortable with your explanation.

KNOW YOUR MAIN QUESTION

So far we have been looking at the big picture: placing your explanation in a larger body of research and ensuring that you have taken account of all the relevant variables. Nevertheless, we should not lose sight of a key point: making sense means always knowing your main question, the fundamental point you are trying to make. It's easy to get lost in all the details of your research, but be careful not to lose sight of the forest for the trees.

Sometimes losing sight of your main goal comes about in another way. You may chance into a treasure trove of data that are only slightly related to your original research question. If you start ransacking this treasure of data for nuggets—there is no end to the interesting things you can find in a good library or survey—after a while you may forget to use the data to answer the original question, and report on all the data instead.

Suppose that you started with a theory that social relations in the workplace primarily influence the job satisfaction of workers. You discover a survey of job satisfaction, which primarily examines the effect of working conditions and economic incentives, but also includes one question on how well people relate to their workmates. The data reveal all sorts of interesting relationships, but only a weak relationship between job satisfaction and workers' relations with their co-workers. Does this finding disprove your original theory? No: in this report, the data are irrelevant. Instead of measuring the key explanatory variable—social relations on the job—in various useful ways, you have measured it in only one way, which may be flawed or irrelevant. Mainly, you have redirected attention to many other possible explanations about which you have no theory. Exploration is not bad in itself; but you should be aware if this activity has caused you to leave an explanatory design for exploration or description. You cannot automatically move back from an unstructured exploration into an effective explanation.

If you have done this, your three choices are clear: rethink your goal and admit it is an exploration, not an explanation, of the dependent variable; find another body of data that better measures social relations on the job; or develop some theories about the likely role of working conditions and economic incentives, about which you have plenty of data.

KNOW HOW YOUR MAIN QUESTION RELATES TO SECONDARY QUESTIONS

You can never go too far in thinking about your main question of interest and secondary, related questions. You should address these questions with data if possible, or at least admit that these related questions deserve later research. Examples might include explanations of why particular intervening or contextual factors are important, or discussions of paradigm-related issues.

Imagine, for example, that research on television sitcoms found that the central characters were always middle-class people living a prosperous, urban lifestyle, and that this portrayal implied to viewers that such a lifestyle was desirable, easily obtainable, and a reward for social conformity. You might then analyze the component parts of this portrayal. What does it mean that these characters hold certain kinds of jobs, wear certain kinds of clothes, or have certain kinds of furniture? What meanings do viewers attach to certain roles or material objects in our environment, and where do these meanings come from? Why, for example, are doctors usually portrayed as heroic, unselfish, and helpful? What is the social meaning of "doctor" in our culture, how did it arise, and how is it maintained despite our first-hand experience that doctors, like everyone else, are just as likely to be unheroic, selfish, and unhelpful? These secondary questions will help you draw some conclusions about the main findings of the initial research.

EXPLORE AT DIFFERENT LEVELS OF ANALYSIS

The social sciences involve research at several different levels of analysis, as the examples in this book suggest. Social scientists study societies, organizations, communities, and individuals—social formations characterized by different levels or degrees of complexity. We should make two points about levels of analysis.

AVOID REDUCTIONISM

Although some important theorists have argued to the contrary, events at one level of analysis cannot be easily broken down, or reduced, to a larger number of smaller events at a lower level of analysis. Such a strategy, called *reductionism*, is not acceptable.

Take, for example, an examination of the reasons people form social movements: why do people join together to protest economic, religious, or other types of discrimination or inequality? This question cannot be answered simply by moving down to the individual level of analysis and studying the psychology—the attitudes and motives—of participating protesters. A sense of outrage at the individual level may be *necessary* for a social movement of form, but it is far from *sufficient*. For protest to occur, the outraged people must mobilize: there must be leadership, communication, a shared consciousness, and often material resources—money, food, an office, posters, and many other things. Therefore, the rise of a protest movement does not prove that people have just become outraged: they may have just mobilized. Also, the absence of protest does not prove people are not outraged, but may prove that they are not organized.

This example shows that a social phenomenon can—and often must—be examined at various levels of analysis simultaneously if we are to understand it fully. We may discover that forces working at different levels of analysis are pulling in opposite directions. For example, at the individual level people may feel outraged at their own and other people's unemployment. Yet unemployed people tend to be politically inactive: they do not protest their condition to demand a remedy. Part of this problem is organizational as we have just described it: a shortage of leaders, resources, and communication. However, part of it is cultural: our value system holds people responsible for their own fate. In Canada we are brought up to believe that what happens to people is their own fault: they have earned their success and failures and must live with them. Thus, on the psychological level, all the conditions may be met for social action against unemployment, but on the cultural level, the opposite conditions prevail. With problems at the social-organizational level, cultural (or ideological) factors work against the behavioural expression of forces working at the psychological, or individual, level.

TEST THEORIES AT ALL LEVELS OF ANALYSIS

To say that we should test theories at all levels of analysis may seem to contradict what we have just said about opposing forces at different levels. Indeed, analyses at different levels will often give different results. But this is not always the case.

Consider the issue of punitiveness. Societies vary in their degree of punitiveness: how severely they punish wrongdoers. Canada is, and has historically been, much less punitive than many societies, in the sense that people in this country are not banished, tortured, or executed for minor (or even major) offences, as often happens in other societies. Yet Canada does imprison a higher proportion of convicted criminals than many other modern nations. What accounts for Canada's punitiveness compared with that of many other countries?

We might think that this punitiveness is the result of internal instability: societies (as well as groups, communities, and individuals) that feel insecure are more likely to punish severely, to increase their internal cohesion by reaffirming moral boundaries.

At what level should this hypothesis be tested? The answer is that it should perhaps be tested at all levels of analysis. If the hypothesis is valid, we should find that individuals who are most socially or economically marginal or insecure will express the most punitive sentiments toward wrongdoers. At the societal level, rates of punitiveness (i.e., prison terms for convicted criminals) should increase in times of war, economic depression, or internal unrest, in response to perceived threats to the society. At the cultural level, racism, nationalism, xenophobia, and other declarations of preference for people like oneself should, along with punitiveness, increase when the culture is being threatened by massive immigration or foreign domination of the mass media.

If we find that these changes do occur as predicted, there is reason to believe that we have found the basis for a general theory of punitiveness. Our work is far from done, however. Without examining the process by which punitiveness increases at each level under conditions of internal instability, we run the risk of two grave methodological errors, both connected with improper movement between levels of analysis: the ecological fallacy and the fallacy of misplaced concreteness (for a detailed discussion of these, see "Pitfalls to Avoid" below). However, if we can avoid these fallacies, our multi-level theory will be more compelling than a theory that holds good at only one level of analysis.

PREDICTIONS

KNOW WHAT NEW IDEAS YOUR THEORY SUGGESTS

The essential purpose of a theory is to explain, or clarify, how variables are related to one another. One way to test the truth of a theory is to make predictions based on the theory and to test them with data.

Prediction is not the only test of a theory, for several reasons. We cannot immediately test certain theories with data—some of Einstein's theories in physics waited decades for testing, until the appropriate technology was available. As well, a theory-based explanation that may be correct may fail to yield valid predictions because of faulty measures, incomplete data, or unrecognized intervening or contextual factors.

Conversely, we can make good predictions even without a proper, well-developed theory. For example, traffic engineers can accurately predict the flow of traffic through a particular intersection for a given day or week. They base their predictions on many past observations, not on a theory about traffic. This kind of predicting uses what we sometimes call a *black-box approach*. Researchers can use data to make accurate predictions, but what happens in the "black box," where causes produce these predictable (but not understood) effects, is largely unknown. For many practical purposes, we need not know it.

As well, predictions based on historical explanations are rarely testable. An explanation or theory about the causes of the Russian Revolution cannot do better than persuade the reader through its logical, believable handling of existing information. A comparison with other revolutions may attempt to verify the theory by developing a general theory of revolutions. However, this enterprise is different and full of problems of comparability among societies.

Nevertheless, if prediction is not the perfect test of an explanation, it is nonetheless desirable. People often accuse social science of merely restating the obvious in difficult jargon. To get past this criticism, researchers should aim to show that their theories can produce ideas, understanding, or findings that are not possible using common sense alone.

Consider the question of how families deal with the stresses produced by chronic illness. Common sense tells us that different families will deal with their difficulties in different ways—a true prediction, but vague. Systematic observation and theory show us *which* families cope better than others and *which* coping strategies work better than others. They show that adjustment goes on through a series of stages, each with its own problems and resolutions, before people can attempt the next stage. If we are trying to understand why a particular family is coping in the way it is and how we can help it to cope better, we are far better off with a theory to help us than with common sense alone. With theory we can hope not only to predict the future course of a family's problems, but also to predict which interventions will work best at given times for a given family.

STATE YOUR EXPECTATIONS IN ADVANCE

Creating a flow chart is the best way of stating your expectations, but it is not the only one. Even without a flow chart, you should be clear about what you expect the data to reveal and why. This will help to clarify your theoretical assumptions, suggest appropriate research methodology needed to test your theory, and point to missing variables that might explain or interpret your result.

Anticipating your findings means you win whichever way the data turn out when you analyze them. If the expected result occurs, you can reasonably claim that this supports your theory, since that theory was able to make the correct prediction. If, on the other hand, unexpected results show up, the analysis becomes even more interesting. If you have developed your theory carefully, linking your explanation to questions and findings in the literature, you are right to have expected what you did. The fact that your result is unexpected points to a need for rethinking, or for considering other variables you and others have overlooked. We ignore many useful findings in social science because they fail to support our theories; however, finding a negative relationship where you had expected a positive one or a weak relationship where you had expected a strong one might lead you to a conclusion that is even more interesting than your prediction.

MOVING INTO A RELATIONAL DESIGN

When unexpected results occur, your analysis should move out of an explanatory design into a relational one. The search is on for intervening variables that make sense of the unexpected relationship between the independent and dependent variables. A deviant-case analysis may be in order, for example (see Chapter 2).

Suppose you had predicted that in a particular election, blue-collar workers would vote for one party and white-collar workers for another, based on the belief that different parties protect different class interests. The results, however, show something different: many blue-collar workers voted for the "white-collar party." Your theory of class voting may indeed be wrong, but other key variables may also play a part in making the theory correct. For example, blue-collar voters may have *believed* the "white-collar party" would protect working-class interests. If so, you should modify, not discard, your original theory of class voting. We find that people will vote for their class interests as they *see* them, and as they *see* the platform of the party they're voting for. In this way you come to focus on a new, interesting problem of political misinformation or manipulation, and you can collect new data on people's perceptions not previously considered.

In Canada, we find a complicated relationship between "class voting," "ethnic voting," and "regional voting." Higher educations and incomes tend to predict votes for the NDP, while lower incomes predict votes for the Conservative Party. This is mediated by whether the voter is a union member (which increases the likelihood of voting NDP at any education or income level). Medium levels of income predict votes for the other parties: for the Liberals if the voter lives in Ontario or is an immigrant or a member of an ethnic minority; for the Bloc Québécois if the voter lives in Quebec; for the Conservatives if the voter lives west of Ontario.

This example shows that, even with a simple activity like voting, the explanation may require you to understand how many of variables interact with one another.

KNOW THE CONDITIONS UNDER WHICH YOUR THEORY HOLDS TRUE

All explanatory studies contain elements of a relational design. None can rightly ignore the context within which the data are collected, nor the factors likely to make the explanation stronger or weaker.

The most obvious examples are the historical and cultural contexts. A social fact or social law can be shown to hold true in a particular time and place, but showing that something is universal and timeless requires a great deal of data. In one factory, social relations on the job may exercise an important influence on job satisfaction, but we cannot automatically generalize this to all factories. This relationship may be stronger in unionized factories than in non-unionized factories, where concerns about job security, working conditions, or pay are greater. It may be stronger in a period of prosperity than in one of mass unemployment, for similar reasons. It may be stronger in small-scale, traditional workplaces or in newly industrializing societies than in modern, highly bureaucratized or mechanized workplaces in industrialized societies.

Specifying the conditions under which your theory holds true is important in several ways. First, it helps you clarify what is going on in the situation you are examining, and why. Second, it helps you and others judge the generality of your findings and their applicability to other situations.

Generalizability is sometimes important in applied research, where decisions affecting others are based on research findings. Imagine a demonstration project to decide how we might improve relations between citizens and the police in a particular city. Someone theorizes that such relations are improved when citizens with inquiries have easier, less formal access to police officers. On this basis, the theorist suggests taking some police out of their centralized police station and putting them into a storefront "mini-station," where people can come to ask questions, lodge complaints, and mix with police officers in a relaxed way. Such a mini-station is set up for a trial period of six months, and then community members are surveyed to learn whether their views of the police have improved. The data show no change in views.

What conclusion can we draw from this finding? Further, should we continue the experiment or even extend it to other neighbourhoods? Our answer depends in large part on the characteristics of the neighbourhood in which the mini-station was situated: for example, on whether the community members had originally been fearful of the police, had tended to misinterpret their motives and behaviours, and felt reluctant to make initial—let alone subsequent—contacts. The results have a different meaning if found in an unreceptive community than in a receptive one.

PREPARING TO MAKE AND TEST THEORIES: THE LITERATURE REVIEW

"Science" as a cultural and social institution has certain norms or rules. One of the most important of these is public disclosure of results. Researchers are expected to fully disclose the findings of their work to their colleagues and submit these findings, in the form of journal articles or books, to qualified referees who will then challenge the work. Only if the work passes this testing process will it find its way into reputable publications. From there, the work is abstracted—boiled down—for inclusion in professional databases like "Sociological Abstracts", which are increasingly available in electronic form. In practice, then, a researcher in Calgary or California or Calcutta can go online and find out, almost instantaneously, which researchers around the world have been studying a particular problem and what they have found out.

Of course, the published knowledge may be a little outdated by this time (often by as much as two or three years, owing to delays in publication), which is why serious researchers regularly attend conferences, where they can hear the most up-to-date findings from the mouths of the people who have done the research. But outdated or not, the published research is the best record of what is known in a particular field about a topic; that is where all new work has to begin.

There are many reasons for doing a literature review before setting out to make and test theories. First, another researcher may have already discovered the answer to the question you are asking. Or other researchers may have taken steps to answer the question, and you can build on the work they have done. Second, someone may have demonstrated that it is almost impossible to answer the question you are asking. For these reasons, no serious scholar or student would fail to review and interpret the literature before embarking on his or her own project.

What, then, is a literature review? The literature review found in any scholarly article, dissertation, or book is an interpretation, a synthesis and critical analysis of published literature relevant to a study. As noted, the purpose of conducting a literature review is to benefit from the results of other relevant studies (Fraenkel and Wallen, 1996), to link your study to the larger body of literature (Marshall and Rossman, 1989), and to provide a "framework for establishing the importance of the study, as well as a benchmark for comparing the results of a study with other findings" (Creswell, 1992:21–22). A researcher who does not conduct the review of relevant literatures risks focusing on a trivial problems, duplicating a study which has already been conducted, or repeating other's mistakes (Merriam, 1998:61).

SEARCHING FOR ARTICLES

Before discussing how to write a literature review, it is important to know where to look for relevant material published about a topic and how to assess it. Researchers can find books and articles about their topics in the libraries and on the Internet. Most university libraries have either searchable databases on CD-ROMs available for student use or have subscriptions to online databases. You may even be able to access the online databases via the Internet by logging on to your library's computer system from home. For specific information on how to access the resources at your school, visit your library.

Fraenkel and Wallen (1996:65–6) suggest three sources of information to draw on for literature reviews: general references, primary sources, and secondary sources. They describe *general references* as the starting point, since they tell researchers where to look for similar and related studies. Examples of general references include indexes and abstracts (for example, Sociological Abstracts, Medline, or Psychinfo). *Primary sources* are the complete recorded findings of individual studies, which are found in monographs or scholarly journals. *Secondary sources* mainly consist of authors' analyses and reports on other people's work. A textbook is one example of a secondary source, if it discusses and describes primary sources. A literature review, like a textbook, is mainly based on primary sources.

A researcher who has only a vague sense of the published literature about a topic is well advised to start with an overview by making use of general references. Reading relevant encyclopedia articles, handbooks, and abstracts of journal articles will help the researcher identify major theories and studies (Merriam, 1988:65). But before searching even for general references, it's wise to spend some time thinking about what search parameters to set. The researcher might look for articles in specific publications or published within a certain time frame. Another strategy is to begin with articles by the best known scholars in the field, and to expand the search to include authors cited by those scholars. Be aware that if the topic is too narrowly defined, the search may result in very few articles. A better way to start is by conducting a broad search of all the different terms and variables relevant to the topic.

In compiling material for the literature review, the researcher should always work backward from today, reading the material from this year first, then the material from last year, and so on. Often material more than five to ten years old is completely outdated. It is equally important to know when to stop searching. When any further search turns up familiar results or when the researcher does not find any new significant studies, it is time to stop searching and time to start synthesizing and writing.

WRITING UP THE LITERATURE REVIEW

Like any other scholarly piece of work, a literature review is composed of three parts: an introduction, a body, and a conclusion. The introduction to a literature review gives a brief description of the problem and a short outline of published literature about the topic. The body of the review consists of a detailed discussion of relevant published studies. It is here that similar studies are grouped according to common themes or variables. In this way, literature reviews can be used to summarize the current thinking about a particular topic or problem; for a prime example, see the *Annual Review of Sociology*, the *Annual Review of Anthropology*, the *Annual Review of Psychology*, and so on. These annual publications all contain articles by leading figures, synthesizing the knowledge in particular problem areas of the field. In analyzing the literature, pointing out strengths and weaknesses, the researcher will be able to identify gaps in the literature that can be filled with further research. Thus, the body of the literature review leads the reader to the new research question, which is usually stated at the end of the review in a closing paragraph.

Remember that a proper literature should integrate, synthesize, and critique the relevant literature. A list of articles with summaries is no more than an annotated bibliography. Cooper (1984) identifies three types of literature review: (1) the integrative form, which is the summary of the published literature; (2) a theoretical review, in which the researcher highlights theories related to the problem that is being studied; and (3) a methodological review, in which the researcher focuses on methods that have been used. A good review of literature should contain aspects of all three types.

A good literature review is also one that is organized around ideas, not sources. Organizing the literature review around themes and trends is the proper approach. With quantitative studies, both dependent and independent variables can work as organizing themes. Too many paragraphs that begin with the name of researchers ("Ludwig and Martin report . . .", "Johannes and Mutabo have found . . .") is a hint that a literature review is organized too much around sources and not enough around ideas.

PITFALLS TO AVOID

Once we have identified a problem and the main theories and problems surrounding that problem, we are ready to make and test our own theory. The process of making and testing theory is full of pitfalls. Some are so common that they have become classic social science problems with names to identify them.

Social scientists have spent a great deal of time discussing these pitfalls, and you can read more about them in the literature. What follows is a brief account of classic problems to avoid.

THE ECOLOGICAL FALLACY

The ecological fallacy is the mistake of drawing a conclusion at one level of analysis and applying it to another. Social science analyzes data at several different levels of complexity: those of the individual, the group, the institution, the society, and the culture. Moving between levels of analysis can lead to errors.

For example, imagine that research has found that juvenile delinquency rates are highest in those parts of a city where the average household income is lowest. This does *not* necessarily prove that children from low-income families are more often delinquent than children from higher-income families. Children from high-income families may be the delinquents in both parts of town, but in the wealthier parts, their delinquency less often results in detection, arrest, or conviction.

Also, we are not justified in doing what Emile Durkheim (1951) did in his classic study of suicide. He studied suicide rates for various countries and, noting that the rates were higher in countries that were predominantly Protestant, inferred that Protestants were more suicide-prone than Catholics. However, he did so without any direct evidence that Protestants, not Catholics, were committing the suicides in question.

To repeat, we run a serious risk of error when we infer individual behaviour from ecological or aggregate data (i.e., rates of behaviour in entire neighbourhoods, cities, or nations). Usually, aggregate data merely *suggest* relationships that we can test with other data. They may also be used to explain other aggregate data. We cannot automatically assume, for example, that people who live in modern cities will have "modern" ways of thinking. Nor, for that matter, can we assume that modern ways of thinking will automatically give rise to modern institutions. Please note, however, that research by Heckelman (1997) shows that, under some circumstances, estimated coefficients from aggregate data can be directly related to true underlying micro-coefficients, so interpretations can be made. Though this is not always the case, it is becoming clear that in certain situations, the ecological fallacy does not pose a problem for researchers.

MULTICOLLINEARITY

Often many independent variables are correlated with one another: that is, they vary together. We know this phenomenon as *multicollinearity*.

Consider the problem of explaining the dramatic decline in average family size noted throughout the Western world in the late nineteenth and early twentieth centuries. The decline is correlated with many changes that are also correlated with one another: the spread of literacy, urbanization, industrialization, increased standard of living, reduced child mortality, and so on. These variables tended to change together (and to change one another), which is why we often lump them together under the general term of "modernization." To say which of these was the key influence on childbearing is difficult, almost arbitrary. It is therefore arbitrary to identify one of these variables as *most* important in producing the observed effect. As a researcher, then, you should avoid making any strong claims about the causal influence of a particular variable in such a situation.

THE FALLACY OF MISPLACED CONCRETENESS

You commit the fallacy of misplaced concreteness if you assign to some abstract entity (for example, "society" or "the community") thoughts or behaviours of which only individual humans are capable. Like the ecological fallacy, this mistake results from confusion about the proper level of analysis.

For example, to characterize some societies as more warlike or militaristic than others is both implausible and imprecise. Societies do not make wars: people do. "Society" is an abstract or theoretical idea and therefore incapable of acting. When we say that a society is warlike, we are implying that all its citizens like wars, or that its major institutions or dominant classes are filled with people who are itching for a fight. More likely than not, however, it is only a few people who are promoting military activity, and often for practical reasons (such as profit making, broadening their power, or increasing their prestige) rather than because they like war for its own sake.

Thus, misplaced concreteness combines several serious errors. It assigns actions and motives in a way that is sloppy and too general. It reduces social structure to individual traits, as though each member of society were identical and a miniature version of the entire society. It fails, in this example, to identify who is militaristic and why; and further, why these people are often successful in causing wars. Finally, this imprecision leads us away from an analysis of distinct conflicting individuals, groups, and classes, toward a nearly mystical belief in an acting, consensual society.

This error is common even in simpler social units. Some would argue, for instance, that the notion of "family" results from misplaced concreteness, particularly when we use it in a way that suggests a common will, goal, or interest. We can easily identify the members of a particular household, and even which members of that household are related. But when we use the term "family" to refer to such a group, we make certain assumptions about dependency, love, sexual relationship (or lack of it), commitment, and identification that may or may not be present in the particular household or kinship group. We should be careful not to assume a group of people forms a "family" in all senses without studying the relationships involved.

TAUTOLOGY OR CIRCULARITY

Relationships that are true by definition are not worth researching, since they tell us nothing new and cannot be falsified by data. Exploring such circular— or *tautological*—relationships adds nothing to our understanding of an issue.

For example, the theory that criminal behaviour results from "social maladjustment," "character disorder," or "undersocialization" is tautological if all we mean by these terms is a tendency towards criminal behaviour. (Or, just as bad, we may think that maladjustment, character disorder, and undersocialization mean something more than mere criminal behaviour, but we cannot measure what this something more consists of.)

Such obvious tautology is rare; other kinds are more common. Consider the theory of status attainment that says that in modern societies, a person's adult job status will be determined mainly by his or her educational attainment, whatever class he or she is born into. This theory proves largely tautological when we discover that "job status" here is measured in part by the average educational attainment of people in a particular job. Thus, the theory states, "Attaining a job with a high average educational requirement will be accomplished by gaining a high level of education." This is tautology.

UNMEASURABLES

Theorizing about things you cannot measure—*unmeasurables*—will be useful under few circumstances. Admit if you are exploring or speculating about a topic and not really theorizing. You may have a tight, well-defined theory that can yield predictions well ahead of the technology to test them. Mathematical theories in physics have these properties, but such theories are rare in social science.

Variables are often more complicated than you imagine. You should avoid theorizing about variables you cannot measure clearly and meaningfully, since there is no way of telling whether you are right or wrong. You worsen this problem if your theory contains "escape clauses" to explain away results that are opposite to what you had predicted.

Consider two classic examples: Marx's theory of alienation and Freud's theory of repression. Marx argued that, in a capitalist society, workers lack control over the labour process: over what they will make, how they will make it, and to whom the profits will flow. The result is a sense of alienation or estrangement from work, from the product of work, from oneself, and from others. This leads to the prediction that as we vary worker control over the labour process, the expressed sense of alienation should vary. Yet studies have shown that many workers in (objectively) alienating work settings do not feel (subjectively) alienated. They do not express feelings of estrangement from themselves or from others. A Marxist would counter that such workers show a false consciousness (a false view of the class situation) that causes them to deny their true feelings. Since we cannot discover their true feelings, we must conclude that this theory is unprovable, at least right now.

Freud's theory of repression is similar in many ways. He argued that people have certain natural or inborn drives: for example, drives toward expressing sexual or aggressive impulses. However, most societies have prevented or repressed the free expression of these drives, some especially strongly. The theory seems to predict that people will sublimate, or redirect, these impulses in ways that would not result in punishment; express the impulses in fantasy (for example, dreams or art); or suffer neurotic symptoms if they do not express the impulses at all. However, many people show low levels of sexual or aggressive impulse in any form and yet do not appear neurotic. A theorist from a contending school of psychology would say that the existence of these exceptions proves Freud wrong: that we learn aggression and sexuality, it is not instinctive, and that low levels of such expression are proof of learning, not repression. A Freudian would respond that the apparent absence of expression shows denial, and that the instinctive impulses find their outlet in another way—in smoking, overeating, loud laughter, or a strong devotion to work. Nevertheless, the Freudian theory is unprovable as it stands, since it contains no limit on the number of possible exceptions to the rule.

Methodological and conceptual problems such as these lead to poor predictions that are either untestable or, when tested, wrong. In large part, they have resulted in a wholesale rejection of Freudian and Marxist thought in the late twentieth century. Freudian and Marxist metaphors survive better in the humanities, where they are not subjected to testing, than in social science, where an observable empirical reality determines their usefulness.

MISUSE OF CONSTANTS

Constants are, as their name suggests, unchanging: they never vary. Thus, a constant can never be used to explain anything; only variables can explain one another. More bluntly, no one can explain a variable by a constant, nor a constant by a variable, nor a constant by a constant. A constant just *is*.

The uselessness of constants in explanations should be obvious; unfortunately they enter many explanations nonetheless. A prime example is the use of "human nature" to explain things, whether wars, divorces, discrimination, or the production of art. The statement "Wars are caused by human nature" is untestable as it stands. It seems likely, at first glance, that data could disprove this statement, since wars come and go, yet human nature presumably remains constant. However, someone might respond that wars are caused by a combination of human nature and another factor (for example, a shortage of agricultural land, resulting in population pressure). In this event, the researcher might just as well treat the other (variable) factor as the true explanation. So, in the end, referring to human nature is never a useful way of making a social science theory, and you should ignore human nature as an explanatory variable.

NON-EVENTS

Non-events did not happen. Yet researchers try to study them all the time: why released prisoners do not go straight; why countries did not have revolutions; why cities are not situated in particular places.

There are two reasons why you should be cautious when studying non-events. One is that there are no data, since nothing happened. If it is true that people did not evolve to look like ostriches, we can have little to say about the conditions under which they would or could evolve to look like ostriches. (This is the unlikely example the philosopher Thomas Malthus used in his *Essay on Population* [1798] to discourage idle speculation about the future.) And, if Canada has never had a revolution, we can say little about the circumstances under which it would or could have one, except under conditions we will specify shortly.

You are in a better position to explain why things *did* happen, since data can be plausibly arranged in an explanation. Take the example of young people who run away from home. We have many convincing theories about what makes family life pleasant and what makes parenting better or worse. Children flourish in homes that are loving and cohesive, under parents who are supportive, consistent, moderate, and caring. Our theory would be that children run away from homes that are the opposite of this. We should expect to find an under-representation of children from happy homes on the streets of our major cities, engaged in begging, prostitution, and crime. The research finds that this is the case: most runaways are children escaping dysfunctional families. Abuse aside, children who run away tend to come from "chaotic/aggressive families" and reveal a mixed pattern of youth aggression and parental skill deficiency (Teare, Authier, and Peterson, 1994). Running away is often a response to neglect, abandonment, and physical or sexual violence (Côté, 1992). Abused runaways are even more likely than those who were not abused to describe their parents in ways that suggest their parents suffer from drug problems and have serious antisocial personality traits (Stiffman, 1989).

Running away is an example of an event that does happen (and happens often). We can develop explanations and even try to find the causes of runaway behaviour because we can collect data on this situation. Non-events do not produce data, so we cannot study them in the same way. The only way we can make a non-event the subject of our study is if we have a similar event to compare it with. Success must be compared with failures to see what factors are always present in the successes and always absent in the failures. Also, we must always compare non-events with events, to see what factors are present in the one case and absent in the other.

Failing that, we must study non-events in relation to a general theory about events (and non-events). For example, understanding why Canada has not had a revolution requires us to start with a general theory of revolutions, specifically a theory about the conditions needed to produce one. Making such a theory requires, as we have already noted, an investigation of both revolutionary and non-revolutionary societies: a comparison of non-revolutionary Canada with revolutionary Russia, France, or the United States, for example.

Our conclusion is that you should not study a non-event for purposes of explanation without either a general theory about corresponding events or data on corresponding events.

NON-FINDINGS

We stated earlier that the unexpected discovery of a non-finding may be cause for rejoicing. If a predicted result fails to appear, this may motivate the researcher to refine a theory, not discard it. However, consider again Figure 3.2, exploring the relationships between various measures of CEO satisfaction and firm performance, which found that every predicted relationship but one was significant in the predicted direction. The one exception was the relationship between CEO satisfaction and firm performance. Although several of the relationships turned out as predicted, we did not find out what influences firm performance using this model. In this sense we produced a non-finding. What conclusion should we draw?

One possibility is that a bad theory led the researcher to measure the wrong variables. If so, we must reject the initial theory as unhelpful. Another possibility is that the researcher failed to consider contextual or intervening factors, and that a good explanation will be much more complex than originally thought. Instead of adding up in some simple way, the various influences may interact or multiply together in any of what might be thousands of different ways. Such a conclusion, while conceivably the right one, must in the short run lead to despair. No one is able to study thousands of possible combinations among dozens or hundreds of independent variables. The researcher is, in effect, reduced to starting all over—making a new, simple theory—or giving up the problem altogether.

The final, and perhaps the best, explanation of a non-finding—and its most dangerous meaning—is that we did not measure one or more key variables correctly. The researcher did not manage to predict firm performance because he or she did not know what the term was supposed to mean, or because what the researcher meant was not what other people mean, or finally, because the questions asked of respondents were badly chosen.

If so, the theory may be right or wrong, and there is no way of telling from the data available. Bad measurement has defeated us. Ultimately, developing any scientific discipline rides on the quality of its measurements. Much of scientific work is taken up with devising and refining measuring instruments and then reporting on the observed measures: at what temperature does water boil? how many children are born per mother? at what income does a family fall into "poverty"? While these issues may seem boring to some, in the end they are the essentials of science, including social science. That is why two entire chapters of this book are devoted to measurement. In the next chapter we consider quantitative measures, and in the chapter after that, qualitative measures.

CLOSING COMMENTS

This chapter has discussed the research cycle and the importance of clarity about the purposes of the research. We have examined explanations, paradigms, theories, and predictions—the analytical framework of any research undertaking. If you are unclear about what you are trying to prove, you cannot hope that anyone else will be clear about what you have found out.

We have also examined eight classic problems of logical organization. Avoiding them will help you launch your research toward findings that will make sense. Yet still our job is only half done: we have our hypotheses in hand, but we have yet to measure the key variables in ways that will produce conclusive findings. This is the subject of the next two chapters.

chapter 4

USING QUANTITATIVE DATA

TYPES OF RESEARCH

Most social science consists of trying to answer questions. Gathering the information to answer these questions is social research. For different kinds of questions there are different kinds of research.

Consider poverty as an example. We may read in newspapers or see reported on television that poverty is a serious problem in our society. We may suspect that this is true, but we are not sure whether it is true, or what the size of the problem may be. At this point we engage in *exploratory research* to find out whether poverty is an issue that warrants further research, or what information is already available on poverty, or what further research needs to be done.

If the information we collect suggests that poverty is an issue that needs to be studied further, we will ask many more questions: What is considered poverty in our society? How many people are poor? Who are these people? Where are they living? Here we engage in *descriptive research* to find out what is going on. Descriptive research gives us the answers to specific questions about people, events, or conditions in which we are interested. We may also want to find out *why* some people are poorer than others. Then we engage in *explanatory research*, which we design to find the *cause* of an effect.

EXPLANATION AND PREDICTION

Formally defined, an *explanation* is something that provides reasons or interpretations for something else. Consider the issue of poverty: why are some people poorer than others? While looking for an explanation, we make informed guesses or suggest probable explanations, called *hypotheses*, which we then test with data. A hypothesis, as we defined it earlier, is a statement about the presumed relationships between two or more variables, which we can test through research.

Research has suggested that some people are poorer than others because they have not received enough formal education to get a well-paying job. It may be that they have failed to learn crucial facts and skills, or perhaps it may be that they have learned these facts and skills, but because they did not gain their knowledge at a proper academic institution, they do not have the certificate that shows they have the learning. If our hypothesis is correct, the more education a person receives, the higher his or her income should be. We can now examine the data to verify the hypothesis—to test it with facts. If the data show that people with more education always earn higher income than people with less education, then we have come part of the way toward an explanation.

However, explanation does not end when we show a connection between two events, conditions, or variables, X and Y. We must also understand the reasons for that connection: *why* more education leads to higher earnings. Without understanding the process, we have only gained an ability to predict Y from X. *Prediction* is the act of forecasting an outcome. In predicting, we infer the outcome of an event or series of events from scientific—especially statistical—analyses of known events.

For example, suppose we were trying to guess whether Hector earns more money than Angelo. We know that Hector completed Grade 12 and Angelo only completed Grade 9. Remembering our hypothesis that higher education usually means higher earnings, we predict that Hector earns more. If the hypothesis is valid, other things being equal, our prediction will be right. Nevertheless, we still have not explained the relationship.

In social research, the real world is more complicated. We almost never find an X that always causes Y or a Y that always results from X. Most of the processes social scientists study are *multi-causal* and *conditional*. By multi-causal, we mean that many Xs—independent variables—combine in complicated ways to produce a single Y—the dependent variable. By conditional, we mean that a particular X will cause Y under some conditions but not others.

The relationship between education and earning power is a case in point. Education is not the only factor to influence earnings. Many others, including gender, race, geography, and even physical appearance, also affect how much money a person makes. In addition, education has more influence on earnings in some kinds of work than others. Consider two people making hamburgers at a fast-food outlet. One has a Grade 9 education, the other a Grade 12 education. They are doing the same job and earning the same amount of money, so education does not affect earnings here. Higher education has the greatest effect when it allows a person to enter a restricted line of work—such as a skilled trade, a profession, or a managerial position—that pays higher-than-average wages. The benefits of education vary from one sector of the economy to another.

For these reasons, it's not easy to predict something as simple as how much money a person will earn. Explaining a finding is even harder. Explaining something well means understanding the entire process that ties X and Y together. So, to explain these relationships, social scientists collect data.

TWO KINDS OF DATA

Social scientists work with two types of measured data: quantitative and qualitative. Quantitative data are data to which number values can be assigned; qualitative data are those to which such values cannot be assigned. Some researchers regard qualitative data as inferior to quantitative data, capable of yielding little understanding of the phenomenon under study. Others, however, regard qualitative data as capturing more fully and accurately the "meaning" of observed phenomena than do numerical measurements that have been artificially imposed on reality.

On the one hand, it is clearly inadequate to say that Jani is taller than Marcus if we can accurately measure the difference with a number scale showing that Marcus is 200 centimetres tall and Jani is only 175 centimetres. On the other hand, it is undesirable to avoid topics simply because numerical measurement is impossible. For example, researchers may reasonably argue about whether the English Revolution arose out of religious, rather than political, dissatisfaction, without being able to attach numbers to the extent of each type of dissatisfaction.

Qualitative data, then, may be less precise, but in a certain sense more accurate, whereas quantitative data enable us to use the rigorous statistical methods common in the natural and physical sciences. Some believe the differences between these two types of data are even more encompassing: that the differences represent paradigms, or ways of viewing data and the world. We provide a comparison of these contrasting paradigms in Figure 4.1.

We have sharpened the distinction between these two paradigms here for the sake of comparison. In actual research, social scientists move back and forth between these two approaches, since each paradigm has particular strengths and weaknesses. Moreover, it may be possible to dispute some of the particulars in this model: for example, "obtrusive" does not always apply to the quantitative method—quantitative research can be unobtrusive too. Likewise, we might argue that one approach is not always subjective and the other objective, or that one is holistic and particularistic while the other one isn't. However, in broad strokes, most researchers would agree to these distinctions.

FIGURE 4.1 THE QUALITATIVE AND QUANTITATIVE PARADIGMS COMPARED

Qualitative Paradigm	Quantitative Paradigm
Advocates the use of qualitative methods.	Advocates the use of quantitative methods.
Naturalistic and uncontrolled observation.	Obtrusive and controlled measurement.
Subjective.	Objective.
Close to the data: the "insider" perspective.	Removed from the data: the "outsider" perspective.
Grounded, discovery-oriented, exploratory, expansionist, descriptive, and inductive.	Ungrounded, verification-oriented, confirmatory, reductionist, inferential, and deductive.
Process-oriented.	Outcome-oriented.
Valid: "real," "rich," and "deep" data.	Reliable: "hard" and replicable data.
Ungeneralizable: single case studies.	Generalizable: multiple case studies.
Holistic.	Particularistic.
Assumes a dynamic reality.	Assumes a stable reality.

SOURCE: Reichardt and Cook (1979). Reprinted by permission of Sage Publications, Inc.

Qualitative data are most appropriate when the question to be answered is a *how* question: *how does*, or *how did*, something come about? Quantitative research, as typified by the survey or experiment, is better at answering *what* and *why* questions. The first type of question—the *what* question—asks about stable properties or relationships: *What* kind of people vote for the Conservative party, buy SUVs, or marry outside their own ethnic group? *What* are the characteristics of societies that enjoy a high level of political participation, high productivity, or freedom of speech? Such research is hard pressed to explain *how* these characteristics came about, but it can accurately generalize about the chances that they will occur.

Quantitative research answers the question *why* (or *when*, or *where*) by specifying the conditions under which such events will occur. However, it will not show *how* they occurred in a particular time or place; for this, we depend on qualitative research. For example, quantitative research will show that college-educated women are twice as likely as high-school-educated women to marry outside their own ethnic group, but only qualitative research can help us understand *how* the women made the marriage choices they did: why these women were attracted to their spouses, and how they overcame their own and their families' prejudices.

This is not to argue that quantitative research can never enlighten us about the processes of interest to social scientists. The quantitative and qualitative paradigms, like most other paradigms, are best used as complements to one another, not as opponents. From qualitative research come rich insights and new ideas to be tested by rigorous quantitative methods. From quantitative research come generalizations to be fleshed out by the close study of single cases, especially cases that deviate from the general rule.

Social science research requires an interplay between these different types of data and data analysis. As Mahoney (1999) notes, the choice among different techniques of causal analysis reflects the role of scholarly tastes and skills, the research question, and ongoing research cycles. We will focus on quantitative approaches for the remainder of this chapter and look at qualitative approaches in Chapter 5.

QUANTITATIVE DATA

USES OF QUANTITATIVE RESEARCH

Data on amounts of education and earnings are examples of *quantitative data*. They are based on precise measurements in recognizable units. We can say exactly, in dollars and cents, how much a person earns. We can say exactly, in years, grades, or degrees and diplomas, how much education a person has completed. What is more, everyone knows what dollars and grades are, so we can easily share and discuss our findings. With such quantitative data, it is easy to *replicate* a study another researcher has done—to copy it to see if we get the same results. We know exactly what the earlier researcher was measuring and how.

In addition, such precise and clear-cut measures allow us to evaluate the results with powerful statistical methods. They allow us to judge whether our findings could have occurred by chance alone. Quantitative measures also let us compare the relative importance of the different independent variables that affect the dependent variable. Finally—and perhaps most importantly—they let researchers create mathematical models for their theory. In short, quantitative measures allow sociologists and political scientists to do research that is similar to research in economics and the physical sciences.

It is not simply that quantitative social science uses numerical measures of social variables. Beyond that, quantitative research is associated with a particular way of thinking about social life. Typical quantitative studies are narrowly focused on one part of the social structure. The researcher assumes that reality is stable and knowable, that reality does not flip around randomly: that precise hypotheses, when tested in a rigorous way, will yield reliable and replicable findings. Finally, the researcher assumes that such work will produce conclusions that we can generalize over time and from one social situation to another.

Much of quantitative research is obtrusive and controlling: the researcher sets the agenda through the questions being asked and the way he or she puts these questions. Concepts, when measured empirically, become variables in the model, and hypotheses are developed for empirical testing. The researcher then tests the hypotheses about these relations by collecting quantifiable data and examining relations between the variables. Statistical tests are used to decide whether the hypotheses are valid or not.

The result is a set of findings that is clear and unarguable (though there may be some shortcomings unaccounted for that must be "argued"). Consider, for example, the theory that people today place little importance on their extended family largely because they have less extended family—fewer uncles, aunts, nephews, nieces, and cousins—than people had a century ago. This is due to a continuing decrease in fertility over the last hundred years. There cannot be many uncles, aunts, and so on without many brothers and sisters a generation earlier, so low fertility always means fewer kin. In turn, fewer kin means more importance for the nuclear family. It may also mean more demands being placed on spouses and children for economic or emotional support. Perhaps it means a growth in the importance of friendship over kinship. It may also mean a growth in the value placed on relationships with those few relatives outside the nuclear family.

Note that these speculations, or hypotheses, are all logically related, testable with data, and possibly even correct. The best way of testing this theory is by collecting survey data on kinship relations in the past and comparing it with survey data on kinship relations in the present. Once the data are in, we can draw firm conclusions; there will be little room for doubt.

TYPES OF MEASUREMENT

Quantitative researchers rely on four levels of measurement: nominal, ordinal, interval, and ratio:

Nominal level. Nominal-level measures consist only of named categories, such as "Anglophone/Francophone/Other" or "male/female." These categories cannot be *arrayed* (i.e., displayed or arranged) on a scale running from most to least. They are incomparables, like apples and oranges.

Ordinal level. Ordinal-level categories can be arrayed on a scale from most to least, since they are all measured in the same units. For example, "big, bigger, biggest" is a range of sizes whose order we can know and communicate. We have no doubt that "biggest" has more size units (whatever these may be) than "big." What we don't know is whether the difference in size between "biggest" and "bigger" is the same as the difference in size between "bigger" and "big." For some purposes, this information may not be important. Often we cannot get the information. Typically, qualitative research is more likely to be carried out on variables at the nominal and ordinal levels of measurement.

Interval level. Interval-level measures are the ones most commonly used in quantitative social science research. Their categories are an equal distance, or interval, from one another. An example is the IQ test score. The *average* score for a population is 100. We assume the distance between the score of 100 and 110 has the same meaning as the distance between a score of 110 and 120. However, one never hears a researcher claiming that someone with an IQ of 140 is twice as smart as a person with an IQ of 70. For IQ scores, there is no absolute zero, meaning a complete lack of intelligence. Only such an absolute zero allows the comparison of two levels in the way just mentioned.

To state the same ideas another way, an interval scale is one in which we know where people rank on some attribute (such as intelligence); we know how far apart the people are from one another with respect to the attribute; but no information is available about the absolute size of the attribute for any person. Thus, an interval scale is an ordinal scale to which we have added information about the distance between ranks. What distinguishes the interval scale from the ratio scale is the lack of an absolute zero; this means that in an interval scale, we can only measure people in relation to one another.

Ratio level. Ratio-level scales measure such phenomena as height, weight, and income. Describing someone as twice as tall or rich as someone else is meaningful because we can imagine (and measure) a complete absence of height or money. Researchers often set up attitude measures to contain a zero score, so it is possible to claim that one person is twice as satisfied, for example, as someone else (since being "not at all satisfied" is possible).

To review these ideas about different scales, suppose that you are a teacher evaluating student papers. You may choose to put them into categories, labelling some "creative," others "well organized," others still "full of good information." These categories or labels are *nominal* measures of the students' achievement: they do not rank or grade them in relation to one another.

You would achieve a true *ordinal* measure if you graded the papers from best (first ranking) to worst (last ranking), with no or few ties at any rank. These are ordinally measured in the sense that you have ordered them from best to worst, but there is no hint either of how far apart the ranks are or of what absolute scores correspond to particular performances.

You would provide a *ratio* measure if you assigned each paper a grade from zero to one hundred. In this way, you would provide information not only on rank but also on how close students were to one another in their performance and how close they were to the minimum score of zero.

Finally, you would provide an *interval* measure if you graded each paper in relation to the group average. You might, for example, select the middle-ranking paper and assign it a score of 65 per cent. In a normal distribution, or what is sometimes called a "bell curve," two-thirds of the cases are one standard deviation away from the mean, and 95 per cent of cases are within two standard deviations. The teacher might arbitrarily decide to make the standard deviation 10 per cent, so that two-thirds of all student papers that surround the middle-ranking paper will receive grades between 55 and 75 per cent, and 95 per cent of all papers submitted will receive grades of between 45 and 85 per cent, with the remainder receiving grades of 40 to 90 per cent. Here, you have met the conditions for interval measurement: students are ranked in relation to one another, and we have specified the numerical distance between them. However, the relation between their grade and a true zero is not known (or is positively hidden). Teachers often grade on a curve in this way precisely because they do not believe that a test or assignment can validly include a score of zero.

Most statistical procedures in common use are designed for ratio or interval-level measures. However, ways of dealing statistically with ordinal- and nominal-level variables are coming into wider use.

SECONDARY ANALYSIS: READING A TABLE

Much of what the student researcher does is secondary data analysis: interpreting quantitative data that someone else has collected, often for other reasons. You may want to do a secondary analysis because no one has ever brought together the data you are collecting from separate studies, as you are doing. Or you may wish to verify or reinterpret someone else's conclusions. To do a proper secondary analysis, you should be able to read the tables in which such data are usually presented and arrange your own data in similar fashion.

The data in a table are arranged according to certain conventions. The dependent variable—the phenomenon to be explained—is represented in the horizontal rows of the tables, while the hypothesized cause is shown in the columns. Researchers then list the data as percentages down columns and compare percentages across rows to see the effects of the independent on the dependent variable. Table 4.1 presents imaginary data on the different tendencies of college- and high-school-educated women to marry within their ethnic group.

The data show that 40 out of 200 high-school-educated women (or 20 per cent) married outside their own ethnic group, whereas 80 out of 200 college-educated women (40 per cent)—twice as many—did so. This finding might support the explanation that higher education reduces prejudice and promotes attitudes that are more favourable to mixing ethnic, religious, and other distinctive social groups.

However, other explanations are reasonable. We can test them by adding variables to the table and rearranging the data. We call these extra variables *control variables*. Consider the counter-explanation that education does not so much change values as bring people from diverse origins into contact with one another. If this explanation is true, the role of higher education in ethnic assimilation is to prolong contact with people of diverse origins. Let us assume that we have data on whether these women met their spouses at school or elsewhere. We add this information and rearrange the data as in Table 4.2.

The data in this table show that when we control for where women met their spouses, the original difference in likelihood of a woman's marrying outside her ethnic group disappears. Women who met their spouses at high school are just

TABLE 4.1   THE LIKELIHOOD OF MARRYING OUT, BY LEVEL OF EDUCATIONAL ATTAINMENT

| | LEVEL OF EDUCATIONAL ATTAINMENT | | |
	High School Completed	College Completed	Total
Woman Marries In	160 (80)	120 (60)	280
Woman Marries Out	40 (20)	80 (40)	120
Total	200 (100)	200 (100)	400

*Percentages are in parentheses.

as likely to marry outside their group as women who met their spouses at college. Conversely, women who met their spouses elsewhere are just as *unlikely* to "marry out," whether or not they received higher education. This shows that the second hypothesis (that education prolongs contact with potential mates from different ethnic backgrounds) is the better explanation, and the first hypothesis (that education reduces prejudice) has no support in these data.

GETTING GOOD DATA

Much of the work you will do as a student will involve taking measurements from existing research studies and using them in your own research paper. Doing this well requires you to understand the basis of good measurement. Only with such an understanding can you judge which data are trustworthy (and worth using) and which are not. We will continue our discussion as though you were starting from scratch to design and carry out your own study. Here, too, you should keep in mind that it is just as important to apply these principles to the work of other researchers as it is to apply them to your own.

TABLE 4.2   THE LIKELIHOOD OF MARRYING OUT, BY LEVEL OF EDUCATIONAL ATTAINMENT AND WHERE WOMAN MET SPOUSE

	WHERE WOMAN MET SPOUSE			
	At School		Elsewhere	
	LEVEL OF EDUCATIONAL ATTAINMENT			
	High School	College	High School	College
Woman Marries In	25 (60)	75 (50)	135 (90)	45 (90)
Woman Marries Out	25 (50)	75 (50)	15 (10)	5 (10)
Total	50	150	150	50

*Percentages are in parentheses.

SUITING DATA TO YOUR THEORY

Suiting your data to your theory means doing two things. First, you must make sure that every variable in your hypothesis is measured by at least one set of data. For example, to test the explanation that age, education, and an overall awareness of political issues influence a person's tolerance of free speech on controversial matters, you must collect at least four pieces of information from each respondent: his or her age, educational attainment, stated level of political awareness, and stated tolerance of free speech.

Second, you must make sure you collect no more data than you need to test the theory. You can relax this rule as you become more experienced in research. For the newcomer, however, collecting too much presents two major dangers: it increases the time and other costs of the study, and it threatens to divert attention from the key variables. As a result, you may give too little attention to collecting good measures of your key variables. It is far better to collect two or three measures of each key variable and few extra pieces of information than to collect one measure for each of many variables that are less significant for the theory.

OPERATIONALIZATION

Operationalization is the part of the research cycle that takes the researcher from concepts to measures. More precisely, it is the process of specifying procedures or operations that will measure a concept named in the hypothesis to be tested. Indicators are selected to measure the conceptual variables

So, for example, the hypothesis that students who are more intelligent will have higher career aspirations than students who are less intelligent cannot be proven true or false until we define the key concepts "intelligent" and "career aspirations" *operationally* (i.e., as we intend to use and interpret them in the course of our research). If we define "intelligence" as "the score obtained by a student on the Wechsler IQ Test at the age of 14" and "career aspiration" as "the job a student hopes to hold at age 35, as measured by the Blishen occupational-status scale," we can then survey a sample of high-school students, calculate the correlation between measured intelligence and measured career aspiration, and determine whether that correlation is large or small. If large, we consider the data to have supported the hypothesis.

Researchers must take care to maintain a distinction between the concept and its measure. Some researchers and reviewers might argue that "intelligence" is more than what an IQ test measures: that it includes creativity and resourcefulness, for example: two qualities that many believe are penalized by the standard IQ test. Likewise, they might argue that "career aspiration" means more than a student's wished-for job status at age 35. To them, "career aspiration" may mean an entire pattern of work plans, not one attainment, or a concern with job satisfaction and autonomy, not merely income and prestige (which the Blishen scale measures).

Here the quarrel is not about the value of operationalization, but about whether the designated operations faithfully capture the meaning of the concepts the researcher has in mind. As a researcher, you must always take care, in doing your own work and in evaluating the work of others, to decide whether the planned operations for collecting data are enough to address the hypothesis as you originally imagined it.

PLAN WHERE YOUR DATA WILL COME FROM

Once you have decided what your key concepts and intended operations are, you must still specify where and how these operations are to be done. Things can get out of hand if more than two or three concepts are involved, with several measurements intended for each. You will find it useful to make a table to keep track of what you are doing. Let's try this now.

In the first column, list all the key concepts in your hypothesis. Consider the following hypothesis as an example: "The probabilities of migrating are proportional to the job opportunities in the place of destination and inversely proportional to the opportunities in the place of origin." The key concepts are "probability of migrating," "job opportunities," "place of destination," and "place of origin."

In the second column, list the corresponding measures or operations to be performed on the data. By "probability of migrating," do we mean chance based on a projection of migration figures for a given year, or chance based on the stated aim of current residents to migrate in the year ahead, or both, or neither? By "job opportunities," do we mean "job vacancies" or "expected job vacancies"? In either event, do we mean "all job vacancies" or "job vacancies in the line of work the respondent is used to doing"? When we speak of "place of destination" and "place of origin," do we mean to compare countries or smaller units—cities or provinces, for example? How we answer these questions will determine where we look for our data and how we measure them.

In the third column, specify the data source for each operation. If, for example, you are interested in measuring the chance of migration in terms of the measured migration between two countries (for example, Italy and Canada) during the past year, published or unpublished government statistics will be enough. If, however, you are interested in measuring intended migration in the coming year, you will need a survey; government statistics will not be adequate.

After completing the third column, you will know all the data sources that you must tap. You can then reorganize your information, putting the measures from column two into boxes defined by the data sources noted in column three. By doing this, you decide which two, three, or more questions you need to find answers to in the government statistics; which two, three, or more questions to ask in a survey of current residents; and so on.

If certain data sources (such as the plans and attitudes of Italian residents) are not available, certain operations are going to be impossible. You must then decide whether what remains possible—here, an analysis of government statistics—will be enough to answer the question you originally set out to answer.

Once you have created a means of collecting information, such as a questionnaire, you will find it useful to go through it and label all the questions to see how they contribute to testing your hypothesis. Remember that one or more items should be used to measure all concepts, and that you should eliminate items that have no relevance to your theory.

DEFINE YOUR CATEGORIES BEFOREHAND

Before designing questionnaires or other devices for collecting information, good researchers list the categories of their variables and may even draw up mock tables based on their expected results. These steps direct them to proper measurement; for example, to the proper wording of questions. With complex, multi-dimensional ideas such as social class, job satisfaction, or quality of life, doing so may even suggest added questions to ask.

SURVEY DESIGN

The survey is the most common type of quantitative research in social science. Its purpose is to generalize about the relationships among variables in a population. That population can be an entire nation or city, or some designated portion of all people: for example, all voters, car buyers, parents, schoolchildren, and so on.

Survey reasoning begins by showing differences in the likelihood that certain subgroups will behave in certain ways: that college-educated women will marry out proportionally more often than high-school-educated women, for example, or that labourers will be more likely to vote NDP than owners of small businesses, or that people will more readily migrate out of areas of higher unemployment.

The data are tabulated as in Table 4.1. Then we introduce control variables, as in Table 4.2, for one of two purposes. If the first bivariate (two-variable) table shows a relationship between the independent and dependent variable, the purpose of introducing a control variable is to make that relationship decrease or disappear. If repeated attempts to make the relationship disappear fail, we assume the first relationship is valid. If introducing a control variable weakens the original relationship, this means either that the control variable is intervening in the effect of the independent variable on the dependent variable, or that it is before both. This fact will force us to refine our theoretical model to include the new variable.

In the example given earlier, our data show that attendance at an educational institution is one of possibly many experiences that will increase a person's exposure to people of other ethnic groups. This does not eliminate educational attendance from our model. It merely changes its meaning and forces us to look for other experiences that would also increase exposure to potential mates from different ethnic groups.

There is a second reason for adding control variables, especially where the original table reveals no relationship between the independent and dependent variable. That is to learn what factors, if any, may be suppressing a relationship we had expected to find in the data. Recall the example (page 14–15) of the effect of marriage on suicide-proneness. The data showed that suicide rates are highest for married women and unmarried men. Thus, in a survey of equal numbers of men and women, marriage will have no clear effect on suicide; but, if we control for the gender of the respondent, the effect will be strongly positive for women and strongly negative for men.

A recent survey by Plotnick and Hoffman (1999) used an ingenious method to discover the relative effects of family and neighbourhood on young people's social and economic outcomes. To control for the effects of family of origin, it compared sisters who lived in different neighbourhoods. Each pair of sisters would have had a common family, even if they later lived in different neighbourhoods.

Finding a third variable that will help to reveal, elaborate, or interpret a first relationship between two variables is an important part of survey-data analysis. Increasingly, researchers rely on social science computing programs, or software, to carry out such analysis.

SOCIAL SCIENCE COMPUTING PROGRAMS

To a large degree, twentieth-century changes in survey (and other quantitative) research in social science were driven by the development and spread of computers, especially small personal computers. They enable researchers to carry out data exploration and analysis well beyond what was possible for the founders of social science in the nineteenth and earlier centuries.

However, computers are merely machines. What makes computers useful is their software, and here also we find revolutionary advances. In the last 30 years, the development and spread of a few easy-to-use software packages, like SPSS and SAS, has revolutionized the way researchers—professionals and students alike—analyze data. These packages are important because they make it easy for people with little or no understanding of computers to define their variables of interest in a data set and then carry out sophisticated data analyses, of which they may have no technical (but a reasonable conceptual) understanding. What's more, these analyses are often carried out nearly instantly and at no cost (once we factor in the cost of the computer and a license to use the software).

Students just starting out in social science will have little sense of how radical, and recent, these developments are, but their professors will probably remember the days of punchcards and mainframe computers. In the 1950s, much social analysis was done with mechanical adding machines. In the 1960s, analysis was carried out by punch cards in large mainframe computers, which required a detailed understanding of "machine language" that few social scientists had. In the 1960s and 1970s, the first user-friendly social science languages appeared, enabling researchers to create tables and perform basic statistical analyses with relative ease. It was not until the 1980s, with the rapid development and falling cost of personal computers, that new software made data analysis truly "democratic."

Small, affordable machines were faster and much more powerful than the early mainframe computers. With the new software, it was possible to analyze huge amounts of data—many thousands of cases, with hundreds of variables—in various different ways. Like word processing software, which has made revising manuscripts quick and painless, new software designed for data analysis has made data exploration quick and painless, enabling people to explore more data more thoroughly.

The downside of such innovations is that when technology makes something affordable and easy, some people are likely to use it in foolish, thoughtless ways. For instance, the explosion in word processing has produced more—and, perhaps, even better-edited—books and articles, but it hasn't produced more Shakespeares. It has probably produced more potboilers though, since it has lowered the cost of entering into "authorship" for people who may be untalented.

Also, the democratization of data analysis through easy-to-use software has improved the speed at which we analyze data and may have increased the quality of good research by good researchers. However, it has probably increased (by a larger fraction) the proliferation of poor research by poor researchers, since it has dramatically cut the cost of data analysis. Under most circumstances, it costs no more to produce ten thousand correlation coefficients than to produce one. This means we are deluged by more correlation coefficients, as well as more tables, charts, diagrams and—at the other end—more complex, confusing statistical models and their outputs. Besides, the laws of probability tell us that mere chance will throw up convincing relationships in any body of data if we calculate enough correlations. Thus, not only do we run the risk of wasting our time with too many calculations, we also risk fooling ourselves.

For better or worse, developing SPSS and other data analysis packages has transformed social science within the reader's lifetime. Statistics software designed to help data analysis can be of great help to the professional or student social scientist, but only if used to support a well-reasoned argument. Technology can assist, but should never replace, the methods used to conduct proper research.

CHOOSING STATISTICAL SOFTWARE

Much research has now been done on these statistical packages. This research reveals that, because of differing assumptions, different packages will sometimes produce different p (probability) values from the same set of data (see, for example, Bergmann, Ludbrook, and Spooren, 2000). They vary in general ease of use and flexibility in formatting (Moshiri, 1999), and differ in their target audiences, interfaces, capabilities, and approaches (Oster, 1998). An entire issue of *The American Statistician* was devoted to assessing the reliability of statistical software packages in such routine operations as random number generation, correlations, and analysis of variance (see McCullough, 1998, 1999). Since then, assessments of statistical packages have become available in a variety of sources on the Internet. Even more impressive is the variety of free non-commercial software found easily on the Net. For example, see http://www.hmdc.harvard.edu/micah_altman/socsci.shtml.

The conclusion: the software used to analyze survey data, like any other software, is available in a wide assortment of packages that vary in what they will do and how well they will do it. New packages and features are changing all the time, making them difficult to cover in a book revised only every few years. To get the package that best suits your needs, you have to be a wise consumer of statistical software. Do some research online, or through discussions with your instructors, to discover the differences among the various packages. Once armed with this information, you can go out and get the software package that is best for your needs.

TYPES OF SAMPLING

No one carries out surveys on entire populations; that would cost too much. Researchers typically sample from the population they are interested in to get a representative picture of certain relationships in it. The science of statistics has refined sampling procedures to a high degree. Armed with the proper know-ledge, researchers can know in advance how large an error they are likely to make in generalizing to total populations from small samples.

Sampling statistics tell us how much confidence to have in our findings from a survey sample and, conversely, how many people would have to be sampled to raise our confidence to an acceptable degree. Repeated use of samples in polit-ical polls, market surveys, and other purely academic research has shown that we can attach a high degree of credibility to the findings of a well-conducted sample survey.

Central to conducting a good survey is drawing a good sample. Not only must the sample be large enough to provide the level of confidence needed, given the size of the population, it must be selected by procedures that are un-biased. The least biased surveys are based on random samples, in which respon-dents are drawn in a way that minimizes the under-representation of certain types of people.

There are several types of random sampling. Some are more suitable (or more practical) in certain types of research than others:

Pure random sampling. The researcher begins with a listing of all the people in the population, assigns each person an identification number, and then uses a table of random numbers (or a computerized random-number generator) to select the specific cases to be studied.

Systematic random sampling. In this equally unbiased procedure, the researcher randomly selects the first case and then every n^{th} case after that. So, for example, if we were randomly sampling the telephone directory, which we knew contained 600,000 entries, and we wanted to sample 500 cases, we would select the first case randomly from the first 100,000 numbers, then take every thousandth case after that one.

Stratified random sampling. Here the researcher divides the population into subpopulations of interest, such as male and female, and samples randomly within each subpopulation. This procedure ensures the resulting sample will contain a pre-decided number of males and females (which we cannot ensure with simple random sampling), yet will be unbiased in other respects.

Random sampling is not always possible, however. In such cases, the fol-lowing sampling techniques are used:

Quota sampling. Consider the problem of drawing an unbiased sample of unemployed workers: there is no list of all workers who are unemployed at a given moment for the researcher to draw on. Therefore, the best strategy is to sample the population randomly and reject all cases that do not meet the needs of the study: those who are nonworkers or who are workers and are employed. This technique, though not strictly random, is unbiased and can be used, with certain adjustments, to represent adequately the population of unemployed workers.

Availability sampling. This procedure, which is inexpensive and commonly used but far from random, consists of selecting respondents who are available to a researcher standing on a street corner or in a shopping mall. The results obtained by this method can only be considered suggestive, since all sorts of potentially important factors will enter into determining who happens to pass by the researcher on a given day. On the other hand, if you are studying people who are normally hard to find through standard sampling and interviewing techniques—for example, young male members of minority groups who live in poor neighbourhoods—you can carry out this sort of sampling in locations where you think you are most likely to find these people, who might be difficult to involve in your sample otherwise.

Snowball sampling. This technique is also not random and is potentially biased. A starting sample of respondents gives the researcher the names of others who might participate in the study, and the sample grows like a snowball rolling downhill. This technique is widely used where the behaviour under study is rare or illicit—for example, drug use or criminal activity—although it is not limited to these cases. Like availability sampling, it provides findings that are suggestive but far from conclusive; it is useful where cost and time, and other reasons for the inaccessibility of cases, would otherwise make the research impossible. It is potentially biased because it will only sample people who are members of the networks that contain the first few people sampled. At worst, if you begin the sampling with atypical or unusual people, you will end up with an atypical or unusual sample overall. At best, the sample will be unrepresentative, though interesting.

THE ROLE OF TIME SEQUENCE

In using survey data for explanations, time sequence is critical because a cause must come before its supposed effect. Something that happens *after* a particular effect cannot be considered its cause unless we had anticipated or actively sought the effect, and its anticipation is therefore a cause.

Independent variables working at the same time as dependent variables are hard to organize into a causal explanation: they require a systemic design. Independent variables that work before the dependent variable are easier to handle.

Consider the problem of explaining educational attainment. Suppose the independent variables in a particular study are social class at birth, intelligence (or IQ), gender, and parental encouragement. All of these variables influence educational attainment. Some may be more significant earlier in a person's life, some later, but they are all influential before the completion of a university degree. They can, therefore, be causal influences on the completion of a university degree.

Some types of explanatory design deal with time sequence more effectively than others. Experiments and quasi-experiments are best, since by experimentally manipulating the independent variable, the researcher can ensure that the supposed cause precedes the measured effect. Next most sensitive to time are *longitudinal studies*, which follow a particular group, organization, or society over time, to see which changes occur first, which later. The earlier changes are not necessarily the causes of the later ones, but they may be, whereas the later changes can never be the causes of the earlier ones. A problem that arises in the longitudinal study of collectivities—families, groups, or communities, for example—is finding a way to study, simultaneously, changes in the collectivity itself (i.e., as a system of interrelated parts) and changes in each of the parts (for example, the family members as individuals).

Cross-sectional retrospective studies are less sensitive to time sequence. They collect data in the present, but ask people to recall things that happened at earlier times in their lives, so the researcher can analyze the recalled sequence of events. Retrospective studies are less reliable than longitudinal studies because people tend to forget or distort the past, often dramatically. They have often created their own explanation about why something happened, and their theory may lead them to forget or suppress facts that violate it. Recent developments in oral history and sociology suggest methods of collecting retrospective data that may minimize recall bias (Blane, 1996).

Cross-sectional correlational studies are the least sensitive to time sequence, but they are the most common because they are the least costly and difficult to carry out. Some of these ignore time sequence entirely and look only for strong associations between variables, from which causation is assumed. Thus, if highly paid workers prove to be more satisfied with their jobs than poorly paid workers (other things being equal), researchers might infer that higher pay *produces* greater satisfaction: that an increase in pay would result in an increase in employee satisfaction. However, the data justify none of these inferences, since they do not show that satisfied, highly paid workers were dissatisfied before receiving an increase in pay.

A more satisfactory version of the cross-sectional design compares units (i.e., people, groups, organizations, or societies) at different stages. For example, if older workers (or people with more job seniority) are more satisfied than younger ones (or people with less seniority), we might infer that aging (or increasing seniority) increases job satisfaction. In a similar sense, if industrial societies value education more highly than non-industrial ones, we might infer that, over time, the process of industrialization has changed the value placed on education. In each instance, the researcher assumes the unit at a later stage was once identical in all important respects to the current earlier-stage social unit, but changed with the passage of time: with aging, seniority, industrialization, and so on. Such assumptions are rarely warranted, but are often made. They are at the root of all evolutionary theories of society, most stage theories of human behaviour, and many theories of organizational change.

The survey design that we have been discussing in much of this chapter is, typically, a cross-sectional design, based on data collected on a single occasion. It is therefore subject to all the problems about attributing causation that we have been discussing. You should understand these problems because, as a researcher, you will be bombarded daily with the results and interpretations of survey data. And while some of the problems of survey analysis are resolved or reduced by qualitative data collection, this basic issue of attributing causation remains a problem, as we shall see.

CLOSING COMMENTS

In this chapter we have explored issues that quantitative researchers must address before, during, and after gathering their data. When well conceived and properly executed, quantitative research can reveal complex relationships between multiple variables and provide powerful insights into social phenomena. However, such research—even when flawlessly performed—has its limits.

In the next chapter, we will explore qualitative research. Although less objective than quantitative research, qualitative research—by dealing with people as people, not statistics—can provide many answers and insights that quantitative research can never reveal.

chApter 5

USING QUALITATIVE DATA

Qualitative data analysis, or what is more often called the "interpretive approach to social science research," has become much more popular in the last twenty years. Inductivist, process-oriented, and rooted in the constructionist paradigm, it is an approach that examines the *what*, *how*, and *why* of social life.

Researchers following the qualitative model, as opposed to the quantitative model, hardly ever use numbers to measure the variables in their theories; in fact, they rarely talk about "variables." They are, partly because of this, more open to understanding the real world in terms of unique cases to be studied individually rather than as a mere set of units or events. Qualitative researchers are more inclined to use their data to explore and describe these individual cases than to produce statistically sound conclusions. They are more concerned with how an entire pattern of thinking and acting fits together, with the uniqueness and changeability of the situation they are studying, and with the strange interplay between their own consciousness as observers and the consciousness of the people they are studying.

While quantitative data may tell us objectively that variables X and Y combine to produce result Z, this objectivity comes at a high price—the removal of the very subject of inquiry, individual human beings. Statistical research sees numbers, not people; it does not care if people do what they do because they are happy or sad, or if ambition or despair or any one of a million other human characteristics motivate them.

Qualitative research takes the opposite approach, exploring relationships intimately and on many levels. This style of thinking is particularly useful in carrying out case studies, whether the subject is a family, work organization, community, or nation. Qualitative data, as we mentioned in Chapter 4, are most suitable for answering *how* questions: *how does*, or *how did*, something come about? For example, how do Aboriginal people assimilate to city life in Canada? How have small organizations adjusted to the introduction of computers? How did universal literacy affect the everyday life of English working people? How do gays and lesbians deal with living in a world dominated by heterosexuals? We can answer none of these questions without understanding the consciousness of the subjects, their subtle social relationships, and the changes and read-justments these people make at each stage of the process under consideration.

TYPES OF QUALITATIVE RESEARCH

There are various methods of collecting and analyzing qualitative data. The following are a few of them.

INTERVIEWING

Interviews can be used to collect both quantitative and qualitative data. While quantitative researchers use a formal, structured interview to collect precisely the data they need, qualitative researchers use a less structured or even non-directive interview to explore a much broader range of variables: the thoughts and feelings of the subjects.

While considered unscientific by some, informal interviews can reveal much that formal interviews cannot. Consider, for example, a survey designed to explore the reasons some abused women remain in relationships with their abusive partners. It is hard to imagine a survey that could really illuminate the complexities of such relationships. Nevertheless, with an experienced interviewer in the right interview setting, it may be possible for a woman to feel comfortable enough to open up and discuss her fears, hopes, and plans to change her situation.

Such interviewing is difficult: the interviewer must establish a rapport with the subject before he or she will open up. Developing this rapport is essential to qualitative research, yet we cannot teach this skill in any textbook. Researchers must often use their intuition about how to effectively and ethically persuade the interviewee to talk openly. Keep in mind that some interviewees will have an easier time relating to some researchers than to others. To continue with our example of abused women, a female interviewer may have more success drawing out an abused woman than a male interviewer would.

Interviewers must also be aware that, when interviewed, people have a tendency to try to guess what the researcher is looking for and provide the desired answer. They may also (consciously or unconsciously) bias their answers to make themselves look good. Unfortunately, a researcher can do little to prevent this. However, a researcher who recognizes this tendency in the results of a study can take it into account when evaluating the data.

FOCUS GROUPS

Focus groups are used to interview a group of unrelated subjects about their feelings on a certain topic, event, or person. For example, a focus group might be used to collect several people's opinions about a political candidate or a product.

What focus group data lacks in depth, compared to the data a researcher can collect in a one-on-one interview, it makes up for in breadth. The interaction between the individuals creates much more dynamic results than a single interview, with each member continuing, expanding on, or offering counter-examples to the comments of the others. However, often people are reluctant to share personal or confidential information in front of complete strangers. As in interviews, subjects may try to provide the expected answer or express opinions that conform to the prevailing attitudes in the group. The experienced researcher will provide enough direction to a group to ensure that he or she hears various opinions, but not so much direction that natural exchanges are stifled.

Focus groups and group interviews have emerged as a popular technique for gathering qualitative data, both among sociologists and across a wide range of academic and applied research areas. Focus groups may be used as the only basis for a study, or in combination with surveys and other research methods, especially individual in-depth interviews. Under the best conditions, focus groups strengthen the validity of other data-collection methods—for example, questionnaires—by highlighting concerns held by real people that would otherwise have been neglected (Powell, Single, and Lloyd, 1996).

The following are some examples of focus group research:

- Researchers studying gender have used focus groups to examine the reasons adolescent girls in the US are reluctant to take part in outdoor recreation (Culp, 1998); the reasons for son preference among Pakistani women (Winkvist and Akhtar, 2000); and the ways the Chinese define and regard violence against women in Hong Kong (Tang, Wong, and Cheung, 2000).
- Researchers studying sexuality have used focus groups to examine attitudes towards female sex workers (Peracca, Knodel, and Saengtienchai, 1998) and extramarital sex (Vanlandingam, Knodel, and Saengtienchai, 1998) in Thailand; the ways men and women in Zimbabwe talk about sexual matters, with consequences for condom use and HIV/AIDS issues (Kesby, 2000); and dating violence in a New Zealand sample of senior high school students (Jackson, Cram, and Seymour, 2000).
- Researchers studying health have used focus groups to examine knowledge and attitudes among American women from low-income neigh-

bourhoods about the risk factors of cardiovascular disease (Mein and Winkleby, 1998); the choice of child delivery sites among pregnant women in Uganda (Amooti and Nuwaha, 2000); the meanings of traditional healing in Nigeria (Offiong, 1999); and the stigmatizing of tuberculosis patients in Pakistan (Liefooghe, Michiels, and Habib, 1995).

The advantages of focus groups can be increased through careful attention to research design issues. There are, however, some disadvantages to focus group research. For instance, few standards have been developed so far for reporting or evaluating focus group research findings (Morgan, 1996), and there is also a danger that focus groups are misused, for example, as an inappropriate alternative to opinion polls during elections (Gaber, 1996). Among other problems, the findings of focus groups can be manipulated by altering the composition of these groups (Unger, 1999).

However, focus groups allow a fuller range of perspectives to be studied simultaneously. In future, focus group research may even be conducted by video conferencing as "virtual groups" so members will not have to travel long distances to personally attend these meetings (Heather, 1994).

ETHNOGRAPHY

Ethnographic research has many definitions, but in essence it consists of trying to understand a culture from the insider's perspective. From this standpoint, it is a means of learning about social situations, the way they develop and change, and the way other insiders view them (Brunt, 1999). Classically, ethnography has been rooted in the study of real people interacting naturalistically with one another (Adler and Adler, 1999).

Unlike participant observation, to which it is related, ethnography is sometimes also concerned with setting up new research ethics and inventing new moral discourses (Gans, 1999). Often, ethnographers are immersed in the injustice and oppressions of their time, and they try to challenge the reader to reconsider his or her moral outlook (Denzin, 1999). To do ethnographic research, the researcher abandons strict objectivity and gets inside the study environment. Ethnography, in this way, accomplishes the twin goals of scholarship and engagement.

If the researcher is not already a member of the subculture being studied, guides or informants must be used to gain entrance to the community and to learn its rules of conduct so that the researcher will not immediately reveal him- or herself as an outsider. Long-term intensive fieldwork is the main method of ethnography, which is interactional, interdependent, and collaborative (Trujillo, 1999). However, ethnography is often effectively combined with interviews of members of the subculture to gain a deeper understanding of the norms, folkways, mores, and rules of the society and the observed behaviours of its members. Document and content analysis (discussed below) can add another dimension to the researcher's understanding. The ethnographic researcher is, in anthropologist Levi-Strauss's sense of the term, a *bricoleur*—someone who uses whatever is at hand to solve problems (Hammersley, 1999).

Fieldwork, which we discuss further in the next section, is essential to the study of culture and to defining anthropology as an ethnographic discipline (Mintz, 2000). However, ethnography is not limited to anthropology: sometimes we cannot do social science research any other way. We cannot understand many subcultures without reliable ethnographic data. It is ethnographic research that gives us, for example, insights into how articles of clothing or jewellery can show gang affiliation or sexual orientation. Similarly, ethnographic research gives us a bottom-up sense of poverty and how welfare policy actually works, by using case studies, interviewing, and naturalistic observation (Curtis, 1999).

Consider, as an example, studying a radical underground political movement. Information gained by attending and observing meetings could be put in a more detailed context by talking to others at the meetings and examining any literature (pamphlets, posters, etc.) being distributed or displayed. However, there is no formula to follow in order to achieve the best results.

Ethnographic research has some drawbacks. It can be used to show that a theory is reasonable, but it can never prove a theory because the research is too specific—it does not lend itself to generalization. There are also many ethical problems associated with this kind of research. For example, what do you do when you learn, through your research on gangs, that someone is going to be robbed, deliberately injured, or even killed? You must also consider that you are doing research without the consent of those being studied, and that you may cause harm to the group or some of its members by doing so.

Other ethical and moral issues are unavoidable. For example, there was controversy surrounding the ethnographic work of one anthropologist, Napoleon Chagnon, and his alleged distortions of fact in writing about the Yanomami Indians of the remote Venezuelan/Brazilian frontier (on this, see Tierney, 1999). In his efforts to prove and publicize the violent inclinations of this indigenous people, Chagnon may have influenced the social environment in a way that made violence more likely. For example, by introducing new resources (and competition for these resources) into an otherwise tranquil situation, it may be that he exaggerated both the violence he saw and the reasons for it. The debate about this among anthropologists illustrates how important it is that ethnography be unobtrusive and self-aware, both to protect the people and cultures studied and to have some chance of discovering "the truth" about cultures.

Many researchers believe that the value and vitality of ethnographic work lies not so much in truth claims as in making interesting connections and in offering new perspectives on important issues. Among other things, the best ethnographies give voice to the experiences of people who might not otherwise be heard and respect the complexity and ambiguity of social life. Ethnographers deal with important questions about the illusion of truth and the impossibility of ever describing reality (Karp, 1999).

As a result, an interesting dynamic has developed at the border between ethnography and narrative. *Narrative analysis* is used to examine the various commentaries, conversations, and stories that are heard in everyday life. Ethnography offers a more long-term study of a group of people to find out about the patterns of their social lives. There is considerable overlap between the two, but there has also been a growing recognition of the difference. The challenge is learning to walk the border between these two disciplines and learn from the tensions between social conditions, voice, and authorial ambitions (Gubrium and Holstein, 1999).

FELD OBSERVATION

All ethnography requires *field observation*—that is, in-place, naturalistic, and unobtrusive observation, as opposed to experimental, manipulated observation. An especially important kind of field observation is participant observation, which is particularly useful for studying small populations that exist outside the mainstream. It relies on the systematic collection and recording of a wide range of observed and overheard data.

Ethnographers using field observation hope to provide detailed, credible accounts of the situations they are viewing: in particular, accounts of the techniques by which participants understand their worlds—that is, the processes and principles by which people make sense of reality (Fine, 1999). Note however, that self-presentation and the elimination of boundaries separating the investigator from those under study pose problems. As a result, the nature of the research enterprise affords only the illusion of inclusiveness and openness: in the end, the researcher is still an outsider.

When you conduct qualitative research in the field, it is important that you record your data carefully and organize them in such a way that you can retrieve them easily for later use. Once again, we must stress how important it is to keep track of the chronology of data collection, for two reasons. First, if the research is concerned with the unfolding of some social process—such as the adjustment of a community to disaster, the assimilation of an immigrant family, or the reorganization of a business enterprise—the timing and stages of the observed process will be as important as the character of the changes. Second, as an observer, you yourself are taking part in the process, and your understanding of it will change with time. Your field notes will record these changes. To keep track of changes in your own understanding, it is important to date all your observations for further reflection.

Field notes, related documents, and collected artifacts (for example, memos, art, photographs) must thoroughly record the experiences and observations of the researcher. Conversations conducted or overheard should be noted in enough detail to both capture the meaning and importance of major events and illustrate them for a reader. Behaviours observed and inferences drawn from these behaviours should be noted and interpreted. Do not leave these notes and other materials for interpretation at the end of the project. Instead, examine them recurrently as you look for major ideas, themes, and symbols by which to characterize the complex environment you are observing.

To make sure that you do not become lost in the mass of detail, it is a good idea to recall the central goals of your project periodically: what you were looking for when you went into the field and what you have found so far. Remember that in the end, you will be summarizing your findings in terms of the underlying structures and central relationships in the group or culture you have studied.

As an example of field observation, consider the study of a juvenile court conducted as a doctoral dissertation. The court was part of a larger network of relationships that included police, truant officers, probation and parole officers, psychiatrists, and school principals, among others. This court was responsible for making hundreds of decisions every year and recommending treatments. It also had to contend with pressures from various sources: from the community, for measures to control delinquency; from children's parents, for leniency; from lawyers, for due process; and so on. Yet the written law provided little guidance on how juveniles should be handled: a juvenile could be dismissed, given a suspended sentence, or sent to reform school, among other things, depending on how the judge and others viewed the child, the child's record of offences so far, and his or her prospects for reform.

What made the situation even more complex was that professional participants brought conflicting expectations to their decision making. The police, for example, were part of a professional subculture with values and behaviours different from—indeed, opposed to—those of the psychiatrists. Where the police were dispassionate and inclined to punish "for the child's own good," the psychiatrists were typically more theoretical, tolerant, and concerned with the child's mental health. Where the lawyers were largely concerned with matters of procedure and evidence, the probation officers were more concerned with family pathology and the overall well-being of the child, whatever the evidence of his or her wrongdoing.

The research asked, How does a judge make decisions in such a confusing context? And how do the various participants adjust to one another's views to make possible the provision of justice and treatment year after year? Answering these questions required the researcher to watch the court for many months, to listen for clues of conflict and accommodation, and to talk to the participants to get their views of what would happen and why. It involved visiting police stations and riding in police cars to get to know the officers, sifting through informal police records on offences unknown to the court, drinking many coffees with probation officers to get a sense of their viewpoint, and becoming a known fixture in the court. Records of past offenders, other people's analyses of this and other court systems, and scholarly writings on juvenile justice all had to be assimilated. Once the researcher had gained a general familiarity with the system, he could ask more pointed questions in private interviews and enjoy a reasonable likelihood of getting honest answers.

Several key problems must be solved in such research. You must get close enough to the situation to understand it, yet stay distant enough to see it objectively. And you must be familiar and friendly enough with the participants to win their trust and co-operation, yet detached enough to avoid being drawn into their intrigues and conflicts. Participant observers always have to take a stance with one section of a community over another, and such choices have political and social consequences.

How the observer gains entry into such a group is itself problematic. If you arrive as a figure of authority or a representative of some institution, some members of the group will be reluctant to reveal their true feelings and attitudes to you for fear of punishment. On the other hand, if you arrive without any group contact or other source of legitimacy, the people you plan to observe will have little incentive to co-operate with you. College and university students are often in the best position to study a group, since they can claim a general interest without having to commit themselves to any particular belief or faction. The prevailing view in social science today is that a researcher should let the group know that he or she is a researcher on a data-gathering mission (for example, with the purpose of writing a term paper for a course). Secrecy about identity and general purpose is unacceptable; however, the researcher is under no obligation to provide a detailed description of his or her purpose, theories, and expectations—in fact, doing so would be inadvisable.

Once inside the research situation, however, you must move quickly to connect with the main factions, such as the leader or leaders and key informants—people who will give you a rapid introduction to the way things work (from their standpoint) and the key players.

As the discussion of Chagnon shows, it is important to avoid intruding on the way the group normally functions. You must be careful to avoid hints and body language that give away your purposes. You should be quick to listen and slow to talk; present, but not necessarily noticed; and slow to form and express judgments about the group and its members. Nothing sinks a field project faster than interfering with the group's way of thinking and doing things. At the very least, such intrusiveness will change the situation you have come to study; in the worst case, it may result in your expulsion.

Social scientists have long known that their mere presence may influence group functioning. What has come to be called the "Hawthorne Effect" is the production of changes (especially improvements) in group behaviour by the mere process of observation, which is taken as a sign of interest in the well-being of the group. For this reason any researcher (in field situations especially, though not exclusively) should seek to measure the social processes under study as unobtrusively as possible.

DOCUMENT ANALYSIS

Document analysis, or documentary research, is especially common in history and political science. It aims to examine and interpret original written records as data about the activities and beliefs of a person or group not otherwise available to the researcher. Such documents may include speeches, books, and essays by eminent figures; parliamentary debates; pamphlets, magazines, and other popular writing; and even legends, folk tales, and art.

The first concern in documentary analysis is to confirm the authenticity of the document. Did Mister X really give this speech at such and such a time and place, or was it someone else, or at another time and place? Suppose you wish to record the increasing radicalism of some political leader or group by using speeches and other written materials. It will make a lot of difference whether a given speech really was written and delivered by the person to whom we credit it; and, here, whether it came before or after another speech that suggests a greater or lesser degree of radicalism.

The second concern in document analysis is to discover the meaning of the document, which may be obscure. Perhaps the document originally appeared in a foreign language. Can you afford to risk reading a translation, or must you learn to read it in the original language? Another concern relates to references to contemporary events, persons, and writings. You cannot fully understand any document unless you are familiar with the people, events, and ideas it refers to. Without being able to immerse yourself in the place and period you are studying, you must read other sources to get the essential background.

A superficial understanding of the words and references in the document is not enough. You also need to understand the nuances, unstated assumptions, and local meanings hidden in the document. What is meant if the document refers to an eminent figure—the king, for example—as "dashing" and "gallant" but not "wise" or "good," or to parliament as "overcautious" or "foolhardy," or to a piece of legislation as "radical"? Surely what is "good," "overcautious," "foolhardy," or "radical" in one context may not be considered so in another time and place. Therefore you must first understand the shadings of meaning in the document, and then place these shadings of meaning in relation to contemporary views and debates.

Two main approaches are available. One is to examine prevailing interpretations of the document in question: how other researchers have interpreted the document, and the reasons for their interpretations. Every documentary interpretation means applying a theory about what was going on at another time and place. As a theory, it is never the final word on the subject, but it may be helpful or suggestive to the new researcher.

The other approach is to examine supporting documents: other written materials by the same person or group, originating at the same time and place. The concept of "construct validity"—the tendency of measures of the same underlying phenomenon to point in the same direction—is no less important in documentary research than in the survey kind. If you understand one document to say that a certain figure was disloyal, sacrilegious, radical, or ambitious, for example, you should support your interpretation with other contemporary materials affirming the same thing, or at least expressing similar concerns.

When you undertake documentary research, you are in many respects subject to the same constraints as an anthropologist studying a new culture, a sociologist who has begun observing a juvenile gang, or a political scientist trying to make sense of stated attitudes towards a political party by some group with which he or she has little familiarity. Like them, you must learn the language and unspoken assumptions in which the document is grounded; make and test theoretical interpretations about what you are observing; and test these interpretations for coherence against other information you may have: other documents, other types of information about the society in which the document appeared, and other scholarly interpretations of the same document, group, and society.

HISTORICAL ANALYSIS

Developing historical explanations of social life, using historical data, has become much more popular in all the social sciences in the last thirty years. To a superficial degree, we covered the problems of historical analysis in the previous section on document analysis, since most historical research relies on historical documents. However, more needs to be said; historical analysis, like all social analysis, is enmeshed in prevailing ideologies and beliefs. The field of historiography, which we will now briefly discuss, is concerned with the problems we have separating true historical "fact" from mere belief.

Webb (1998) compares the writing of history to the writing of an accident report. In accident reports, as in historical accounts, the outcomes determine the antecedents: that is, we know in advance what we have to explain, and we organize our understanding of past events so they converge in the present. Clearly, such analyses are subject to the purposes and expertise of the observer. The true causes of accidents (and any other historical events) may be infinite in number and go back infinitely far. The framework of our search depends on how we define the event, and the framework we use may contain gaps or distraction. The methods for causal selection are poorly developed and the methods of proof lack objectivity.

Selectivity and subjectivity pervade the writing of historical accounts, from how key facts are chosen to how these facts are combined into a story. The selective and subjective nature of writing historical accounts blurs the boundaries between gossip and historiography, and assessing historical accounts is a subjective exercise, too (Wishart, 1997). Both historians and the archives they use are partial, in the sense of being limited and subjective. Archives are testimonies to past relations between individuals and events or between individuals. The fiction of an objective historical method producing hard historical fact becomes apparent once we recognize that archival research is a dialectical and dynamic process, itself subject to politics and change (Milner, 1999).

Historical analysis has an important social role that is of particular interest to the social scientist. A century ago, English writers used history to develop both a national identity and a unique regional identity for the Cotswolds. In telling the history of the Cotswolds, English historians incorporated ideas of the past—tradition, longevity, history, and discontinuity—to set the past apart from contemporary England (Brace, 1999). This allowed them to celebrate traditional "Englishness" and criticize changes in society and national character. Similarly, much of current Indian writing about India dwells on the gulf between the vision of its founders and what their country has become. Much of the writing finds fault with the founders, and some reflects wistfully on an age of relative innocence and wonders how it can be relived, reflecting India's disappointment with itself (The Economist, 1998).

For these and other reasons, history writing has its own methodology and methodological debates. Historians recognize that knowledge systems, including historical analyses and classifications of past events, contribute to domination of the socially vulnerable, and to supremacy of the West (Lal, 1997). Historical works have, as a result, ideological as well as research interest.

History needs time for all the facts to emerge and interpretations to solidify. It is hard to imagine how historians will interpret the events of 11 September 2001, given the multiplicity of conflicting interpretations shortly after the event itself. For example:

- According to Seyla Benhabib (2002), the September 11 attacks reflect the failures of modernity and modernization, and the worldwide discrediting of communism. Allegedly, these have created an ideological vacuum in the Middle East that radical Islamism has rushed to fill.
- Robin Blackburn (2002) notes that past US policy decisions to strengthen Saudi Arabia, Pakistan, and anticommunist Afghani "freedom fighters" all backfired. All three have supported al-Qaeda and other Islamic jihadists.
- John Michael (2002) denies the validity of viewing opposition to the United States as the product of the Islamic world's misinterpretation of Western values and opposition to modernity, rather than a rational response to US policies of imperialist domination and military aggression.
- S. Ravi Rajan (2002) sees fault on both sides, noting other trends in world history related to this terrorist incident are just as frightening as the attack itself, including the persistence of imperialism, the backing of evil leaders by Western governments, and the gradual dilution of democracy in the US.

As these examples make clear, there are strong links between the writing of history and the political ideology. A historical account—like any story or account—is an imaginative or creative work that endeavours to capture and conform to the agreed-upon "facts" about the past. It provides people with a way of thinking about their lives. Since it has political implications and consequences, the writing and interpretation of historical "fact" is always a contested terrain.

CONTENT ANALYSIS

Data analysis that bridges the gap between qualitative and quantitative data is called *content analysis*. Its goal is to quantify large amounts of qualitative data for generalization.

Imagine that you have read fifty magazine stories about entrepreneurs. How should you analyze these data? You can treat them by giving a general impression of what the articles said. Or you can analyze their content by looking for certain systematic patterns and counting their occurrence: for example, depictions of these entrepreneurs as aggressive or easy-going, successful or unsuccessful, likeable or unlikeable.

To take the latter approach, each story must be coded to produce numerical data. So, for example, if the story presents its central character, an entrepreneur, as aggressive, you assign the number value 3 in the category labelled "aggressiveness." If the story presents him or her as patient, you assign the value 1. If no mention is made of aggressiveness (and you can draw no inference about it from her words or actions), you assign the value 2.

Under the best circumstances, the result of such systematic data coding is a cultural archive. One example is the Human Relations Area File (HRAF), started by George Peter Murdock in 1937 as the Cross-Cultural Survey of Yale University's Institute of Human Relations. The HRAF was a visionary science project, aimed at making an archive of past ethnographies to enable cross-cultural analyses of the world's people, past and present (Marcus, 1998). Researchers have also used content analysis to study such diverse kinds of writing as leaflets, to understand the rhetoric of environmental sustainability (Myers and Macnaghten, 1998); focus group transcripts, to explore the stressful experiences daughters faced in providing care to parents living in a nursing home (Krause, Grant, and Long, 1999); and family sociology textbooks, to examine shifts in content and theoretical perspectives since the 1960s (Mann, Grimes, and Kemp, 1997).

Such data can be analyzed statistically, in the same way as any other quantitative data. Their value rests mainly on the quality of the coding scheme and the objectivity of the person (coder) reading and interpreting the stories. However, the potential drawback or limitation of content analysis lies in the quality of the coding. If the researcher uses an inappropriate or inadequate scheme for coding the textual materials or observed behaviours, the resulting data will be worthless. If he or she employs coders to apply an otherwise good coding scheme but makes no effort to train these coders and ensure their uniform, unbiased application of the scheme, the resulting data will be worthless.

The raw observations do not become data until they have been coded. In the end, therefore, the most important research job in content analysis is good coding—something that is harder to achieve than most people realize.

To establish coder reliability, it is important to have two or more people code the same content independently. A high degree of agreement will show that the interpretations are not flawed by the biases of particular readers. Assessing inter-rater reliability—whereby data are coded by independent researchers and the coded data compared for agreement—is a recognized process in quantitative research. However, its applicability to qualitative research is less clear and questions remain. For example, should researchers be expected to identify the same codes or themes in a transcript, or should they be expected to produce different accounts? Some qualitative researchers argue that assessing inter-rater reliability is an important method for ensuring rigour, while others argue that it is unimportant. In one study, Armstrong, Gosling, and Weinman (1997) found close agreement among six raters on the basic themes in a focus group transcript; however, each analyst "packaged" the themes differently.

However, another study of the coding of focus group transcripts found that three raters failed to agree on between one-third and one-half of the factors. This disagreement occurred despite the fact the raters generated the individual factors (or categories) themselves, based on their reading of a random sample of transcripts, and even though the raters were trained in the use of rating forms. These data suggest that if a single rater evaluates focus group transcripts, as is commonly done, judgments may not be reproducible by other raters. Moreover, a single rater may not extract all the important information contained in the transcripts (Weinberger, Ferguson, and Westmoreland, 1998).

In one respect, these problems will be solved by the spread of new computer-assisted qualitative data analysis software (CAQDAS), which is being used increasingly in content and discourse analysis in different parts of the world (see the issue of *Current Sociology,* volume 44 Winter 1996 on this topic). To date, more than 20 computer programs have been designed to help researchers analyze ethnographic data, and these programs may be used by researchers with various orientations (Dohan and Sanchez-Jankowski, 1998). Use of this software will eliminate the need for human coders and raters, since it works directly from raw text. Thus, the problem of inter-rater reliability will—in the simplest sense—disappear, since the computer itself is the only rater. However, bear in mind that the resulting computerized data analysis will be only as good as the coding scheme devised by the investigator and set up by the programmer. If there are ambiguities in the program, there will be errors in the data analysis.

FEMINIST RESEARCH: QUALITATIVE RESEARCH FOR SOCIAL ACTION

There has always been disagreement on what a feminist research is and what makes it different from mainstream research. There is, however, consensus among most scholars that feminist research is distinct from mainstream research in its aim to create social change that will improve the lives of women, and in the value it puts on subjectivity and the lived experiences of those studied.

A wide range of topics can be explored within a feminist research framework, including issues of difference, social power, and commitment to political activism and social justice (Hesse-Biber, Leavy and Yaiser, 2004:1). Feminist qualitative research has made notable contributions to our understanding of health and education, social movement formation, and policy analysis and organization (Olesen, 2000:216–17). But feminist research does not always depend on qualitative research. Many feminist researchers have used quantitative methods such as surveys to collect data.

It is important to distinguish between the terms *method* and *methodology* as they are used by feminist researchers. A research *method* is merely a way of collecting data; methods are not gender-specific (Hesse-Biber, Leavy and Yaiser, 2004:15). Feminist *methodology*, on the other hand, exists in opposition to mainstream and conventional ways of data collection and analysis, which often reflect andropocentric values. For feminist researchers, the feminist methodology is a theory in itself, connected to the feminist struggle of empowering women and other oppressed people (Sprague and Zimmerman, 1993:266). It represents feminist values and worldviews, highlights the inclusion of women from diverse social and ethnic backgrounds, and values the relationship between the researcher and the subject.

Feminist researchers use a wide range of qualitative and quantitative research methods to collect data, sometimes combining the two methods to obtain data from different perspectives and in different forms. Oral history interviewing is a preferred method of research, since the questions in this method, being less pre-determined, are better at capturing the meanings women attach to their lived experiences. Feminist researchers also favour in-depth interviews, which allow the researcher to develop a connection with the subject, lessening the status difference between researcher and interviewee. By allowing the researcher to gain the subject's trust, the in-depth interview eases the collection of data about sensitive issues. This methodological approach also provides more insight into the lives of subjects and produces a more varied set of responses.

Another reason that feminist researchers prefer this kind of interaction with the subjects to the one-way communication of traditional data collection methods is that it allows them to involve the subjects in the generation of research questions, making them partners in the process of data collection. The researcher does this by sharing results with the subjects who can add their opinions to the research. The researcher may give subjects her own views of the issues and on occasion may even offer advice. Christine Webb, in her study of hysterectomy, faced the dilemma of trying to stay neutral as a researcher while giving advice to patients seeking help:

> I decided to tell women at the beginning that I saw the interview as an exchange of information. I had some questions to put to them but they should ask me anything they wanted at any stage and I would answer as fully as I could, based on my experience as a nurse and what I had learned from my previous study. . . . Therefore I would give information and advice wherever I detected a need or opportunity during the interview. The effect of this had been that at times I talked more than the women but this seems an inevitable consequences of my decision. (Webb, 1984)

Some feminist researchers argue that quantitative methods do not capture the subjective experiences of women. For instance, Anne Kasper (1994) in her study of women with breast cancer writes:

> Central to the methodology of this study is the belief that the essential meanings of women's lives can be grasped only by listening to the women themselves. If, as in more traditional approaches, the terms of the research are imposed on subjects and they are required to respond within the strict confines of the method, personal meanings may be easily repressed or lost. (266)

Nevertheless, feminist researchers have historically used quantitative methods of data collection, such as surveys, to study social changes and social problems. Researchers in favour of surveys argue that this method enables them to show the differences among groups and the changes over time among a large population. Proponents of quantitative research also argue that basing one's assumption only on qualitative research can produce misleading results (Reinharz, 1992:80). For instance, Gondolf and Fisher (1988), in their study of battered women, claim that qualitative approach might lead to untested and undocumented generalizations.

As we can see, there are disagreements among feminist researchers on what methods are suitable for a feminist research, who qualifies as a feminist researcher, and what makes up a feminist research. However, the diversity of viewpoints does not detract from the value of feminist research. In fact, recognizing the presence of conflicting views about feminist research is considered to be one of the strengths of feminist research (Hesse-Biber, Leavy and Yaiser, 2004:4).

COMMUNITY-BASED RESEARCH: QUALITATIVE RESEARCH FOR SOCIAL ACTION

Community-based research is a model used to examine a broad range of issues, including community health, environmental problems, and education. In community-based research, the unit of identity is not the individual but the community. A community can be a geographic area; it can also be shared ethnic, racial, or sexual identity. Research takes place in a community setting and involves its members at different stages of the design and implementation of the research project. This makes community-based research fundamentally participatory (Stringer, 1997:17), with outcomes that should benefit the community.

Depending on the research question and the issue to be explored, both qualitative and quantitative methods of data collection are used in a community-based research design (Blumenthal and DiClemente, 2004). Methods of data collection range from survey to interviews and ethnography. Qualitative and quantitative methods may be combined in a single study, but this approach is not common in community-based research (Blumenthal and DiClemente, 2004).

The feature of community-based research that most sets it apart from other methods of research is its involvement of community members in the design of the project. For example, approaching his class as a community, Stringer (1997) provided students with the opportunity to take part in developing the course syllabus and deciding what kinds of activities and materials should be covered in the class and what forms of evaluation should be considered. Community members may remain involved beyond the earliest stages of the research and can have real influence on directing the research project. By exercising their power to have control over the research, community members can make sure the research is carried out according to its original goals and outlines.

Community-based research should benefit the community by building on the strengths and resources within the community (Schultz, Parker and Becker, 1998). It does this while promoting what Blumenthal and DiClemente call a "co-learning and empowering process that attends to social inequalities" (Blumenthal and DiClemente, 2004:16). Because of its emphasis on the non-hierarchical relationship between the researcher and subjects, researchers and community members learn from each other.

Stringer (1997:17) notes that community-based research also provides group members with a sense of community. Teaching a course on community-based ethnography, Stinger (1997) approached the class as a community and fulfilled the principles of community-based research in the classroom setting. The author writes: "Over time, participants began to accept the reality of their power to question how the class ran and to take increasing control of their own learning. By the end of the semester each group was an active learning community . . ." (Stringer, 1997:26).

Involving community members who are affected by the research helps to promote the "building of confidence, skills, and support networks" (Ristock and Pennell, 1996:17). Community-based research thus becomes "research as empowerment." Nelder and Snelling's research on women's abuse is an example. The researchers used interviews to collect data. They explain that "the interview method of women talking with other women in a safe, familiar environment using a semi-structured format allowed for collecting rich data that may not have been accessible any other way" (Nelder and Snelling, 2000:8). The researchers reported that some women who took part benefited by gaining the knowledge that they were not alone, while others got healing just from the telling their stories.

In general, the purpose behind carrying out a community-based research is to incite action and solve the problem that is under study. The challenge that the participatory model of research often faces is to provide a bridge between research and action. In the case of Nelder and Snelling's research on women's abuse, the researchers were able to report that "hearing the voices of survivors of women abuse has resulted in a meaningful, contextualised piece of research that has important implications for future research and policy" (Nelder, and Snelling, 2000:8).

CLOSING COMMENTS

In this chapter, we have examined some of the methods used by qualitative researchers and looked at how this kind of research differs from quantitative analysis. Qualitative research is concerned with exploring individual cases and events, rather than with quantifying these in order to produce statistically sound conclusions. However, qualitative research should not be seen as exclusive to quantitative research; rather, as we have seen in discussing content analysis, and as we shall see again in the next chapter, the two approaches can be combined to advantage to produce a clearer, more detailed picture of the subject under study. In the next chapter, we will take a closer look at some of the ethical problems social scientists are faced with in the process of conducting research, and some of the ways to handle or avoid them.

chApter 6

EXERCISING JUDGMENT AND GOOD ETHICS

Now that we have discussed how to start collecting data, measuring your concepts, and exploring your research question, it's time to discuss how to analyze your data. First, to produce trustworthy conclusions, the measures used to obtain the data must be both valid and reliable. For this reason it is essential that you know how the research findings—whether your own or those of another researcher—were collected. In the first part of this chapter, we will examine the various ways of judging validity and reliability. We will then look at the inevitable problem of flawed data and suggest some ways of dealing with it. After offering some ideas on how to handle flawed and unreliable data, we will explore some of the kinds of situations that pose ethical problems for social science researchers, and suggest ways of collecting and using data in a fair and proper manner. In the final part of the chapter, we will discuss the importance of being aware of cultural and gender sensitivities, and look at ways of handling these sensitivities in your writing.

JUDGING YOUR DATA

MEASURES SHOULD HAVE FACE VALIDITY

The way a concept or variable is measured should make sense to an objective observer, given their understanding of that concept. This is what researchers mean by the *face validity* of a measure. As an example, consider measuring job satisfaction with questions asked of workers. To an untrained listener, these questions should seem like a reasonable means of measuring job satisfaction. They might include any of the following:

- How do you like your job?
- What things do you like about your job?
- Would you recommend your job to a friend looking for work?
- Would you encourage your child to prepare for a job like this one?
- Would you choose this job again if you were looking for work and knew what you do now?

- Do you look forward to coming to work in the morning?
- Do you feel exhausted and frustrated after leaving the job at night?

All of these questions have face validity in that they adequately address the issue of how satisfied a worker is with his or her job, although each does so in a different way.

MEASURES SHOULD HAVE CONSTRUCT VALIDITY

Measures of the same variable or concept should be correlated with one another in *scales*. A scale is a combination of responses to a series of related questions that are believed to measure the same underlying concept. *Construct validity* is the degree to which all the items in a scale are correlated with one another and the scale, as a whole, is distinct from other scales.

Imagine, then, that you had asked all the questions about job satisfaction mentioned above. You should find that the answers are correlated with one another: a person who answers "yes" to one question should be answering "yes" to the others, too. Researchers have statistical methods to measure how strong that correlation between items is and to help construct a good overall job-satisfaction score from many related items. (Such a score can then be used with confidence as the dependent, or independent, variable in empirical research).

However, common-sense expectations do not always prove correct. There may be many reasons why certain items do not group. The most likely is that one or more items have been badly measured. For example, the categories used may have been inappropriate, or the respondent may not have understood the questions. A second reason is technical. The statistical methods used to construct scales often have strict requirements about the form of the data, especially the distribution of answers. (This issue belongs more properly in a course on statistics.)

A third reason items may not group together is that the concept being measured is *multi-dimensional*: in other words, it has many aspects, so the items group into two or more distinct, uncorrelated scales, each one having construct validity. Such multi-dimensionality can be seen in people's attitudes towards computers in the workplace. One might expect a series of questions about satisfaction with the effects of computerization to reveal a single satisfaction measure—people either love computers or hate them—but they do not. In one study at least, two major dimensions, or scales, appeared: one measured the worker's approval of the increase in efficiency brought about by computerization; another, the worker's concern about the increase in managerial control that computerization made possible. A worker could be favourable towards the computer as an instrument of increased efficiency, but unfavourable towards it as an instrument of increased control. So there may be no single overall measure of satisfaction.

MEASURES SHOULD BE RELIABLE

Measures should be reliable, or stable, over time in the sense that each respondent should answer in roughly the same way six months from now as he or she does today. Marked or frequent changes in response should be explained.

As well, you should ensure a high degree of reliability or agreement in the responses produced by different interviewers (or coders). These two types of agreement—agreement of the respondent with himself or herself over time, and agreement of one coder with another reacting to the same stimulus—constitute what is meant by reliability in social science research.

The need for such reliability is obvious. We cannot reasonably explain something with attitudes or behaviours that are constantly changing. Yet people's attitudes *do* change over time. If they change in a random, unpredictable way, with great frequency, a researcher should not use them in an explanation. If they change in predictable ways, however, the explanation should include variables that predict these changes. So, for example, if people's willingness to save or invest money changes with their job security or their view of political and economic stability, we should include measures of these experiences and views in our explanation of saving.

One common way of being certain about your measures is to adopt the ones that other researchers have often used. Widely used measures of intelligence, anxiety, social status, work satisfaction, and family cohesion, to name just a few, abound. They all have known properties: thoroughly considered face validity, statistically tested construct validity, and measured reliability. A scale with high reliability and validity is easily justified in any research, student or professional; one without these features is used at the researcher's peril, for it may yield inconsistent or unreliable results.

MAKE SURE THE VARIABLES CAN VARY

In Chapter 3, we noted that constants should never be used in an explanation because they never vary, and explanations need variables. Measured variables should be able to vary as widely as reality does. In general, researchers should ensure that respondents are allowed to give a variety of answers wide enough to capture their true range of feeling. The wider the range of variation the questions make possible, the more widely the answers will vary. The more widely answers vary, the greater the possibility for a good explanation. Therefore, questions allowing wide variation offer the best chance for a good explanation.

Variables with only two data points—yes/no; agree/disagree; and so on—are weak. Such limited variables should not be used if others offering a greater range of possible answers can be substituted: yes/no/maybe; strongly agree/agree/no opinion/disagree/strongly disagree; and so on. There is a point of diminishing returns, however, where adding more categories adds nothing to the ability of the respondent to answer truthfully. For example, asking respondents to judge their satisfaction with an undergraduate course on a seventeen-point scale ranging from "immensely satisfied" to "immensely dissatisfied" will probably not produce better results than asking them to judge their satisfaction on a seven-point scale ranging from "very satisfied" to "very dissatisfied." The human ability for gradation is limited, at least in this form.

If fine gradation is needed, a much better strategy is to use many *yes/no* questions. The answers can then be summed together, or scaled (summing weighted values), to give a score that ranges widely from very high to very low. For example, if you want to measure how satisfied people are with their lives, you might ask each respondent to rate his or her satisfaction from 0 to 10, where 10 indicates extreme satisfaction. Or you might ask each to answer ten questions—"Are you satisfied with your work?"; "Are you satisfied with your friendships?"; "Are you satisfied with your sex life?"; "Are you satisfied with your standard of living?"; and so on—where each *yes* answer is worth 1 point and each *no* answer is worth zero. (Different weights can be attached to questions according to their theoretical contribution to the overall result, so a *yes* answer to the question "Are you satisfied with your marital situation?" might be worth more than a *yes* answer to the question "Are you satisfied with your job?") The latter approach, which is preferable, will produce a total score ranging from 0 for some respondents to 10 for others.

If an independent variable does not vary much, it cannot "explain much variance" in the dependent variable: it will not appear, statistically, to have a strong causal effect. If the dependent variable does not vary much, the explanatory model as a whole cannot "explain much variance": it will appear that the independent variables, taken singly or together, fail to provide an acceptable explanation. Failures of these kinds account for many of the non-findings in social science.

There are two solutions to this problem, depending on where the problem originates. If the problem lies with faulty measurement, the researcher should make sure that revised measures adequately reflect the range of variety in the real world, by refining his or her categories to tap the available variance. However, if the problem lies with the real scarcity of extreme or unusual cases in the world (for example, morons and geniuses versus people with ordinary intelligence; or saints and villains versus people with ordinary morality), this should be dealt with at the design or sampling stage. One method is to oversample unusual cases—to select a greater number of extreme cases for study than would normally turn up in a random sample. Such oversampling is justified if the purpose of the research is to examine cases within this entire range of possible variation.

To take an example, suppose we are interested in studying the reasons people hold the views they do on smoking marijuana. A random sample might show that 10 per cent of the Canadian population is opposed to marijuana use under any circumstances and 10 per cent is in favour of its decriminalization. The remaining 80 per cent of the population is sympathetic to both views and undecided, or supportive of marijuana use under only certain specific circumstances (for example, when used for strictly medicinal purposes). With so many people holding down the middle position, there is little variance in our dependent variable (attitude towards marijuana use). As a consequence, no matter how many good independent variables we measure—in other words, no matter how many questions we ask, or how refined our categories are—we will still find a weak statistical correlation between the dependent and independent variables: a weak model of explanation.

If, on the other hand, we compose our sample to include one-third opposing marijuana use under all circumstances, one-third favouring decriminalization, and one-third in the middle, we increase the range of measured variation in the dependent variable. Doing this shows our explanation—the entire collection of independent variables—to work much better than it did before.

PRETEST YOUR OWN MEASURES

Respondents may not always understand the questions asked on a survey. That is why researchers pretest their questions on a small sample before using them in a larger study. Such pretesting often involves asking the respondents why they answered what they did in cases where their answers did not seem consistent with their answers to other questions. Some researchers give the respondents a chance to comment on the survey as a whole and to offer any suggestions on how to make it clearer or more accurate.

In large surveys where, because of the cost, the consequences of mistakes are greater, researchers often pretest questions many times on different groups. This practice has the value of showing whether questions are worded well and whether there are differences among groups that the researcher did not expect, but which may be worth further study.

This strategy was used in the classic study of the authoritarian personality by Adorno, Frenkel-Brunswik, Levinson, and Sanford (1969). Researchers in that study not only pretested their questions and scales on dozens of different groups in various versions, but also checked the responses against other kinds of data through interviews and projective tests. Only items that repeatedly satisfied the criteria of both face and construct validity across many groups and types of data were used in the final measures of authoritarianism.

USE A NATIVE EXPERT OR KEY INFORMANT

Studies designed to examine the views of people from different nations are more common in some social sciences than others. Comparing nations is unavoidable if the unit of analysis is society as a whole, or some institutional feature of society, such as an economy, a polity, or a work force. Comparing societies is also unavoidable if the goal is to show that a certain theory holds universally.

Such comparisons are also useful for cross-sectional correlational studies designed to test stage theories, as discussed in Chapter 4. The effect of literacy on voting behaviour, for example, can be tested within a single society; but since complete illiterates are few—indeed, deviant—in our own society, it is better for researchers to compare the effects of literacy on voting in societies with different literacy and voting patterns. This will typically mean comparing modern with modernizing or pre-modern societies.

The difficulty in cross-national studies is developing comparable measures of the key concepts. Standards of literacy may be higher in one society than in another. Similar problems of measurement attend most social concepts, including urbanization, poverty, satisfaction, freedom, and inequality. One cannot impose the same definition on many different societies. The social meaning of a phenomenon (for example, what it means to earn $25,000 a year, to be poor, or to be aged 16) may vary a lot from one society to another. People's behaviour is largely influenced by the social meaning—not the investigator's meaning—of that variable. A way around this problem is to use indigenous (local) definitions of concepts.

But suppose that poverty for a family of four is defined in India as annual income less than $500 and in Canada as annual income less than $20,000. These different measures give an identical social meaning, but they violate our common sense. There are, after all, certain material differences in lifestyle associated with these different levels of poverty—differences in nutrition and life expectancy, for example.

There is no easy way to solve this problem of the two realities, cultural and material. As a researcher, you must at least be aware of the forms the problem takes. Doing so means familiarizing yourself with the societies and cultures you are studying. The best way to do this, if possible, is through discussion with an indigenous expert or key informant—someone who has lived all of his or her life in the community and is well informed about community activities and sentiments. Such an informant can tell you the ways your key variables are seen in the foreign country, whether your theory is likely to hold there, and whether the measures you plan to use on data from the foreign country will likely have your intended meaning and produce your intended result.

LIVING WITH FLAWED DATA

PREPARE FOR FLAWED MEASURES

Most social science measures are flawed in some respect. However careful researchers may have been, their measures will still be imperfect in important ways.

First, measures may suffer from respondent reactivity. As we discussed in Chapter 5, respondents may react to what they think the researcher is looking for and give answers that are more strongly positive or negative than their true feelings. There are many reasons for such reactivity, some more likely in certain situations than in others. The problem is greatest in research on intimate or deviant behaviour (for example, drug use or premarital sex), attitudes about controversial subjects (for example, capital punishment), or attitudes towards a group that exercises control over the respondents' lives (for example, a work-place manager, the police, or the government).

Some groups are more likely than others to react strongly to certain kinds of questions. For example, immigrants from countries where power is exercised in an authoritarian manner often hesitate to answer survey questions about the police or the government, despite assurances their answers will be treated confidentially. (Sometimes researchers are pleasantly surprised to find that respondents enjoy the opportunity to safely air their grievances, but we can never rely on this reaction.)

Bias on the part of the researcher and, especially, biases built into the data collection will produce flawed results. This problem includes questions not asked, or asked in pointed ways that discourage certain kinds of answers (for example, "Don't you think the government ought to limit the number of Chinese refugees it accepts?"). But such biases also include certain types of under-enumeration: the systematic failure to count, observe, or survey certain kinds of people or behaviours.

Under-enumeration is common in even the best surveys. The national censuses of modern countries always under-enumerate by a large proportion—perhaps 5 to 10 per cent of the total population in North American censuses. People most likely to be missed are the poor, the transient, and the young. Most surveys are likely either to miss these same kinds of people or to find non-random—therefore, potentially biased—pockets of them. Telephone surveys will miss people who do not have their own telephones: again, the poor, the transient, and the young. Door-to-door surveys will tend to select in favour of people who are at home a lot—homemakers, the ill, the unemployed, or the retired—and miss those who are at work, have no fixed address, or are hiding from the authorities (for example, illegal immigrants).

Studies relying on volunteer respondents are also biased; volunteers are known to differ in their characteristics and attitudes, at least towards surveys and experiments, from respondents selected by more random means. Other kinds of biases infect institutionally collected data: for example, police and court statistics on arrests and convictions. These data are well known to over-represent the poor, the young, and the transient, and to under-enumerate offences by the well-off, the middle-aged, and the socially and economically stable. This is because the expectations of rule enforcers, such as the police, determine who will be left alone and who will be processed by public institutions. As well, many crimes go unreported or charges are dropped.

Another government statistic that is often widely doubted and debated is the unemployment rate. Government critics will often argue that this statistic fails to consider people who would be counted as unemployed had they not temporarily dropped out of the workforce (i.e., into school or household duties) or accepted part-time or inappropriate work (the so-called "under-employed").

Questions asked of the people processed by institutions will also reflect institutional theories about what causes a particular behaviour (for example, mental illness, criminality, delinquency, or drunkenness). For example, questions asked at intake of mental patients into hospitals reflect theories about causes of mental illness. This bias may cause us to neglect variables that may be needed to test a theory.

When social scientists are unable to experiment with ordinary people in natural settings, their ability to devise ideal measures, to control the data collection, and to select a representative sample of respondents will be hampered. They are often stuck with analyzing measures that other people have devised, data collected under unsatisfactory or incomparable conditions, and unrepresentative respondents that have been treated as though they were representative.

KNOW THE SOCIAL PROCESSES PRODUCING YOUR DATA

Since data can be biased by the ways they are collected, it is essential that the researcher know how data collection has affected the data: what respondents were expecting in a survey, how interviewers were behaving, and how institutions carried out their data collection.

You may be able to correct biases you know about. For example, if you know that a particular sampling procedure is likely to capture few poor, transient, or young people, you can get a fair measure of some attitudes for all members of society by giving extra weight to the under-enumerated social types.

Usually, however, biases in the data cannot be corrected after the fact. The best cure is prevention.

COMBINE QUALITATIVE AND QUANTITATIVE MEASURES

Understanding why people do or think what they do is difficult. Qualitative data allow us to understand best, since they invite the respondent to speak, answer, or behave in less constrained ways. By contrast, quantitative measures force respondents to answer in certain fixed categories that may not accurately reflect how they feel.

Because of their limited choices, quantifiable answers are easy to analyze with powerful statistical techniques. In this limited sense, quantitative data, because they are more precise, are better measured than qualitative data. But what is gained in precision may be lost in accuracy—in the "true-to-lifeness" of the findings. To solve this problem, researchers try, where possible, to combine both qualitative and quantitative measures of the same thing.

Qualitative measures obtained by field observation, semi-structured interviewing, or analysis of written materials (for example, documents, letters, or diaries) can be combined with quantitative measures in various ways. For example, in the classic study of authoritarian personality by Adorno et al., quantitative data were used to make up scales. Based on these scales, respondents were sorted into high- and low-authoritarianism categories. Then samples of high- and low-scorers were interviewed in a semi-structured, informal way. The respondents also completed projective Rorschach and Thematic Apperception Tests, which required them to make up stories about largely neutral stimuli— in the first case, inkblots; in the second, sparse line-drawings of people.

Then the researchers determined whether, in a general sense, the qualitative data agreed with the quantitative data: whether people who scored high on the quantitative authoritarian scales also appeared highly authoritarian in the qualitative data. The two types of data proved to sort people the same way and, when combined, gave rich picture of the personality type under study.

Research findings from a single project are rarely conclusive. However, our confidence increases if we find the same result independently, using different approaches. Corroboration from different phases of an interview is one example; corroboration of survey findings through equality-tested census data is another. Therefore, whenever possible we should include items in a survey that allow such corroboration.

DEVELOP A SUMMARY MEASURE OR SCALE

To test a theory, it is better to use many flawed measures than one alone, either to see if alternative measures, taken separately, show the same pattern of findings, or to create a summary measure or scale by combining many flawed measures. This approach takes advantage of the virtues of each measure while minimizing the effects of its weaknesses. Combining flawed measures in scales usually makes the final measure of key variables more valid and reliable, and this is as true in the scaling of many quantitative items as in the scaling of quantitative and qualitative items together.

For example, recall the study of family adjustment to chronic illness discussed in the last chapter. "Family adjustment" is a complex notion, difficult to assess with a single measure. The direct question "How well adjusted is your family?" will not produce a valid or trustworthy response in most cases, since respondents may not understand what the question means or may react against it and give false answers. It is better to ask many subtler, less direct questions about the attitudes and behaviours considered characteristic of a well-adjusted family.

Respondents should also be encouraged to speak freely, in whatever way they like, about the way their family functions; from this you can infer whether it is "well adjusted" in the sense you intended. Finally, you might want to watch the family interact. Observing it will allow you to assess the quality of communication and emotional interplay.

All three types of data should be used to cross-check one another. Some families will score well or poorly on "adjustment" regardless of which method is used. In this particular instance, choosing a single summary measure is difficult; but, in principle, it is possible. And such a measure will have taken advantage of many different data sources, each with its own strengths and weaknesses.

The summary measure you select may be a single measure, the one that best correlates with all the others; or it may be the arithmetical sum of scores by a family on various measures. Combining interval- and nominal-level measures arithmetically may prove more trouble than it's worth, but it can be carrried out by statistical scaling techniques too complex to go into here.

EXERCISING GOOD ETHICS

Now that we have considered issues associated with exercising good judgment where your data are concerned, we turn to another problem of judgment: that of exercising good ethics. Although any research you do as an undergraduate will be guided and supervised, it is still important to have an understanding of the ethical implications of your work and of your responsibilities as a researcher.

Codes of professional ethics arise from the need to protect vulnerable or subordinate populations from harm incurred, knowingly or unknowingly, by researchers intervening in their lives and cultures. As a social scientist, you have a responsibility to respect the rights, and be concerned with the welfare, of all the vulnerable and subordinate populations affected by your work.

You must not exploit individuals or groups for personal gain and must recognize the debt you incur to the communities in which you work. You should be sensitive to the possible exploitation of individuals and groups in the research, and you should try to minimize the chance of such exploitation in the conduct of research. You must also be sensitive to cultural, individual, and role differences in studying groups of people with distinctive characteristics.

You must also be sure that you conduct research only within the boundaries of your ability, based on your education, training, supervised experience, or professional experience.

PROBLEMS THAT MAY ARISE

Consider some of the ethical problems that arise when people are doing important social research. Here are a few examples that will help you understand why associations of professional social scientists enact rules of ethical conduct.

STUDYING SUBSTANCE ABUSERS

Imagine you are studying teenage drug users who are in treatment for their addiction. Are they able to give informed consent to participate in your study? Do they feel pressured to co-operate with your research project? What is the danger that what they tell you, the researcher, will get into the hands of treatment personnel; or worse, that it will get into the hands of the police or courts? How can we assess the value of this "dangerous research" and just how valuable does it have to be to justify such risks? These are the kinds of questions raised by Brody and Waldron (2000).

McCrady and Bux (1999) find that most investigators who study alcohol and drug abusers regularly recruit subjects who are susceptible to pressure, but most of them take steps to minimize this pressure. Two-thirds of these researchers use objective means to measure a respondent's competence to understand and complete a consent form. Virtually all investigators have policies to deal with suicidal or homicidal tendencies, or reports of child abuse. Half of researchers interviewing juvenile delinquents used collateral data sources to corroborate the statements of their respondents; of these researchers, only half asked the collaterals (in this case, parents of the respondents) to sign informed consent forms.

Urban adolescents seemingly have their own views on how these ethical issues should be handled. Fisher, D'Alessandro-Higgins and Rau (1996) report that adolescents favour maintaining confidentiality where risky behaviours that are discovered by a researcher are of low perceived severity, or where greater risk might follow from adult discovery. They are less favourable towards maintaining confidentiality, and more willing to see the researcher take action, in instances of child maltreatment and threats of suicide.

ETHNOGRAPHIC STUDIES

Imagine that you are an ethnographer conducting a study of the socialization of children. During your research, you witness one child beating up another. Should you intervene?

Typically, ethnographers consider it inappropriate to interfere in the situations they are studying. In ethnographic research with children, adult researchers must seek to avoid intrusive adult roles of authority—that is, they must avoid intervening in the processes they are observing. So, if one child is fighting with another child, it is not the ethnographer's job to intervene. This allows ethnographic researchers to lessen the power imbalance between themselves and children. On the other hand, it also decreases children's views of adults as advocates on their behalf (Eder and Corsaro, 1999).

Consider a thornier situation: what if ethnographers watch and record the folkways of drug addicts who may be risking contamination from HIV by using infected needles. Ethnographers consider it inappropriate to alter the culture they are watching. Yet it is harmful to observe potentially fatal acts that may be easily prevented (Novick, 1996). Should ethnographers intervene? What is the proper ethical stance?

STUDIES OF VULNERABLE PEOPLE

More generally, researchers must consider ethical concerns that arise when conducting ethnographic research on populations that are vulnerable or submissive to authority. These may include children, disabled people, prisoners, or people living in other "total institutions," such as nursing homes (Schuster, 1996).

How, for example, should a researcher solve the ethical issues presented by issues of informed consent, accountability, and the need to balance the needs and goals of inmates with those of correctional officials when studying prison inmates? Prison inmates in general are characterized by their official lack of power, personal autonomy, and freedom. Anthropological research, if done ethically, encourages a significant degree of empowerment of the subject, since it is often used to promote the cause of a vulnerable group—in this case, prison inmates. Thus, the researcher may find himself or herself in the middle of a conflict that pits the interests of prison inmates against those of correctional officials (Waldram, 1998).

Researchers engaged in emancipatory or empowering research, which is often used to document and publicize the plight of a disadvantaged population, may recognize a conflict between their activities and conventional research activities. Core principles of the emancipatory research paradigm include surrendering claims to objectivity and voicing both the political and the personal. These principles create problems in finding a balance between the twin requirements of political action and academic rigour (Stone and Priestley, 1996). But is attention to the four ethical issues in the use of biographical materials in research—namely, informed consent, autonomy and competence, respect for the ground rules of various biographical approaches, and notions of authenticity and truth in life stories—enough to protect the integrity of the research and the research subject (Kenyon, 1996)?

In Canada and the United States, social science researchers—and, particularly, ethnographers—have little legal protection against being compelled to testify in court or having their data seized. It is necessary for researchers to be aware of this, both for their own good and for that of their subjects. Researchers must be prepared to face jail if they carry out research that involves certain kinds of information from vulnerable sources they wish to protect. One researcher, Rik Scarce, was jailed for 159 days for refusing to reveal the content of confidential research interviews in a federal grand jury investigation into vandalism by an animal rights group (Scarce, 1994).

This risk can be minimized, if not avoided, by the used of a randomized response technique (RRT), which provides absolute anonymity to subjects and "legal immunity" to the researcher. Not only does this RRT protocol afford some protection to both researchers and their subjects, but, in a study of business ethics, use of this RRT protocol led to far higher admissions of proscribed behaviour than the conventional protocol. Subjects were far more likely to admit deviant or illegal behaviour than they would have been under traditional data collection techniques (Dalton, Wimbush, and Daily, 1996).

EVIDENCE OF CHILD ABUSE

What should a researcher do if he or she discovers that a child under study is being abused? Often where there is potential for discovering evidence of child abuse, the professionals involved are outside the categories normally named as legally responsible for reporting that abuse. How far should researchers go in uncovering and reporting suspected abuse in a research setting? What is the proper ethical standard here?

This issue arises in cross-cultural studies on family violence and sexual abuse. Fontes (1998), for example, suggests that attention to the issues of informed consent, the composition of research teams, the definition of samples, and possible harm and benefit is key in the design of ethical cross-cultural research. Ultimately, however, what is at issue is cultural relativism and non-intervention: is violence to be excused if another culture excuses it? Is violence to be overlooked or ignored if we are present, with the permission of the people under observation, only as observers?

RANDOMIZED CLINICAL TRIALS

Ethical standards dictate that patients and clinicians should not consent to randomized treatment for the study of clinical therapeutics unless there is a condition of *equipoise*—uncertainty about whether any of the treatment options is superior to the others. However, true equipoise is rarely present. Most randomized trials, therefore, present challenging ethical problems. Should some subjects—those making up a control group—be deprived of treatment that may improve their health, simply to satisfy the needs of experimental design? Or, as Avins (1998) asks, should more subjects be assigned to treatment conditions the experimenter believes are likely the most effective?

REPORTING UNETHICAL RESEARCH BEHAVIOUR

What should you do if you discover that another researcher is behaving in unethical ways—for example, misusing research funds or reporting fraudulent results. Should you report this to his or her research team, or tell an administrator, dean, journal editor, funding agency, professional society, or reporter (Wenger, Korenman, and Berk, 1999)? Researchers hold differing views on this question, according to their research experience and administrative responsibility.

There is no simple answer to this question, and therefore "grey areas" persist and many ethical rules go unpoliced and unenforced. In professional research communities, as in society at large, many principles are stated and rules passed that cannot be enforced for practical reasons, or because large numbers of community members reject them. The community has to satisfy itself that, for symbolic reasons, it has stated a principle or enacted a rule, though it cannot or will not oversee enforcement. Gradually, ethical rules and principles that enjoy the support of a majority pass into ordinary practice, while rules and principles with little support fall into disuse and are forgotten. Note, however, that these rule-breaking processes of communities are cyclical: ethical concerns return repeatedly, with new solutions being suggested and old solutions being revived. There is no end to the "solutions" of ethical problems, so no final resolutions in research communities.

PROTECTING PEOPLE IN THE RESEARCH ENVIRONMENT

As a researcher, you have a responsibility to ensure that the physical, social, and psychological well-being of research participants is not harmed by your work. You should always strive to protect the rights of those you are studying, as well as their interests, sensitivities, and privacy.

You must tell research participants of their right to refuse participation whenever and for whatever reason they wish. You should also discuss the potential uses of the data you collect, especially where there is a likelihood that data may be shared with other researchers.

Be aware of the possible effects of your work. Wherever possible, you should try to anticipate, and guard against, harmful effects for those who have agreed to take part in your research study. You are not absolved from this responsibility by the consent given by research participants.

INFORMED CONSENT

As far as possible, social research should be based on the freely given, informed consent of those studied. This implies a responsibility on your part to explain as fully as possible, and in terms meaningful to participants, what the research is about, who is undertaking and financing it, why it is being undertaken, and how it is to be promoted. Special care should be taken where research participants are particularly vulnerable because of factors such as age or social status.

You should recognize the possibility of undue influence or subtle pressures on subjects that may arise from researchers' expertise or authority and consider this in designing informed consent procedures.

You must not expose respondents to risk of personal harm. Informed consent must be obtained when the risks of research are greater than the risks of everyday life. This may be the case in a wide variety of situations, particularly when the research threatens to unveil social practices that are illegal. So, for example, to ask respondents to tell you about drug dealers in their community, the people from whom they learned to hack into bank computers, the members of their immediate family who practice incest or violence, their contacts in a spy network, or terrorist acquaintances who are planning to bomb an airport, may be to ask them to risk their lives for your edification. They have a right to know how you plan to use the information they are giving you and what assurances you can provide that they will not be identifiable as sources. This is particularly important for people who live in "total institutions"—prisons, mental hospitals, military bases, residential schools, monasteries, and (for children) families and schools—where they will be continuously at risk of observation and retribution if they are viewed as "snitches" in the interests of research.

You must inform research subjects that they have the right not to answer particular questions or to withdraw without penalty at any point in the research. (This does not apply to cases in which informants have a duty to provide information, such as public servants.)

While obtaining a signed consent form will often serve to verify informed consent, in the study of cross-cultural contexts, illegal activities, or politically sensitive settings, it may be difficult, impossible, or culturally inappropriate to get knowledgeable and voluntary (let alone written) consent from everyone in the field setting. Sometimes the requirement that one obtain signed consent forms from everyone studied may violate anonymity and actually create risks for some groups of subjects. Therefore, the signed consent form may be inadequate or inadvisable in certain circumstances, in which case you should employ culturally appropriate methods to allow subjects to make ongoing decisions to engage in or to withdraw from the research.

For example, imagine a situation in which a researcher is studying people who commit fraudulent acts or other kinds of white-collar crimes for which they have not yet been caught. We have found these people through snowball sampling, and they have informally agreed to take part in our study. However, they may be unwilling to sign a document agreeing to participate, since, in effect, doing so admits to having committed a criminal act. This could, in principle, be used as evidence against them in a criminal trial later.

When informed consent is needed, you should provide research participants or their legal representatives with the opportunity to ask questions about any aspect of the research, at any time during or after their participation in the research.

You must explain that refusal to participate in or decision to withdraw from the research involves no penalty, and then explain any foreseeable consequences of declining or withdrawing. You must clearly discuss confidentiality. When informed consent is needed, you must keep records of this consent confidential.

Despite the paramount importance of consent, you may seek waivers of this standard when (1) the research involves no more than slight risk for research participants, and (2) the research could not practicably be carried out were informed consent to be required.

CONFIDENTIALITY

As a social scientist, you have a duty to ensure that confidential information is protected. When gathering confidential information, you should take into account the long-term uses of the information, including its potential placement in public archives and the examination of the information by other researchers or practitioners.

You must take reasonable steps to ensure that records, data, and other pieces of information are preserved in a confidential manner, recognizing that law or institutional principles may also govern people, the ownership of records, data, and information. When transferring confidential records, data, or information to other people or organizations, you should get assurances that the recipients of the records, data, or information will employ measures to protect confidentiality at least equal to those you have originally pledged.

The duty to preserve confidentiality extends to members of research or training teams and collaborating organizations that have access to the information. To ensure that access to confidential information is restricted, it is the responsibility of researchers, administrators, and principal investigators to instruct staff to take the steps necessary to protect confidentiality.

When confidential information about research participants or clients is entered into databases or other systems of records available to people without the prior consent of the relevant parties, you should take care to protect anonymity, either by not including personal identifiers or by employing other techniques that mask or control disclosure of individual identities. When using private information about individuals collected by other researchers or institutions, you should protect the confidentiality of details that might identify the individual or individuals that it concerns. Information is private when an individual can reasonably expect that the information will not be made public with personal identifiers (for example, medical or employment records).

LIMITS OF CONFIDENTIALITY

When performing research, you must inform yourself fully about all laws and rules that may limit or compromise guarantees of confidentiality and determine your ability to guarantee confidentiality. It is your responsibility to inform research participants or others of any limits to this guarantee at the outset of the research.

During your work, you may confront unanticipated circumstances where you become aware of information that is health- or life-threatening to research participants or others. In these cases, you must balance the importance of guarantees of confidentiality with other principles, standards of conduct, and applicable law.

As a researcher, you should discuss confidential information or evaluative data about research participants only for appropriate scientific or professional purposes and only with people concerned with such matters.

Confidentiality is not needed for observations of people or activities in public places or other settings where no rules of privacy are provided by law or custom. Similarly, confidentiality is not needed with information available from public records.

USE OF DECEPTION IN RESEARCH

Do not use deceptive techniques unless the following conditions apply:

1. the use of deceptive research techniques will not be harmful to research participants and is justified by the study's prospective scientific, educational, or applied value;
2. no equally effective alternative procedures that do not use deception are feasible; and
3. you have obtained the necessary approvals from your academic institution.

Never deceive research participants about significant aspects of the research that would affect their willingness to take part, such as physical risks or unpleasant emotional experiences. When deception is an integral feature of the design and conduct of research, you must try to correct any misconception that research participants may have before concluding the research.

On rare occasions, you may need to conceal your identity to undertake research that could not practically be carried out if it was known that you were a researcher. Under such circumstances, undertake the research if it involves no more than slight risk for the research participants, and then only if you have obtained approval to proceed in this manner.

USE OF RECORDING TECHNOLOGY

Obtain informed consent from research participants or others before videotaping, filming, or recording them in any form, unless these activities involve naturalistic observations in public places and it is not expected that the recording will be used in a manner that could cause identification or personal harm.

OFFERING INDUCEMENTS FOR RESEARCH PARTICIPANTS

Be careful to avoid offering excessive or inappropriate financial or other inducements to secure the involvement of research participants, particularly when it might force their participation. Researchers differ widely in their views on when financial inducements are excessive or inappropriate. Generally, a higher inducement is needed if the researcher requires more time away from home from the research subject, or intends to engage the research subject in activities that are unpleasant. Few interviews or questionnaires fall into this category, so inducements for this kind of research are typically low.

Providing an incentive, whether monetary or not, significantly increases response rates; it also appears to increase response completeness early in the interview (Willmack, Schuman, and Pennell, 1995). For example, an incentive of one dollar raised the response rate in a study of nurse practitioners from 66 per cent to 81 per cent (Oden and Price, 1999). This symbolic one-dollar incentive has proved highly effective in other studies, for example of exercise professionals (Hare, Price, and Flynn, 1998). Although other strategies, such as a letter of introduction or an intensive follow-up, can also significantly increase the response rate (Summers and Price, 1997), the modest one-dollar incentive may prove more effective than a non-monetary incentive (Easton, Price, and Telljohann, 1997).

Where incentives are larger, increasing them—for example, from $10 to $25—may significantly increase compliance with interview arrangements, such as agreeing to be physically evaluated in a clinic and keeping the appointment (Pavlik, Hyman, and Vallbona, 1996). It also seems that people prefer cash inducements to lottery tickets and charitable donations (Warriner, Goyder, and Gjertson, 1996).

The prevailing norms are evident in funding provided by major institutional sources of research funds, such as the Social Sciences and Humanities Research Council of Canada (SSHRCC), or the National Institute of Mental Health (NIMH) in the United States. It is evident from grant application protocols that paid inducements are acceptable, but they must be justified. It is left to the researcher to find the "right level" of payment and then to justify it to the funder. Often researchers choose to provide a small gift or honorarium rather than a dollar amount, which might be interpreted, by the funder or the participant, as signalling a pro-rated fee for time worked. This gift is meant only to show gratitude for help provided. Sometimes, gift certificates (for example, for books) may be provided, rather than cash. Note, too, that respondents are sensitive to issues of fairness in distributing incentives.

Researchers must be aware of the sort of power and influence they wield when using inducements to conduct their research. A small financial incentive may be innocuous when used to secure the participation of research subjects whose only reason for not taking part in a particular study is a lack of sufficient motivation. In other situations, however, inducements can be coercive and even destructive. Such inducements as money offered to poor people, connections offered to isolated people, or a means of expression (or "a voice") offered to ignored people may be impossible to turn down. At best, these people will be overstudied, and their participation will make for an unrepresentative sample; at worst, their dignity will be compromised, their thoughts distorted, and their lives disrupted. The case discussed in the previous chapter of Napoleon Chagnon, whose anthropological study of the Yanomami Indians may have influenced the social environment, is an illustration of how inducements can be harmful to the subjects of study. The social scientist must be aware of this.

DISSEMINATING FINDINGS

As a social scientist, you have a duty to report results openly, unless they are likely to endanger research participants or violate their anonymity or confidentiality. Social scientists have a responsibility to report their findings accurately and truthfully. You should also try to make clear the methodological and theoretical bases of the study and state the limitations of the data.

Research reports must also disclose all sources of financial support for the research and any other sponsorship or special relationship with investigators. However, you must consider carefully the social and political implications of the information you disseminate. Always strive to ensure that such information is well understood, properly contextualized, and responsibly used.

ACKNOWLEDGING THE CONTRIBUTION OF OTHERS

Thank everyone who has contributed to your research and publications. Attribution—ordering and acknowledging contributions—should accurately reflect the contributions of all main participants in both research and writing.

CONFRONTING ETHICAL ISSUES

Finally, if you have any doubts or uncertainties about any ethical problems with your work, talk to a professor or an institutional ethics review committee. They will be able to help you resolve the issue.

WATCH YOUR LANGUAGE

Many people today are aware of the language they use when referring to particular groups of the population, including those defined by gender, race, religion, cultural origin, sexual orientation, and physical and mental ability. As a social scientist, it is your responsibility to be aware of the meanings and implications of the language you are using—and to exercise good judgment in this area of your work, as in all others.

GENDER

"Man" has been used to refer to people in general for a long time, and academia (long dominated by men) has been as guilty as any other institution of perpetuating this use of the word. You may have seen textbooks that refer to "man's impact on the environment" or taken courses with titles like "Man and Society." However, such use of the term is no longer considered appropriate. In fact, using "man" in this way now appears ignorant: women have played as important a role in everything "man" has done—leaving them out makes it appear as though you are not aware of this obvious fact. Using "humankind" or "people" is better, and "women and men" or "men and women" are acceptable substitutes as well.

In addition, "man" is still used in many English compound words that refer to women as well. Such terms are easy to avoid by substituting, for example, "police officer" for "policeman," "fire fighter" for "fireman," "synthetic" for "manmade," and so on. Note, however, that excessive dedication to gender-inclusive language can lead to silly terms such as "horsepersonship" (here it might be better to use something like "equestrian skill"). Also, some words that contain the prefix "man-" are derived from the Latin word *manu*, meaning "hand." Thus, there is no need to find alternatives for words like "manufacture," "manipulate," or "manuscript."

RACE

You should be able to identify and avoid common racist terms that are more often found in street language than academic writing. However, there are subtleties to how you should use terms to identify people by their "race" that you must be aware of.

For example, you must be careful to avoid overgeneralizing based on the geographic origin of racial groups. To simply refer to someone as, for example, "African" shows not only that you have little appreciation for the vast differences between the many different peoples that populate the African continent, but also that you have not taken the time to determine where your subject's national origins lie.

Acceptable words also change with time and place. While the term "Negro" was widely used just a few decades ago, it has been superseded by terms like "African-Canadian" or, less specifically, "people of colour." "Black" is also widely used now, but is by no means universally accepted.

Acceptance of the term "Indian" has also diminished over the last few decades. It is still used in some official capacities to refer to people indigenous to North America: for instance, the U.S. government still has a "Department of Indian Affairs," and some Canadian government legislation still recognizes "status Indians" and "non-status Indians," those who, respectively, are and are not members of bands that have signed treaties with the government. In Canada, the term "Indian" is useful when distinguishing among the three groups of Aboriginal peoples: Indians, Inuit, and Métis. However, even in this capacity the term "Indian" is becoming less and less common, and many of the people themselves prefer alternative terms such as "First Nations citizen." When in doubt, it is always best to find out the term preferred by the people you are discussing and use that term.

CULTURE

While someone is born with certain "racial" characteristics, "culture" is a general term that refers to how people live their lives. No one is born with a culture: a person develops a culture as he or she grows up, based on family and surroundings. When defining a group by its culture, you must consider its language, religion, traditions, clothing, art—even the foods that members of the group eat. These distinctions, in many ways, define who a person is, while their race does not. This is why cultural distinctions are very important; your language should reflect your appreciation of this fact.

Catholics and Protestants would not generally approve of being mislabelled, nor would a Sunni Muslim want to be confused with a Shia Muslim, or vice versa. And while many North Americans may not see the differences between, for example, people of Chinese, Japanese, or Korean origin, members of these cultural groups will not appreciate being confused.

Even within nations, there are sometimes sharp divisions between cultures. Canada is a perfect example of this. To refer, for example, to French Canadians as a particular "race" is incorrect, since they are not racially distinct from the majority of Canadians (most of whom are Caucasians), although they do have some cultural differences. Many French Canadians, however, refer incorrectly to most others in Canadian society as "English," irrespective of their national origins. Be precise: use "race" when it is the appropriate term, and use "culture" likewise. Always respect cultural sensitivities in your work. As a social scientist, it is part of your role to promote understanding of differences between people, not ignorance of it.

CLOSING COMMENTS

With a good design, good theory, good judgment, and good ethics in hand, you are ready to argue the merits of your theory. To a great degree, the argument will make itself. If theory and design have been adequately thought out in advance, data that agree with the theory will persuade the fair-minded reader without any need for rhetoric.

But research results are rarely clear-cut, and inconsistent findings are commonplace. Despite our best efforts, flawed data are the norm, not the exception. To make a persuasive case—to make sense in social science—you must show not only that your explanation is reasonable, but that it is better than any other reasonable explanation. And, you must do this with style. How to do this is the subject of the next chapter.

chapter 7

Arguing and Writing with Style

Now you have the data to test your theory and argue its merit. An argument puts your theory and data together in a coherent, sensible way that can be communicated effectively to others.

This is not the place to discuss the statistical analysis of data in any depth; such a discussion belongs properly to the study of statistics. However, a few general observations about data analysis may be useful as you prepare to make your argument. First, however, we'll take a brief look at "Enlightenment thinking" and its influence on modern academic argument and writing.

THE CLASSICAL IDEAL: CLEAR AND SIMPLE

Modern academic writing style reflects certain cultural assumptions about serious inquiry. Once you understand those assumptions, it will be much more evident why we are giving the advice contained in this book. Let's consider these assumptions briefly, and when and how they arose.

The philosopher René Descartes, who wrote his famous *Discourse on Method* in 1607, believed that anyone is smart enough to learn the truth, so long as he or she breaks down the problem into solvable parts, goes from the easiest to hardest parts, reviews his or her reasoning, omits nothing, and does not accept anything as true unless the evidence shows that it is true. This sounds simple and obvious, but we should consider a little more carefully what this approach assumes.

Descartes' approach reveals a deep belief in human powers of reasoning over religion, faith, or God to show us what is true. That anyone is able to find at least some truth through logic and scientific evidence is a modern, liberal point of view. Taken together, Descartes' views—particularly his belief in reason and science—exemplify the highest ideals of what historians call "Enlightenment thinking."

Enlightenment thinkers like Descartes believed that we can all attain rational knowledge of society that is superior to religion, ideology, common sense, superstition, or prejudice. This knowledge will be universal and objective, cumulative and progressive, and it will be the basis for liberation and human betterment. From this way of thinking comes what we will call the classic stance on writing.

In their book *Clear and Simple as the Truth*, authors Thomas and Turner (1996) describe the classic stance on writing style as including the following assumptions:

- The goal is to tell the truth. Anyone can know and express truth; it is pure and disinterested, eternal and universal.
- Expression of the truth is frank and open, one person speaking to another. We assume that the reader is competent and interested, and the writer is competent and genuine. The goal of the writer is *not* self-examination or self-revelation, only to tell the truth.
- Good prose is a window on the truth: that is, it is seamless, clear, and exact. Anyone can read it. Every word counts: good prose is efficient but not rushed, energetic but not anxious.

These are the common assumptions of post-secondary writing today: that the writer is knowledgeable, calm, honest, and direct; and that the reader is competent and interested. Take these ideas seriously. Not only are these aspects of good writing important in themselves, as means of conveying what you want to say most effectively; they also show that you have understood and accepted conventions of thinking associated with the Enlightenment, which are central to modern post-secondary education.

FACTS DO NOT SPEAK FOR THEMSELVES

Many people are confused about the relationship between "facts" and theories. Historically, many scholars have commented on this relationship. One of the founders of the scientific method, Francis Bacon (1620: Aphorism xxxvi), stated that "we must lead men to the particulars themselves; and their series and order; while men on their side must force themselves for a while to lay their notions by and begin to familiarize themselves with the facts." From this, one of the founders of social science, Auguste Comte (1855), concluded that "all good intellects have repeated, since Bacon's time, that there can be no real knowledge but that which is based on observed facts."

Yet the meaning of any fact is not self-evident. The statesman Disraeli is said to have observed, caustically, that "there are three kinds of lies: lies, damned lies, and statistics." By this he meant that even facts can be twisted to suit a desired interpretation. They make sense only within a given paradigm, or way of interpretation. This relativity of facts holds true from the simplest to the most complex problem. Is the glass half empty or half full? No facts can answer this question. Facts say only how much is in the glass: the rest is interpretation. Do Canadians accept income equality for men and women doing similar jobs? No simple fact or set of facts can answer this question either. To answer it, we must first enter the realm of personal values and conceptual definitions. A complex process of inference from observed facts to conclusions and theories lies between the observed and the observer.

As John Stuart Mill (1859: Chap. 2) wrote, "Very few facts are able to tell their own story, without comments to bring out their meaning." Facts do not speak for themselves: they always need interpreting. Statistics provide forms and standards for examining data so that the reader can have some confidence in the conclusions drawn.

WHAT STATISTICS SHOW

Bacon established that facts—however difficult their interpretation—are needed to really understand the world. The discipline of statistics has provided science with a body of knowledge and tools to analyze facts.

Statistical methods fall into two main types: descriptive and inferential. *Descriptive statistics* are ways of using numbers to describe or convey information about some population or social process. *Inferential statistics* are ways of using numbers, and statistical principles, to determine the true strength of relationships between variables and their degree of significance (or non-randomness). Hypothesis testing relies on inferential statistics. However, in most of everyday life, non-researchers rely on descriptive statistics to tell them about the world.

Descriptive statistics help to summarize data in precise ways. For example, a description of specifically how poor and rich families differ in their spending patterns—how much is spent per week on food, shelter, clothing, entertainment, etc.—is much more informative than the mere statement that rich families lead a more varied, luxurious, or comfortable life than poor people. For this reason, the study of budgets is informative—whether dollar budgets (how people spend their money) or time budgets (how people spend their time).

Inferential statistics allow us to decide whether findings occurred for the reasons we think—because an explanation is correct—or by chance. The testing of "statistical significance" falls into this second category. However, significance tests do not measure the substantive importance of a finding; they only show whether it likely occurred by chance. Thus small effects and weak relationships may be statistically significant, even if their explanatory value is trivial. Inferential statistical procedures help us to judge the relative importance of explanatory variables. Such procedures (including analysis of variance and regression) are far more valuable for understanding the data than significance tests are. Again, we recommend that you take a course on statistics or consult a "user-friendly" text, such as Hays (1970) or Harshbarger (1971).

EXPLORE YOUR DATA

Some researchers believe that statistical testing is cut and dried: that only one or two tests of observed results need to be made before drawing conclusions. Others feel that research findings should be explored thoroughly, to make sure of getting everything out of the data that can contribute to an explanation.

Various techniques for systematically exploring data have been devised. They can never replace creativity and patience on the researcher's part, but the methods devised by statistical researchers are particularly simple—which encourages use—and flexible, which means that they are useful with many types of data and resist excessive influence by a few extreme cases. They provide a good sense of the main story the data have to tell.

Although we can say little about these methods here, we urge you to learn more about them and to use them creatively. The best explanation will be the one that most completely unlocks the story hidden in facts that the researcher has gathered.

TELLING THE STORY

THE IMPORTANCE OF A LITERATURE REVIEW

Whatever your own ideas or findings, you can never undervalue the ideas prevailing in your discipline. If most "professionals" would agree with your explanation, you are on solid ground. To make sure, it's a good idea to do a second review of the literature on your topic. You will already have done an initial review at the beginning of your research, when you were devising an explanatory model. A second review will help you bolster your opinion and refine your argument by making sure the discipline supports you.

As an undergraduate you are at a disadvantage here, since you are less familiar with the discipline and its attitudes than the professor grading your paper. So do the best you can, while recognizing that you may miss something. Your instructor will not expect the impossible. But you invite disaster if you ignore the discipline's thinking entirely. More likely than not, what you have thought and studied has been written about by many others. Make a good attempt to learn what they have said and incorporate their thinking into your own. Your argument will be stronger and more persuasive if you do, and your reader will know there is a body of thinking behind it, and not simply your own.

AT LEAST TWO SIDES TO EVERY STORY

In Chapter 3 we noted that in every social science you will find at least two paradigms, or ways of thinking about the same question. This means that in order to explain your data, you need to take more than one interpretation into account.

Even within a single paradigm, more than one interpretation is possible. This is largely because data in social science research are typically flawed. To be persuasive, therefore, you must either argue both *in favour* of the interpretation you prefer and *against* the best alternative explanations, or attempt to assimilate both into a single explanation.

For example, Canada's observed "conservatism"—its lack of a revolutionary past, and Canadians' greater deference to tradition and authority—can be explained in several ways. One is cultural: Canada has preserved a way of thinking, promoted by eighteenth-century Loyalist settlers and early British immigrants, that was anti-revolutionary and anti-republican (since it was anti-American). An alternative explanation is economic: Canada, always an economic dependency—first of Britain and then of the United States—has a ruling class that has always encouraged subservience. Ordinary Canadians have been taught to accept a subordinate status within their own country and in the world as a whole. This produces the illusion of conservatism.

Any study of Canadian political behaviour—whether a historical study of government institutions or a contemporary study of voting—will need to examine these alternative interpretations of Canada's perceived conservatism. Each points to a different explanation of the phenomenon under study and, equally important, to different predictions about the future. Each would see different possibilities for change and different ways of bringing change about.

Some scholars prefer to argue in a way that sharpens the distinctions between alternative interpretations as much as possible. This approach has the great merit of clarifying one line of theoretical argument through contrast with another. Other scholars prefer to blur the differences, taking elements from different approaches as they seem useful. The philosopher Isaiah Berlin (1953:1, 2) calls the latter thinkers "foxes" and the former "hedgehogs," following the Greek poet Archilochus: "The fox knows many things, but the hedgehog knows one big thing." Berlin describes as hedgehogs those who "relate everything to a single central vision." The foxes, on the other hand, are those "who pursue many ends, often unrelated and even contradictory, . . . moving on many levels, seizing upon the essence of a vast variety of experiences [without] seeking to fit them into . . . any one unchanging, all-embracing . . . unitary inner vision."

As Berlin shows, both camps have historically included great, innovative thinkers, so both approaches are useful and defensible, subject to two warnings. First, write for your reader: if the professor reading your paper is—or wants you to be—a hedgehog rather than a fox (or vice versa), do what is desired, whatever your personal inclination. Second, if you are convinced that fox-work —using a variety of paradigms and approaches—is the best way to go, be sure to demonstrate to the reader both that you are capable of understanding the distinctions you are blurring, and that the purpose of this blurring is to better understand or explain your subject matter. In other words, do not let the reader think that you are a fox because you are not clever enough to be a hedgehog.

A good argument will compare at least two interpretations of the same facts: yours and the best alternatives you can think of. You must be assertive when you present your interpretation, even if the results you obtain do not fit easily within a dominant paradigm, for this may signal an important discovery. Failing to argue forcibly for disconfirmatory findings hurts the discipline by weakening its tendency to renew itself with difficult new ideas.

GOOD ALTERNATIVES ARE USUALLY COMPLEMENTARY

No theory is ever conclusively right or wrong: it is only better or worse than alternative theories. In fact, most good arguments will prove to be complementary: they will fit together, even when they seem to argue opposing sides of the same issue.

Researchers have two related goals in making an argument. The first is to test a theory and show it to be better than another one. The second is to understand thoroughly the phenomenon under study. In order to fully understand a phenomenon, you may have to assimilate the best parts of an alternative theory into your own—recognizing, in the last example, that *both* cultural *and* economic forces help to shape political behaviour. After explaining the subject of your study, try to create a better theory than the one you started with: a theory that persuasively combines alternative theories or paradigms, if possible.

This is how a discipline improves. Researchers start with a question narrowly defined within a given paradigm and try to prove their own hypothesis right (or wrong) and their interpretations better than any others. Observations that their theory cannot accommodate are signs that a new, more comprehensive way of thinking is needed. Existing paradigms are burst open when anomalies become too numerous to ignore and too contradictory to accepted thinking. In time, new, more complete paradigms are created; and so scientific understanding progresses.

COME DOWN HARD

Do not argue half-heartedly. Remember, you may be right and the rest of the discipline wrong. However, if you are really of two minds about a question, be of two minds assertively. Say clearly why a resolution is not possible. Ambivalence is justified if competing interpretations are equally suitable to your data yet cannot be assimilated in a single explanation. Like disconfirmatory results, ambivalence points to the need for new thinking, and a new, broader paradigm.

DEALING WITH DISAPPOINTMENT

ACKNOWLEDGE SHORTCOMINGS

Ignoring weaknesses in your argument—logical flaws, or data that do not support your case—will not make them go away. Therefore, you should always assume that your readers will challenge you on any weak point that you fail to address.

In fact, your readers will be looking for weak points, and will see your failure to address them as an admission that you *cannot* deal with them. Readers who share your viewpoint may make allowances and simply judge your work as sloppy. Others, however, may dismiss your whole argument as weak, in which case all your work will have been wasted.

BITE THE BULLET

Your research findings may prove your argument dead wrong. If so, admit it. Do not try to deny what will be obvious to any reader as qualified in data analysis as you are, or more so.

Suppose, for example, that you had studied the effects of industrialization on people's behaviour. You theorized that the more people interact with machinery at work, the more likely they are to adopt modern attitudes in other parts of their lives: towards politics, social relations, family life, and so on. Accordingly, you collected data in Third-World countries from farmers, small artisans living in cities, and factory workers. You predicted that factory workers would appear the most modern of all your respondents, and measured a great many attitudes and behaviours to test this.

A statistical analysis of the data found that experiences with modern machinery had a statistically significant (i.e., non-random) effect on modernity, but one that was much less important than the effect of education. What *most* appears to modernize people is education, not working with machinery. You were right in a small way, but not to the degree you had hoped. The best thing to do is admit it.

NEVER LET A LITTLE DATA SPOIL A GOOD THEORY

Researchers respond to disconfirmatory findings in different ways. You may conclude, and admit, that you were wrong; or you may refuse to do so. You might also look for the source of the problem in your measurement. This is reasonable, since flawed measurement is the norm in social science, not the exception. The problem may indeed lie here. But if it doesn't, you're back to biting the bullet or adopting another strategy of data analysis.

You could move into a relational-study design and look at deviant cases. To take the previous example, you might compare the highly modern workers with the less modern ones to find conditions under which modern machinery does and does not modernize attitudes and behaviours. In so doing, you might find that although modern machinery has no modernizing effect within an essentially traditional factory organization, where tribal loyalties and traditional forms of authority prevail, such effects may be *facilitated* by a work organization that rewards expertise, productivity, and excellence, and undermines those old loyalties. In other words, the effect of machinery interacts with—is suppressed or magnified by—the form of work organization. In this case, you will have improved on the original theory and largely salvaged the argument that modern machinery modernizes people. (Your finding does *not* prove that only the form of organization has an effect.)

However, suppose that no conditions can be found under which the theory holds true. The most useful and honest thing to do is admit that the theory is wrong. Perhaps the error traces all the way back to fundamental assumptions about human nature or social organization. If so, a lot of research based on the same assumptions needs reinterpreting and may in fact be proven wrong.

In this way, admitting that you were wrong may yield more understanding in the long run than excusing the findings on the grounds of poor measurement or conditional (i.e., limited) corrections.

ADMIT THE STRENGTHS OF OPPOSING ARGUMENTS

Deal thoroughly and honestly with opposing points of view. Assume that your reader will challenge you if you do not. Failure to give your opponents their due will seriously weaken the credibility of even your best findings.

It is hard to admit the merits of an opposing argument, let alone think creatively within its framework. Yet this is exactly what you should be learning to do as an undergraduate in social science. Ideally, once your education is complete, you will be able to take any problem within your field and ask, "What would _____ (Marx, Weber, Durkheim, Malinowski, Freud, Skinner, Milton Friedman, Mill, Toynbee, Adam Smith, Rousseau, etc.) have said about this?" And you will be able to give a reasonable answer. In this sense, your education in social science should train you to play a wide variety of intellectual roles. You must learn the strengths and weaknesses of all the important theoretical positions in your discipline and be prepared to address them when they run counter to your argument.

The point of this kind of education is not to make you into a parrot of other people's views, but to arm you with the best thinking of the past. Knowing the problems you are likely to encounter and the ways of arguing around them is a valuable tool. And you must use it honestly, for your readers have trained in the same way, and can spot dishonesty at three hundred paces.

Remember the immense study of authoritarian personality discussed in the last chapter. Researchers framed, then tested, the theory that authoritarian adults grew up experiencing emotional repression. According to this theory, a person becomes a racist because (normal) childhood fears and hostile impulses are denied expression. In adulthood, the authoritarian takes every opportunity to direct (or project) hostile impulses onto vulnerable racial groups, which he or she fantasizes are subhuman, immoral, and deserving of punishment. This is a Freudian theory, which requires that we assume each person has a subconscious mind capable of changing childhood rejections and disappointments into adult punitiveness.

A learning theorist opposed to Freud, however, would favour a simpler explanation, arguing that racist behaviour was learned and rewarded from childhood on: that authoritarians are bred by other authoritarians, without the intervening processes of repression and projection.

Good researchers will consider the alternatives to their own explanations. To make an effective argument you must examine the data to see whether they support alternative arguments. In the example above, if the data showed that authoritarian adults are no more likely to have had authoritarian parents than non-authoritarian adults, that evidence would rule out the learning-theory argument.

THINGS TO REMEMBER

DO NOT BE INTIMIDATED BY OTHER PEOPLE'S IDEAS

Admitting that other people's ideas have merit does not mean giving up your own ideas. It can, however, be especially difficult to defend your argument against other points of view if your ideas are unpopular. You must steel your resolve: make your points carefully and clearly and give the opposition its due. If you hold distinctly unpopular views and can defend them, do so.

There is no shortage of unpopular ideas that may or may not be true. In particular, ideas about inequality generate a lot of angry response—for example, the ideas that members of certain racial groups are less intelligent than people from other racial backgrounds; that unemployed people show less initiative (are more apathetic) than employed people; or that well-paid people work harder than poorly paid people. Each of these ideas is controversial, not only because each points to inequality but, more important, because there are people who might try to use these inequalities to justify a broader social inequality: higher pay, higher job status, or greater social acceptability for some people than others.

Yet empirical studies have found support for each of these unpopular ideas. Many equate intelligence with the score on an IQ test, and certain racial groups test lower than others in many studies. Similarly, many unemployed people *are* often apathetic; and well-paid people *do* in many cases work harder. The important thing is not to deny such data, but to draw appropriate conclusions from them.

If some racial groups have lower-than-average IQs, this may result from poorer education or from cultural biases in the questions IQ tests ask. The appropriate conclusion is not that members of these racial groups deserve less pay or respect than others, but that they should be given better education and fairer (less biased) tests.

If unemployed people are more apathetic, this may tell us less about the *causes* of unemployment than about the deadening, disheartening *effects* of unemployment. Far from deserving less help, unemployed people may need more help in feeling worthy, in mobilizing politically, and in finding a job.

Finally, if well-paid people work harder than poorly paid people, this may direct our attention to the reasons why people work hard. If hard work is something we want to stimulate in our society, we may need to pay ordinary workers more and give them more challenges and satisfaction in their work than they presently enjoy.

By addressing the unpopular idea creatively rather than fleeing from it, you may contribute something socially as well as theoretically valuable. But to get to this stage you must keep your head. Do not be put off by other people's aggressive reactions against what you are saying. They may think they know where you are headed; but you have every right to demand a full hearing.

DEAL FAIRLY WITH THE DATA

Just as you should not be intimidated by other people's ideas and by the aggressive way they are put forward, neither should you argue in an intimidating, obnoxious fashion. Emotional appeals to decency, morality, or common sense count for nothing in a logical argument. In fact, they undermine your credibility by supplying unnecessary rhetoric and excitement instead of calm reason.

Our goal is objectivity and value-neutrality. This does not mean that we should be indifferent towards topics of research or research outcomes. As human beings and citizens, we should invest ourselves fully—our hearts, as well as our brains—in the things we study and debate. This means choosing to study and argue for things that matter. We cannot easily be unemotional about such things. We may want it to be true that an underprivileged group is more deserving than a privileged group; or that some malfunctioning social institution is recognized as bad and is forced to change; or that a cruel society is censured. Defending Nazism or ethnic cleansing, or justifying police brutality or the starvation of the poor on welfare do not rate a high place on many people's research agendas.

However, once you have chosen a problem that is personally significant, you must deal with it fairly, remaining unbiased and unemotional in your data collection, analysis, and argument. This objectivity is the essence of scientific truthfulness. Valid results established in this way can then be used confidently in the emotional, political world of action.

DON'T RALLY STRANGE BEDFELLOWS

Be fair in reporting the literature. If the literature goes against your argument, say so and deal with the problem honestly. If you have not read the literature, do not pretend a false knowledge. In any case, do not let disappointment, haste, sloppiness, or an unwillingness to accept your own findings lead you to fake footnotes or make other assertions that can easily be shown to be false. Unfortunately, this kind of practice is not uncommon. If your reader takes the time to check your references and finds them incorrect, your entire work will be thrown into question. Make sure that you always footnote and cite your sources thoroughly *and* scrupulously.

Another form of fakery is the use of tainted authorities to bolster your argument: published works that lack scholarly acceptance, are taken out of context, or are misinterpreted to your benefit; published data you know to be untrustworthy or irrelevant; and earlier theories that are so general or vague as to be open to almost any interpretation. Published social science research is so diffuse that you can find studies or theories to support any position. A few selected authorities supporting your argument are no substitute for good theory and good data. At best, authorities can make your good theory and good data look better. They cannot turn a bad argument into a good one.

A second point to remember is that individual authorities have often said a great many things. If they are great thinkers, they have changed their thinking over time, modifying and even rejecting earlier ideas. How to deal with the early ideas—what status to give them in the field—is a problem to consider.

For example, Marx's early unpublished manuscripts were much more concerned than later writings with the psychological aspects of alienation. However, the legitimacy of his later work cannot be used to legitimize the earlier work, especially if we cannot show a clear connection between the two. Marx, after all, made no explicit attempt to connect his early manuscripts with his later conclusions in the masterwork *Capital*.

A third point is that authorities should not be used indiscriminately. Using Marx to support one part of your argument, Freud to support another, and Adam Smith to support a third will not necessarily result in a convincing argument. In fact, your three selected authorities in this case are so different, their concerns, assumptions, and conclusions so at variance with one another, that unless you are exceptionally brilliant you cannot bring them together in a single argument. It is better not to try. This is a good reason for working with a familiar paradigm, rather than across several. That way at least you can try to do justice to one way of thinking.

A final point is that, although instructors vary in this regard, it is often permissible to defend your argument with references to scholars from other disciplines—to cite sociologists in an anthropology paper, for instance, or economists in a political science paper. But the majority of your references should be to scholars within the discipline you are writing for. Doing otherwise is not only unlikely to convince your professor; it may also suggest that you are submitting the same work for two different courses.

LET OTHER PEOPLE JUDGE YOUR ARGUMENT

Try your arguments on the people you have been studying. Once researchers feel they understand the people they have studied, they sometimes tell them what they have concluded. This procedure helps to refine their argument by confronting additional, unnoticed facts or facts that do not fit into their argument. It is dangerous because it tests the researcher in the hardest possible way, but if the argument passes *this* test, it has a good chance of passing every other. If at all possible, therefore, you should try to perform it.

Confronting the people studied is more common in applied research than in basic research. It is also not foolproof, since the subjects may not understand themselves as well as the researcher does. Still, one is likely to learn something useful in this process. Consider, for example, a study of Canada's declining fertility. Annual birth records show that fewer children are being born to Canadian women now than in past decades, and that the women bearing them are, on average, older than mothers were in the past. How do we explain this fact?

We might begin by analyzing existing survey data on fertility decisions to develop and test a theory about the timing and numbers of children that women are bearing. But to find out whether this theory is valid, the researchers would do well to conduct intensive interviews with selected samples of women: for example, women who have followed the typical pattern (few children, borne in their thirties) and other women who have violated the pattern (women who have borne many children early in life, or no children at all). These interviews may not be numerous enough to be persuasive statistically, but they are useful in checking the theory, illustrating various child-bearing decisions with quotes and anecdotes, and most important, getting a reaction to the researcher's theory. Such a procedure—less common than it should be—has the dual advantage of confronting a theory with the people theorized about and corroborating a finding with various types of data.

TRY THE "LAUGH TEST"

In Chapter 1, we recommended using the "laugh test" to see how credible and persuasive your argument is. Tell your explanation to a disinterested person, such as a friend or relative. If doing so makes you feel ridiculous or, worse, provokes laughter in your audience, your argument may be deficient.

The laugh test is not a sure thing. It may prove only that you feel uncomfortable presenting your ideas out loud, or that your listener is not taking the exercise seriously. If so, find another listener, take a deep breath, then try again. You may find that another listener has no difficulty following your argument. He or she might even be able to point out where your argument is not as persuasive, or where your reasoning seems flawed or unclear. Take these suggestions seriously. Chances are good that problems detected by your disinterested listener will not go unnoticed by the instructor or TA who will be grading your work.

WRITING WITH STYLE

Writing with style does not mean stuffing your prose with fancy words and extravagant images. Writers known for their style are those who have infused their own personality into their writing; we can hear a distinctive voice in what they write. It takes time to develop a unique style. To begin, you have to decide what general effect you want to create.

Taste in style reflects the times. In earlier centuries, many respected writers wrote in an elaborate style that we would now consider much too wordy. Today, journalists have led the trend towards short, easy-to-grasp sentences and paragraphs. Writing in an academic context, you may expect your audience to be more reflective than the average newspaper reader, but the most effective style is still one that is clear, concise, and forceful.

BE CLEAR

Since sentence structure is dealt with in Chapter 11, this section will focus on clear wording and paragraphing.

CHOOSE CLEAR WORDS

The key to good writing is using clear words. Two tools that will prove indispensable in this regard are a dictionary and a thesaurus.

A dictionary is a wise investment. A good dictionary will not only help you understand unfamiliar words or archaic and technical senses of common words, but also help you use these words properly by offering example sentences that show how certain words are typically used. A dictionary will also help you with spelling and questions of usage: if you are uncertain whether or not a particular word is too informal for your writing, or if you have concerns that a word might be offensive, a dictionary will give you this information. Be aware that Canadian usage and spelling may follow either British or American practices, but usually combine aspects of both; you should check before you buy a dictionary to be sure that it gives these variants.

A thesaurus lists words that are closely related in meaning. It can help when you want to avoid repeating yourself, or when you are fumbling for a word that is on the tip of your tongue. But be careful: make sure you remember the difference between denotative and connotative meanings. A word's denotation is its primary or "dictionary" meaning. Its connotations are any associations that it may suggest; they may not be as exact as the denotations, but they are part of the impression the word conveys. If you examine a list of "synonyms" in a thesaurus, you will see that even words with similar meanings can have dramatically different connotations. For example, alongside the word *indifferent* your thesaurus may give the following: *neutral, unconcerned, careless, easygoing, unambitious,* and *half-hearted.* Imagine the different impressions you would create if you chose one or the other of those words to complete this sentence: "Questioned about the experiment's chance of success, he was _____ in his response." In order to write clearly, you must remember that a reader may react to the suggestive meaning of a word as much as to its "dictionary" meaning.

USE PLAIN ENGLISH

Plain words are almost always more forceful than fancy ones. If you aren't sure what plain English is, think of the way you talk to your friends (apart from swearing and slang). Many of our most common words—the ones that sound most natural and direct—are short. A good number of them are also among the oldest words in the English language. By contrast, most of the words that English has derived from other languages are longer and more complicated; even after they've been used for centuries, they can still sound artificial. For this reason you should beware of words loaded with prefixes (*pre-, post-, anti-, pro-, sub-, maxi-,* etc.) and suffixes (*-ate, -ize, -tion,* etc.). These Latinate attachments can make individual words more precise and efficient, but putting a lot of them together will make your writing seem dense and hard to understand. In many cases you can substitute a plain word for a fancy one:

Fancy	Plain
accomplish	do
cognizant	aware
commence	begin, start
conclusion	end
determinant	cause
fabricate	build
finalize	finish, complete
firstly	first
infuriate	anger
maximization	increase
modification	change
numerous	many
obviate	prevent
oration	speech
prioritize	rank
proceed	go
remuneration	pay
requisite	needed
subsequently	later
sanitize	clean
systematize	order
terminate	end
transpire	happen
utilize, utilization	use

Suggesting that you write in plain English does not mean that you should never pick an unfamiliar, long, or foreign word: sometimes such words are the only ones that will convey precisely what you mean. Inserting an unusual expression into a passage of plain writing can also be an effective way of catching the reader's attention—as long as you don't do it too often. And, of course, writing clearly does not mean that you should automatically avoid all words that have specific scientific meanings. In many circumstances, such words are invaluable for conveying precise and appropriate meanings, and using them correctly will indicate your understanding. Just remember that when you use technical language, your instructors will not be impressed by the mere presence of such words: appropriate disciplinary terminology must be used correctly.

BE PRECISE

Always be as precise or exact as you can. Avoid all-purpose adjectives like *major*, *significant*, and *important*, and vague verbs such as *involve*, *entail*, and *exist*, when you can be more specific:

orig.   The survey <u>involved</u> ten questions.

rev.   The survey <u>asked respondents</u> ten questions.

Here's another example:

orig.   Granting public-service employees the right to strike was a <u>significant</u> legacy of Lester Pearson's years as prime minister.

rev.   Granting public-service employees the right to strike was a <u>costly</u> legacy of Lester Pearson's years as prime minister.

(or)

rev.   Granting public-service employees the right to strike was a <u>beneficial</u> legacy of Lester Pearson's years as prime minister.

AVOID UNNECESSARY QUALIFIERS

Qualifiers such as *very*, *rather*, and *extremely* are overused. Experienced writers know that saying something is *very poor* may have less impact than saying simply that it is *poor*. For example, compare these sentences:

Bangladesh is a poor country.

Bangladesh is a very poor country.

Which has more punch?

When you think that an adjective needs qualifying—and sometimes it will—first see if it's possible to change either the adjective or the phrasing. Instead of writing:

The bank made a very big profit last year.

Write:

The bank made an unprecedented profit last year.

or (if you aren't sure whether or not the profit actually set a record):

The bank's profits rose 40 per cent last year.

In some cases qualifiers not only weaken your writing but are redundant, since the adjectives themselves are absolutes. To say that something is *very unique* makes as little sense as saying that someone is *rather pregnant* or *very dead*.

AVOID FANCY JARGON

All academic subjects have their own terminology or jargon. It may be unfamiliar to outsiders, but it helps specialists to explain things to each other. Precise disciplinary jargon is appropriate for informal audiences, such as your instructor and other students. The trouble is that people sometimes use this sort of special, technical language unnecessarily, thinking it will make them seem more knowledgeable. Too often the result is not clarity but complication. The guideline is easy: use specialized terminology only when it's a kind of shorthand that will help you explain something more precisely and efficiently to a knowledgeable audience. If plain prose will do just as well, stick to it.

CREATING CLEAR PARAGRAPHS

Paragraphs come in so many sizes and patterns that no single formula could possibly cover them all. The two basic principles to remember are these:

1. A paragraph is a means of developing and framing an idea or impression; and
2. The divisions between paragraphs aren't random, but indicate a shift in focus.

With these principles in mind, you should aim to include three elements in each paragraph:

1. the topic sentence, to indicate to the reader the subject of the paragraph;
2. a supporting sentence or sentences, to convey evidence or to develop the argument; and
3. a conclusion, to indicate to the reader that the paragraph is complete.

Keep these points in mind as you write. The following sections offer additional advice.

DEVELOP YOUR IDEAS

You are not likely to sit down and consciously ask yourself, "What pattern shall I use to develop this paragraph?" What comes first is the idea you intend to develop: the pattern the paragraph takes should flow from the idea itself and the way you want to discuss or expand it. (The most common ways of developing an idea are outlined in Chapter 8.)

You may take one or several paragraphs to develop an idea completely. For a definition alone you could write one paragraph or ten, depending on the complexity of the subject and the nature of the assignment. Just remember that ideas need development, and that each new paragraph signals a change in idea.

CONSIDER THE TOPIC SENTENCE

Skilled skim-readers know that they can get the general drift of a book simply by reading the first sentence of each paragraph. The reason is that most paragraphs begin by telling the reader what the paragraph is about, stating the idea to be developed or the point to be made.

Like the thesis statement for the essay as a whole, the topic sentence is not obligatory: in some paragraphs the controlling idea is not stated until the middle or even the end, and in others it is not stated at all but merely implied. Nevertheless, it's a good idea to think out a topic sentence for every paragraph. That way you'll be sure that each one has a definite point and is clearly connected to what comes before and after. When revising your initial draft, check to see that each paragraph is held together by a topic sentence, in which the central idea of the paragraph is either stated or implied. If you find that you can't formulate one, it could be that you're uncertain about the point you are trying to make; it may be best to rework the whole paragraph.

MAINTAIN FOCUS

A clear paragraph should contain only those details that are in some way related to the central idea. It must also be structured so that the details are easily *seen* to be related. One way of showing these relations is to keep the same grammatical subject in most of the sentences that make up the paragraph. When the grammatical subject is shifting all the time, a paragraph loses focus, as in the following example (based on Cluett and Ahlborn, 1965: 51):

orig.   Students at our school play a variety of sports these days. In the fall, football still attracts the most, although an increasing number now play soccer. For some, basketball is the favourite when the ball season is over, but you will find that swimming or gymnastics are also popular. Cold winter temperatures may allow the school to have an outdoor rink, and then hockey becomes a source of enjoyment for many. In spring, though, the rinks begin melting, and so there is less opportunity to play. Then some students take up soccer again, while track and field also attracts many participants.

Here the grammatical subject (underlined) changes from sentence to sentence. Notice how much stronger the focus becomes when all the sentences have the same grammatical subject—either the same noun, a synonym, or a related pronoun:

> rev. Students at our school play a variety of sports these days. In the fall, most still choose football, although an increasing number now play soccer. When the ball season is over, some turn to basketball; others prefer swimming or gymnastics. If cold winter temperatures permit an outdoor rink, many students enjoy hockey. Once the ice begins to melt in spring, though, they can play less often. Then some take up soccer again, while others choose track and field.

Naturally it's not always possible to retain the same grammatical subject throughout a paragraph. If you were comparing the athletic pursuits of boys and girls, for example, you would have to switch back and forth between boys and girls as your grammatical subject. In the same way, you will have to shift when you are discussing several examples of an idea or exceptions to it.

AVOID MONOTONY

If most or all of the sentences in your paragraph have the same grammatical subject, how do you avoid boring your reader? There are two easy ways:

- **Use stand-in words.** Pronouns, either personal (*I, we, you, he, she, it, they*) or demonstrative (*this, that, those*) can stand in for the subject, as can synonyms (words or phrases that mean the same thing). The revised paragraph on school sports, for example, uses the pronouns *some, most,* and *they* as substitutes for *students*. Most well-written paragraphs have a liberal sprinkling of these stand-in words.
- **"Bury" the subject by putting something in front of it.** When the subject is placed in the middle of a sentence rather than at the beginning, it's less obvious to the reader. If you take another look at the revised paragraph, you'll see that in several sentences there is a word or phrase in front of the subject, giving the paragraph a feeling of variety. Even a single word, such as *first, then, lately,* or *moreover,* will do the trick. (Incidentally, this is a useful technique to remember when you are writing a letter of application and want to avoid starting every sentence with *I.*)

LINK YOUR IDEAS

To create coherent paragraphs, you need to link your ideas clearly. Linking words are those connectors—conjunctions and conjunctive adverbs—that show the *relations* between one sentence, or part of a sentence, and another; they're also known as transition words because they bridge the transition from one thought to another. Make a habit of using linking words when you shift from one grammatical subject or idea to another, whether the shift occurs within a single paragraph or as you move from one paragraph to the next. Here are some of the most common connectors and the logical relations they indicate:

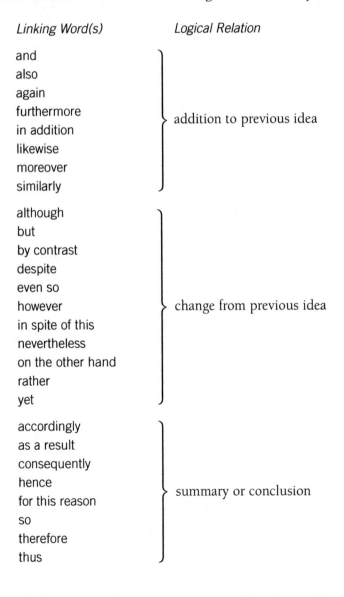

Linking Word(s)	*Logical Relation*
and also again furthermore in addition likewise moreover similarly	addition to previous idea
although but by contrast despite even so however in spite of this nevertheless on the other hand rather yet	change from previous idea
accordingly as a result consequently hence for this reason so therefore thus	summary or conclusion

Numerical terms such as *first*, *second*, and *third* also work well as links.

VARY THE LENGTH, BUT AVOID EXTREMES

Ideally, academic writing will have a balance of long and short paragraphs. Avoid the extremes—especially the one-sentence paragraph, which can only state an idea, without explaining or developing it. A series of short paragraphs is sometimes a sign that you have not developed your ideas in enough detail, or that you have started new paragraphs unnecessarily. On the other hand, a succession of long paragraphs can be tiring and difficult to read. In deciding when to start a new paragraph, remember always to consider what is clearest and most helpful for the reader.

BE CONCISE

At one time or another, you will probably be tempted to pad your writing. Whatever the reason—because you need to write two or three thousand words and have only enough to say for one thousand, or just because you think length is strength and hope to get a better mark for the extra words—padding is a mistake. You may fool some of the people some of the time, but most professors will not be impressed with unnecessary verbiage.

Strong writing is always concise. It leaves out anything that does not serve some communicative or stylistic purpose, in order to say as much as possible in as few words as possible. Concise writing will help you do better on both your essays and your exams.

USE ADVERBS AND ADJECTIVES SPARINGLY

Avoid the scatter-gun approach to adverbs and adjectives: don't use combinations of modifiers unless you are sure they clarify your meaning. One well-chosen word is always better than a series of synonyms.

orig.   As well as being <u>costly</u> and <u>financially extravagant</u>, the venture is <u>reckless</u> and <u>foolhardy</u>.

rev.   The venture is <u>foolhardy</u> as well as <u>costly</u>.

AVOID NOUN CLUSTERS

A recent trend in some writing is to use nouns as adjectives, as in the phrase *noun cluster*. This device can be effective occasionally, but frequent use can produce a monstrous pile-up of nouns. Breaking up noun clusters may not always result in fewer words, but it will make your writing easier to read.

orig.   word processor utilization manual

rev. manual for using word processors

orig. pollution investigation committee

rev. committee to investigate pollution

AVOID CHAINS OF RELATIVE CLAUSES

Sentences full of clauses beginning *which*, *that*, or *who* are usually wordier than necessary. Try reducing some of those clauses to phrases or single words:

orig. The solutions <u>which</u> were discussed last night have a practical benefit <u>which</u> is easily grasped by people <u>who</u> have no technical training.

rev. The solutions discussed last night have a practical benefit, easily grasped by non-technical people.

TRY REDUCING CLAUSES TO PHRASES OR WORDS

Independent clauses can often be reduced by subordination. Here are a few examples:

orig. The report was written in a clear and concise manner, and it was widely read.

rev. The report, written in a clear and concise manner, was widely read.
(or)

rev. Clear and concise, the report was widely read.

orig. His plan was of a radical nature and was a source of embarrassment to his employer.

rev. His radical plan embarrassed his employer.

STRIKE OUT HACKNEYED EXPRESSIONS AND CIRCUMLOCUTIONS

Trite or roundabout phrases may flow from your pen without a thought, but they make for stale prose. Unnecessary words are deadwood; be prepared to hunt and chop ruthlessly to keep your writing vital:

Wordy	*Revised*
due to the fact that	because
at this point in time	now
consensus of opinion	consensus

in the near future	soon
when all is said and done	[omit]
in the eventuality that	if
in all likelihood	likely

AVOID "IT IS" AND "THERE IS" BEGINNINGS

Although it may not always be possible, try to avoid *it is* or *there is (are)* beginnings. Your sentences will be crisper and more concise:

orig. There is little time remaining for the employees and management to reach a settlement before a strike is called.

rev. Little time remains for the employees and management to reach a settlement before a strike is called.

orig. It is certain that crime will increase.

rev. Crime will certainly increase.

BE FORCEFUL

Developing a forceful, vigorous style simply means learning some common tricks of the trade and practising them until they become habit.

CHOOSE ACTIVE OVER PASSIVE VERBS

An active verb creates more energy than a passive one does:

> *Passive:* The ball was thrown by her.
> *Active:* She threw the ball.

Moreover, passive constructions tend to produce awkward, convoluted phrasing. Writers of bureaucratic documents are among the worst offenders:

orig. It has been decided that the utilization of small rivers in the province for purposes of generating hydroelectric power should be studied by our department, and that a report to the deputy should be made by our director as soon as possible.

The passive verbs in this mouthful make it hard to tell who is doing what. This passage is much clearer without the passive verbs:

rev. The Minister of Natural Resources has decided that our department should study the use of small rivers in the province to generate hydro-electric power, and that our director should make a report to the deputy as soon as possible.

Passive verbs are appropriate in four specific instances:

1. When the subject is the passive recipient of some action:

   The politician <u>was heckled</u> by the angry crowd.

2. When you want to emphasize the object rather than the person acting:

   The anti-pollution devices in all three plants <u>will be improved</u>.

3. When you want to avoid an awkward shift from the subject of a sentence or paragraph. Using the passive will sometimes help you maintain focus:

   The contractor began to convert the single-family homes to apartments but <u>was stopped</u> by the police because a permit had not been issued.

4. When you want to avoid placing responsibility or blame:

   The plans <u>were delayed</u> when the proposer became ill.

When these exceptions don't apply, make an effort to use active verbs for a livelier style.

USE PERSONAL SUBJECTS

Most of us find it more interesting to learn about people than about things. Wherever possible, therefore, make the subjects of your sentences personal. This trick goes hand in hand with use of active verbs. Almost any sentence becomes livelier with active verbs and a personal subject:

orig. The <u>outcome</u> of the union members' vote <u>was</u> a <u>decision</u> to resume work on Monday.

rev. The <u>union members voted to return</u> to work on Monday.

Here's another example:

orig. <u>It can be assumed</u> that an <u>agreement was reached</u>, since <u>there were</u> smiles on both management and union sides when the <u>meeting was finished</u>.

rev. <u>We</u> can assume that <u>management and the union reached</u> an agreement, since both <u>bargainers were smiling</u> when <u>they finished</u> the meeting.

(or)

rev.   Apparently <u>management and union</u> <u>reached</u> an agreement since, when <u>they</u> <u>finished</u> the meeting, both <u>bargainers</u> <u>were</u> smiling.

USE CONCRETE DETAILS

Concrete details are easier to understand—and to remember—than abstract notions. Whenever you are discussing abstract concepts, therefore, always provide specific examples and illustrations; if you have a choice between a concrete word and an abstract one, choose the concrete. Consider this sentence:

> The French explored the northern territory and traded with the Native inhabitants.

Now see how a few specific details can bring the facts to life:

> The French voyageurs paddled their way along the river systems of the north, trading their blankets and copper kettles for the Indians' furs.

Suggesting that you add concreteness doesn't mean getting rid of all abstractions; it's simply a reminder to balance them with accurate details. The additional information, if it is concrete and correct, can improve your writing.

MAKE IMPORTANT IDEAS STAND OUT

Experienced writers know how to manipulate sentences in order to emphasize certain points. Here are some of their techniques:

PLACE KEY WORDS IN STRATEGIC POSITIONS

The positions of emphasis in a sentence are the beginning and, above all, at the end. If you want to bring your point home with force, don't put the key words in the middle of the sentence. Save them for the last:

orig.   People are less afraid of losing wealth than of losing face in this image-conscious society.

rev.   In this image-conscious society, people are less afraid of losing wealth than of losing face.

SUBORDINATE MINOR IDEAS

Small children connect incidents with a string of *ands*, as if everything were of equal importance:

> Our bus was delayed, and we were late for school, and we missed our class.

As they grow up, however, they learn to subordinate—to make one part of a sentence less important in order to emphasize another point:

> Because the bus was delayed, we missed our class.

Major ideas stand out more and connections become clearer when minor ideas are subordinated:

> orig. Night came and the ship slipped away from her captors.
>
> rev. When night came, the ship slipped away from her captors.

Make your most important idea the subject of the main clause, and try to put it at the end, where it will be most emphatic:

> orig. I was relieved when I saw my marks.
>
> rev. When I saw my marks, I was relieved.

VARY SENTENCE STRUCTURE

As with anything else, variety adds spice to writing. One way of adding variety, which will also make an important idea stand out, is to use a periodic rather than a simple sentence structure.

Most sentences follow the simple pattern of subject—verb—object (plus modifiers):

> The <u>dog</u> <u>bit</u> the <u>man</u> on the ankle.
>   S   V   O

A *simple sentence* such as this gives the main idea at the beginning and therefore creates little tension. A *periodic sentence*, on the other hand, does not give the main clause until the end, following one or more subordinate clauses:

> Since he had failed to keep his promises or to inspire the voters, in the next election <u>he</u> <u>was defeated</u>.
>   S   V

The longer the periodic sentence is, the greater the suspense and the more emphatic the final part. Since this high-tension structure is more difficult to read than the simple sentence, your readers would be exhausted if you used it too often. Save it for those times when you want to create a special effect or play on emotions.

VARY SENTENCE LENGTH

A short sentence can add punch to an important point, especially when it comes as a surprise. This technique can be particularly useful for conclusions. Don't overdo it, though. A string of long sentences may be monotonous, but a string of short ones can make your writing sound like a children's book.

USE CONTRAST

Just as a jeweller will highlight a diamond by displaying it against dark velvet, so you can highlight an idea by placing it against a contrasting background:

> *orig.* Most employees in industry do not have indexed pensions.
>
> *rev.* Unlike civil servants, most employees in industry do not have indexed pensions.

Using parallel phrasing will increase the effect of the contrast:

> Although she often spoke to university audiences, she seldom spoke to business groups.

USE A WELL-PLACED ADVERB OR CORRELATIVE CONSTRUCTION

Adding an adverb or two can sometimes help you to dramatize a concept:

> *orig.* The suggestion is good, but I doubt it will succeed.
>
> *rev.* The suggestion is good <u>theoretically</u>, but I doubt it will succeed <u>practically</u>.

Correlatives such as *both . . . and* or *not only . . . but also* can be used to emphasize combinations as well:

> *orig.* Professor Miceli was a good lecturer and a good friend.
>
> *rev.* Professor Miceli was <u>both</u> a good lecturer <u>and</u> a good friend.
>
> (or)
>
> *rev.* Professor Miceli was <u>not only</u> a good lecturer <u>but also</u> a good friend.

USE REPETITION

Repetition can be an effective device. It adds emphasis and can help stir the emotions:

> He fought injustice and corruption. He fought complacent politicians and inept policies. He fought hard, but he always fought fairly.

Of course, you would only use such a dramatic technique on rare occasions.

USE YOUR EARS

You ears are probably your best critics: make good use of them. Before producing a final copy of any piece of writing, read it out loud, in a clear voice. The difference between cumbersome and fluent passages will be unmistakable.

SOME FINAL ADVICE: WRITE BEFORE YOU REVISE

No one would expect you to sit down and put all this advice into practice as soon as you start to write. You would feel so constrained that it would be hard to get anything down on paper at all. You will be better off if you begin concentrating on these techniques during the editing process, when you are looking critically at what you have already written. Some experienced writers can combine the creative and critical functions, but most of us find it easier to write a rough draft first, before starting the detailed task of revising.

chApter 8

Planning and Organizing an Essay or Report

If you are one of the many students who dread writing an academic essay, you will find that following a few simple steps in planning and organizing will make the task easier—and the result better.

THE PLANNING STAGE

Some students claim they can write essays without any planning at all. On the rare occasions when they succeed, their writing is usually not as spontaneous as it seems: in fact, they have thought or talked a good deal about the subject in advance and have come to the task with some ready-made ideas. More often, students who try to write a lengthy essay without planning just end up frustrated. They get stuck in the middle and don't know how to finish, or they suddenly realize that they are rambling.

In contrast, most writers say that the planning stage is the most important part of the whole process. Certainly the evidence shows that poor planning usually leads to disorganized writing. In the majority of essays written by students, the single greatest improvement would not be better research or better grammar, but better organization.

This insistence on planning doesn't rule out exploratory writing. Many people find that the act of writing itself is the best way to generate ideas or overcome writer's block. The hard decisions about organization come after they've put something down on the page. Whether you organize before or after you begin to write, however, at some point you need to plan.

READING PRIMARY MATERIAL

Primary material is the direct evidence—usually books, articles, or research studies or reports—on which you will base your essay. Surprising as it may seem, the best way to begin working with this material is to give it a fast initial skim. Don't just start reading from cover to cover: first look at the table of contents, scan the index, and read the preface or introduction to get a sense of the author's purpose and plan. Getting an overview will allow you to focus your questions for a more purposeful and analytic second reading. Make no mistake:

a superficial reading is not all you need. You still have to work through the material carefully a second time. But an initial skim followed by a focused second reading will give you a much more thorough understanding than one slow plod ever will.

A WARNING ABOUT SECONDARY SOURCES

Always be sure you have a firm grasp of the primary material before you turn to secondary sources (commentaries on or analyses of the primary source). Some instructors discourage secondary reading in introductory courses because they know the dangers of relying too heavily on it. As we have pointed out earlier, it is always a good idea to review recent literature on the topic you have chosen to see where your views stand in relation to those of the experts in your discipline. However, if you turn to commentaries as a way around the difficulty of understanding the primary source, or if you base your argument solely on the interpretations of others, your essay will be trite and second-hand. Your interpretation could even be downright wrong, since at this stage you may not know enough about a subject to be able to evaluate the commentary. Secondary sources are an important part of research, but they can never substitute for your own active reading of the primary material.

ANALYZE YOUR SUBJECT: ASK QUESTIONS

Whether the subject you start with is one that has been assigned or suggested by your instructor or one that you have chosen yourself, it is bound to be too broad for an essay topic. You will have to analyze your subject in order to find a way of limiting it. The best way of analyzing is to ask questions that will lead to useful answers.

How do you form that kind of question? Journalists approach their stories through a six-question formula: *what? where? when? why? how?* and *who?* These six questions will lead you to six answers that will, in turn, lead to other questions. Most initial questions and the answers to them tend to be too general, but they will stimulate more specific questions that will help you refine your topic and formulate *the* basic question. The most important question can be posed within your statement of purpose or transformed into a thesis statement, perhaps as a hypothesis. Remember to make your statement limited, unified, and exact.

TRY THE "THREE-C APPROACH"

A more systematic scheme for analyzing a subject is the "three-C approach." It forces you to look at your topic from three different perspectives, asking basic questions about *components, change,* and *context:*

Components:

- What parts or categories can you use to break down the subject?
- Can the main points be subdivided?

Change:

- What features have changed?
- What temporal and spatial patterns can be observed?
- Is there a trend?
- What caused the change?
- What are the results of the change?

Context:

- What is the larger issue surrounding the subject?
- In what tradition or school of thought does the subject belong?
- How is the subject similar to, and different from, related subjects?

WHAT ARE THE *COMPONENTS* OF THE SUBJECT?

In other words, how might the subject be broken down into smaller elements? This question forces you to take a close look at the subject and helps you avoid over-simplification. Suppose that your assignment is to discuss the policies of Mackenzie King. After asking yourself about components, you might decide that you can split the subject into (1) domestic policies, and (2) foreign policies. Alternatively, you might divide it into (1) economic policies, (2) social policies, and (3) political policies. Then, if these components are too broad, you might break them down further, splitting economic policies into (a) fiscal, and (b) monetary policies; or splitting political policies into (a) relations with the provinces, and (b) relations with other countries.

WHAT FEATURES OF THE SUBJECT REFLECT *CHANGE*?

For example, did Mackenzie King alter his policies in a certain area over a period of years? Did he express contradictory views in different documents? What caused changes in policy? What were the effects of these changes?

WHAT IS THE *CONTEXT* OF THIS SUBJECT?

Into what particular school of thought or tradition does it fit? What are the similarities and differences between this subject and related ones? For example, how do Mackenzie King's policies compare with those of other Liberal prime ministers? With Conservative policies?

General as most of these questions are, you will find that they stimulate more specific questions—and thoughts—about the material, from which you can choose your topic and formulate a thesis. Remember that the ability to ask intelligent questions is one of the most important, though often underrated, skills that you can develop for any work, in university and outside.

ANALYZING A PRESCRIBED TOPIC

Even if the topic of your essay is supplied by your instructor, you still need to analyze it carefully. Try underlining key words to make sure that you don't neglect anything. Distinguish the main focus from subordinate concerns. A common error in dealing with prescribed topics is to emphasize one portion while giving short shrift to another. Give each part its proper due—and make sure that you actually do what the instructions tell you to do. To *discuss* is not the same as to *evaluate* or to *trace*; to *compare* means to show differences as well as similarities. These verbs tell you how to approach the topic; don't confuse them. The following definitions will help you decide how to approach your assignment:

outline   state simply, without much development of each point (unless asked).

trace   review by looking back—on stages or steps in a process, or on causes of an occurrence.

explain   show how or why something happens.

discuss   examine or analyze in an orderly way. This instruction allows you considerable freedom, as long as you take into account contrary evidence or ideas.

compare   examine differences as well as similarities.

evaluate   analyze strengths and weaknesses to arrive at an overall assessment of worth.

DEVELOP A HYPOTHESIS

As we have seen in Chapter 3, the hypothesis plays an essential role in the research cycle. But a hypothesis can also be useful when you are writing an essay that does not require a specific thesis. In fact, most students find it helpful to think of any academic essay as a way of demonstrating or proving a point, since the argumentative form is the easiest to organize and the most likely to produce forceful writing. In such cases, your hypothesis need be nothing more than a working thesis—an intended line of argument, which you are free to change at any stage in your planning. It works as a linchpin, holding together your information and ideas as you organize. It will help you define your intentions, make your research more selective, and focus your essay.

At some point in the writing process, you will probably want to make your hypothesis into an explicit thesis statement that can appear in your introduction. Even if you do not, however, you should take the time to develop your working thesis carefully. Use a complete sentence to express it, and above all, make sure that it is limited, unified, and exact (Trimmer, 1998: 18).

MAKE IT LIMITED

A limited thesis is one that is narrow enough to be examined thoroughly in the space you have available. Suppose, for example, that your general subject is the Canadian Alliance party in Canada. Such a subject is much too broad to be handled properly in an essay of one or two thousand words: you must limit it in some way and create a line of argument for which you can supply adequate supporting evidence. Following the analytic questioning process, you might find that you want to restrict it by time: "The Canadian Alliance party in the 1990s was indistinguishable in its monetary policies from the Progressive Conservative party." Or you might prefer to limit it by geography: "The development of the Canadian Alliance party in Alberta had less to do with its politics than with its political opportunities."

To take an example from anthropology, suppose that your general subject for a two-thousand-word essay is the role of religion. You might want to limit it by discussing a prominent religious ritual in one or two societies. So, for example, you might discuss how ritual dancing in one society directly expresses a prayer for divine interpretation in a hunt or battle, whereas in another society dancing has no obvious goal but to promote a sense of ecstasy and social communion. Whatever the discipline or subject, make sure that your topic is restricted enough that you can explore it in depth.

MAKE IT UNIFIED

To be unified, your thesis must have one controlling idea. Beware of the double-headed thesis: "Brian Mulroney introduced some of the boldest economic policies in Canadian history, but his failure to bring Quebec into the Constitution led to his downfall." What is the controlling idea here? The boldness of Mulroney's economic policies or the reason for his downfall? The essay should focus on one or the other. It is possible to have two or more related ideas in a thesis, but only if one of them is clearly in control, with all the other ideas subordinated to it: "Although Mulroney was widely applauded for his efforts to bring Quebec into the Constitution, his eventual failure in this endeavour was the cause of his downfall."

MAKE IT EXACT

It is important, especially in a thesis, to avoid vague terms such as *interesting* and *significant,* as in "Helmut Schmidt was Germany's most interesting chancellor." Does "interesting" mean effective or daring in his policies, or does it mean personally charming? Don't simply say that "Freud's analysis of dreams is an important feature of his writing" when you can be more precise about the work you are discussing. In this case, you can focus on the kind of dreams Freud analyzed, and what he inferred from them: "In his study of the 'Wolf Man' Freud uncovered important clues about the ways people repress and reinterpret childhood experiences, which come to light in dreams and bizarre behaviour."

Remember to be as specific as possible when creating a thesis, in order to focus your essay. Don't just make an assertion—give the main reasons for it. Instead of merely stating, "Many Westerners are resentful of central Canada," add an explanation: ". . . because of historic grievances, such as tariffs and freight rates." If these details make your thesis sound awkward, don't worry: a thesis is only a planning device, something to guide the organization of your ideas. You can change the wording of it in your final essay.

RESEARCH YOUR TOPIC

If your topic requires more facts or evidence than the primary material provides, or if you want to know other people's opinions on the subject, you will need to do some research. Some students like to read about the subject area before they decide on an essay topic. For them, the thesis comes after the exploration. You may find this approach useful for some essays, but it's better to narrow your scope and plan a tentative thesis before you turn to secondary sources—you'll save time and produce a more original essay.

EXPLORE THE WEB

The Internet is a rapidly expanding, remarkably diverse, and, at times, frustrating resource. It can be an extremely useful research tool if used correctly, but it can be overwhelming for novice users. If you aren't used to surfing the Net, it's a good idea to pick up one of the hundreds of books that now exist on how best to use this important resource. Your college or university may also offer a course in using the Internet for academic purposes. Electronic research materials fall into two main categories: those that are in the public domain and those that aren't. You can quickly find huge amounts of material in the public domain using a search engine like Google. Type in "arranged marriage," for example, and you will find thousands of links to websites of varying value. Some will be academic, others will be commercial, and others—blogs, for instance—will be personal. Surprisingly, many in each category are likely to contain useful ideas and references.

Research materials in the private domain are usually accessible through your college or university website, by means of your library system. Typically, your college or university library will have subscribed to scores if not hundreds of electronic databases, portals, and e-journals. So, for example, you will likely be able to access such databases as Sociological Abstracts or PsychInfo or Medline electronically, even from the comfort of your own home. This enables you to carry out a thorough, lengthy literature review at any time of day or night, in your pyjamas or your underwear, if you like. Such previously unheard-of convenience is not to be laughed at: it has revolutionized scholarship over the last twenty years. More important, it has raised the expectations of your graders and instructors. You will now be expected to provide appropriate, up-to-date references on any topic you are writing about. And remember, it is just as easy for your grader to find references online as it is for you to do so; you can't get away with using mouldy references from 1972 and 1985 any more, just because your older sister (or mother) used them.

EXPLORE THE LIBRARY

Even with the abundance of research material available online, it's always a good idea to get to know your way around the library. You don't want to be so overwhelmed by its size and complexity that you waste time and energy trying to find information. Most academic libraries have orientation seminars specifically designed to show you where and how to find what you want. Take advantage of these services. Librarians will be glad to show you the bibliographies, indices, online databases, and other reference tools for your field of study. Once you are familiar with these basic resources you will be able to check systematically for available material.

TAKE GOOD NOTES

Finding your research material is one thing; taking notes that are dependable and easy to use is another. With time, you will develop your own best method, but for a start you might try the index-card system. Record each new idea or piece of evidence on a separate card. The number you need will depend on the range and type of your research. When you've finished with your note-taking, you can then easily arrange the cards in the order in which you will use them.

McRoberts, Kenneth. 2001. *Catalonia: Nation Building Without a State*. Toronto: Oxford.

- Compares the "Catalan Law" to Québec's *Charte de la langue française*:

    "The *Charte* requires that <u>all</u> outdoor advertising be exclusively in French; the *Llei de Política Lingüística* applies to advertising only in public institutions." (pg. 157)

    [DP302.C68 M32]

More and more, students are using computers for this kind of note-taking. A disadvantage of this approach is that a computer can crash, taking all of your data with it, and is more likely to get stolen more than a modest set of cards; moreover, not everyone has continuous access to a computer. However, most post-secondary students do have computer access most of the time, and the advantages of taking notes on a computer far outweigh their disadvantages. For one thing, using a computer to keep your research material enables you to revise and reorganize this material endlessly in little time, with almost no trouble. What's more, you can easily access your computerized notes using keywords, so you can rapidly find everything you collected on the topic of, say, Karl Marx, or single-parent families, or NAFTA. Existing software programs like NUDist are designed to do exactly that with large bodies of research data collected by professionals. You can keep your notes in a text box the same way you would write them out on an index card. Remember that if you're taking notes from an online source to include the full URL and the date you accessed the site.

So get used to using your computer creatively. It will make your research process faster and much easier.

Whatever method you follow, remember that exact records are essential for proper footnotes. For every entry, check that the bibliographic details are complete, including the name of the author, title of the source, place and date of publication, and page number, as well as the library call number. For online sources, record the URL in full and the date you accessed the site. Nothing is more frustrating than using a piece of information in an essay only to find that you aren't sure where it came from. If you take several ideas from one source, you can put the main bibliographic details about the author and work on one card, and then use a separate card for each particular idea or theory.

Also remember to check that quotations are copied precisely and include page numbers for every reference, even if you paraphrase or summarize the idea rather than copy it word for word.

RESEARCH REPORTS

Research reports in the social sciences follow certain conventional patterns. They differ in many respects from essays and book reports and are more similar to scientific or technical writing in the "hard sciences." A typical report consists of four sections—*Objectives*, *Background*, *Methods*, and *Results*—that mirror the stages of the research project itself as we have outlined them in this book: design, theory, measurement, and argument. We will discuss each of these in turn as they relate to the writing of a research report.

OBJECTIVES (DESIGN)

The first section of a research report is typically called *Objectives* or *Goals* or *The Research Problem*. It corresponds to the part of the research project we have called *design* in that it provides a general overview of the structure of the research task. This section states the topic to be discussed or the question to be answered. It also indicates whether the goal of the report is an unstructured description and exploration or one of the more highly structured approaches we have discussed at length: explanation, prediction, examination of conditional relationships, or study of a system of relationships.

An author may use this section of a report to indicate the anticipated practical or theoretical value of the research he or she has done. Where the research is justified on the grounds of its social utility, the author may want to provide some facts about the magnitude of the problem to be solved and the ways in which the research may help to solve it. Where the value of the research lies in its contribution to a scholarly debate, the author can lead directly into the next section of the paper, the "literature review," which is a close discussion of these debates.

So, for example, you might begin a research paper on teenage suicide by stating that your purpose is to gather and analyze comparative cross-national data on recent trends. You could note that in many countries teenage suicide is rapidly becoming a leading cause of death among young people; that the rise in teenage suicide rates is considerably higher in certain countries than in others;

and that the purpose of your paper is to understand the reason for this difference in trends. You might then suggest some practical benefits that may flow from such knowledge—for example, steps that governments or schools might take to reverse the trend in countries with the fastest growing suicide rates; or theoretical benefits that may follow—such as a better understanding of the ways certain social or cultural factors (e.g., excessive competitiveness in school performance) may contribute to the problem.

BACKGROUND (THEORY)

The next section of the paper, typically called *Background* or *Previous Research* or *Literature Review*, reflects the *theory* behind research. Its purpose is to review, in a brief but systematic manner, the current state of knowledge about the problem under consideration.

To write this section of the report you must first review the literature. In many areas, the existing literature is extremely voluminous, running to hundreds or even thousands of books and articles. Worse, these materials may be spread through dozens of different sources. For example, you could look for literature on teenage suicide in journals and books in the fields of sociology, psychiatry, psychology, social work, family studies, epidemiology, and family medicine, to name only a few! It is certainly not possible to carry out a credible literature review using the hit-and-miss method of rummaging through a few textbooks in a single field of social science.

LITERATURE REVIEWS

For most secondary research in the social sciences, the best way to start is with a literature review. As we discussed in Chapter 3, a literature review will inform you of the current state of knowledge in your chosen topic area. All good primary research begins with a literature review to ensure that a study being contemplated has not already been done elsewhere.

Literature reviews may also reveal far more than the results of previous research. They may indicate trends in research and show what questions are being asked and why. They may also illustrate gaps in the existing research, which may give you some ideas for a research topic. As many outstanding scholars have been inspired by questions that have not yet been asked as have worked to expand upon research done by their intellectual predecessors.

Literature reviews, until recently, required considerable time and effort. Today, however, with the availability of so much information on the Internet, comprehensive searches can be done quickly and easily. Students, take note: as secondary research becomes increasingly easy, more professors will expect you to demonstrate that you've done a thorough review of the literature.

PROBLEMS WITH ONLINE DATABASES

Although searching online databases is easy, these databases do have limitations. Perhaps the greatest of these is the fact that online databases are not very current—even less current than academic journals. Only after an article has been written, submitted to a journal, reviewed, and printed will it be archived to a database.

Second, most databases contain only the article abstracts, and these may not even be the abstracts that the authors originally provided. The abstracts may have been edited for content, size, consistency, or any one of a number of other factors. This can make it more difficult to determine if the articles returned from your search are actually relevant to the topic you're researching.

Finally, you will need to have some idea of what you're looking for. Many databases contain hundreds of thousands of abstracts. Trying to browse until you find something of interest to you may make your search far longer and less productive than it should be.

PROBLEMS WITH INTERNET SOURCES

Academic articles may not supply all of the information you're looking for, especially if you want the depth that usually only qualitative data can provide.

Imagine, for example, that you are conducting research on the proliferation of websites with information about the prevention of AIDS. You want to find out what information is available, what types of organizations are disseminating it, and who is accessing it. Web-based content is changing all the time, and any academic journal articles that exist on the subject may already be out of date. In this case, you may be better conducting your research online.

Be aware that unlike academic journals, which are peer-reviewed and tend to be reliable sources of information, many websites do not have editorial boards and publish material which has not undergone any review process. Anyone can publish online, as the current proliferation of blogs will attest. You need to be sure that the author or publisher of any material you use has the necessary authority to lend credibility to the site.

Here are some tips for evaluating websites:

- Look for a statement identifying the site host and giving the author's qualifications and contact information.

- Check the URL. For example, a tilde (~) indicates a personal page where you are likely to find expressions of opinion; and you would expect a *.edu* (education) or *.gov* (government) domain to be more factual than a *.com* (commercial) domain, which might be trying to sell something, or a *.org* (organization) domain, which might have a particular bias.
- Determine the currency of the site. There should be a clear indication of the date when the material was written, the date when it was published, and the date when it was last updated.
- Evaluate the accuracy of the information by checking facts and figures with other sources. Data published on the site should be documented in citations or a bibliography, and research methods should be explained.
- Be wary of blogs. Although some companies have official blogs that can offer good advice about subjects like the stock market and real estate, many are simply online diaries published by a rapidly increasing number of people who are expressing personal opinion and nothing more. Using such unverified material can seriously undermine your essay, as many students have discovered.
- Assess the overall quality of the site as indicated by its level of correctness and writing standard.

METHODS (MEASURES)

The next section of the research report, typically called *Methods*, may include subsections called *Indicators* (or *Measures*), *Sampling*, and *Data Collection*. This is the section in which you put your hypotheses to the test.

Continuing with our example, your goal will be to collect thorough and reliable data on teenage suicide in different times and places. To do this, you will have to look in published official statistics. You will have to make sure that these statistics are comparable: for example, that they define death by suicide in the same ways and provide statistics in the same age groupings. Where the data are not strictly comparable, they must be adjusted to be as comparable as possible. This section of the paper is often long and complex, especially if you have had to create a special data-collection instrument or procedure for coding published statistical data. Since scientists assume that the quality of research findings is no better than the research methods used to produce them, your readers will want a great deal of information about what you did to get your results. For this reason, the "measures" section of a research paper may be the longest one of all.

RESULTS (ARGUMENT)

The final section of a research paper is typically called *Results* or *Findings*, with subsections often headed *Data Analysis*, *Conclusions*, and *Discussions*. Taken together, these make up the portion of the report that we have called the *argument*. Its purpose is to present and interpret the data collected; to judge whether they supported the hypotheses; and, based on that judgment, to draw conclusions about the theory that gave rise to the hypotheses. This section—and the report itself—may end with a modified version of the original theory and suggestions for further research that will test the revised theory.

To continue our example of teenage suicide, we may find that our hypotheses are partly valid and partly invalid. The data may show that although teenage suicide rates were higher during the recession of 1975–85 than during the boom of 1955–65, both rates were higher than during the Depression of 1929–39. Likewise, they may show that although teenage suicide rates are consistently higher in Japan and France than in Canada and the United States, they are not higher in England than in Canada; and further, that the difference in rates between Canada and the United States is as great as that between the United States and Japan. These findings, while partly supporting our theory, contain too many anomalies for comfort.

The next task would be to attempt to account for these anomalies. Was the original theory wrong? Or do some other factors, yet unexamined, also enter into the explanation? If the latter, what might these factors be, and how might we conduct a project to determine whether they really are contributing to teenage suicide?

In this way a good research project reaches backwards and forwards: backwards, by situating itself in the existing literature of competing findings and theories; forwards, by contributing new findings, revised theories, and suggestions for further research that will refine our understanding of the topic. It may be too much to expect that a student research paper will provide a breakthrough in knowledge, or even a significant reinterpretation of the problem. However, it is not too much to expect that it will demonstrate a grasp of the purposes, conventions, and techniques of social science research, however miniaturized.

You will note that almost every article in a scholarly journal is preceded by a brief *abstract*, which provides a capsulized version of the entire report. About one double-spaced page in length, this section is extremely useful for the reader, as you will understand once you have conducted a literature review. Although abstracts are not always required for student work, writing an abstract may also help you to see more clearly what you have accomplished. In an applied-research project written for government or business, such an abstract is expanded to several pages and is called an *Executive Summary*. Since it is often the only part of the report read closely by most readers, it assumes a great deal of importance for the researcher. This is another reason for learning how to write a proper abstract: it may come in handy later on in your report-writing career.

We should finish this brief discussion by reminding you that it is far better to do a good job on a small problem (or a small portion of a big problem) than to do a poor job on too big a problem. Remember, too, that every research project will get bigger than you had anticipated as you carry it out. So start small and let the project grow. If you do this with a problem worth researching, you cannot fail to produce something of value.

MAKING THE BEST USE OF YOUR COMPUTER

Computers are invaluable at all stages of the research process, from the literature review, through data collation and analysis, to the final production of your report. Computers cannot make you a better writer, but they can be extremely useful by letting you revise your work quickly and easily. They will also help you produce clear and attractive tables, charts, and graphs to present your results. In this section, we discuss the features of some common programs that will be of use to social science researchers. We encourage you to explore these tools and learn to use them to help make your data as professional in its appearance as it has been in its collection.

BACK UP YOUR FILES!

Murphy's law says that what can go wrong, will. What seems more common to professors is that what can go wrong the night before a paper is due, will. The trick is not keeping all of your eggs in one basket. Save your work regularly in case of a power outage or system crash and make copies on disk at the same time. If you don't have a disk handy, you can e-mail yourself a copy of the file, thereby storing it on your e-mail server. There are also Web sites that let you store files on them. Accounts are free, and it's not a bad idea to store copies of current projects this way. It can be handy to be able to access your files from any computer with Web access, so that no matter where you are, you can get to your work if you have to.

USING WORD PROCESSORS TO EDIT YOUR WORK

Most word processors will let you track changes to your documents. This feature is handy when you are co-authoring a report, revising successive drafts of a document, or even just letting a friend or colleague proofread your work. It enables you to see exactly what someone thought should be added or cut, and then you can decide to keep—or delete—the proposed changes.

Your word processor will have a built-in spell-checker and grammar-checker, but be warned: computers find only the obvious mistakes. Computers can't catch the *wring* word, only *works* that aren't in its dictionary—see what we *bean*? Always proofread your work thoroughly, and always have someone else proofread your work as well. Your work usually (we hope) makes sense to you; another reader will help you find places where you have not been clear.

USING SPREADSHEETS

A spreadsheet program lets you input data into a table and perform calculations on it. You can enter a column of numbers and have the spreadsheet determine sums and averages, among hundreds of other functions. Perhaps most usefully, the table updates all of its calculations as you work with the data, so you'll immediately be able to observe the effects of manipulating the data across all of your work.

Spreadsheets also come with features that let you produce charts and graphs of your data in seconds. You select which data you would like to represent graphically and in what form you would like to present it (e.g., pie chart, bar graph, etc.), and the computer does the rest. Your graphics will also be updated automatically as you work with the source data in the tables.

Spreadsheet software is indispensable in social science research. Not only does it allow you to sort and update your data, it gives you a tool to enhance your assignments with graphs and charts.

USING GRAPHIC PRESENTATION SOFTWARE

Graphic presentation software, such as PowerPoint, enables you to place text and graphics in slides that can be projected onto a screen and shown in sequence to an audience, or else displayed to a smaller group on a computer monitor. Throughout your academic career and beyond, you will need to present information to different audiences. Spending some time now to learn how to do it effectively using the latest technology is a worthwhile investment.

The following are some things to keep in mind when using presentation software:

- Be consistent in the styles you use for lettering and formatting.
- Use colour wisely. Certain colours—yellow and orange, for instance—are hard to read unless you're using a plain, dark background. Don't overuse colours by using different colours for each slide. A consistent use of colour makes a stronger impression.
- Choose a simple, clean, readable font, one that can be read easily from the back of a room. Sans serif fonts such as Tahoma or Arial are among the better ones to use.
- Use a size of type that can be read with ease from the back of a room. You may wish to try several sizes before identifying the best size for your purpose.
- Don't overload any slide with too many words. Use point form to create succinct statements, and avoid embellishments. Don't include anything that is not essential to the information being conveyed.
- Finally, don't be seduced into using only the ready-made templates available with your software. Think differently. Spend some time considering exactly what you want to show and how you want it to appear. Formatting the slides yourself guarantees that you will get the look you want.

DON'T LET THE SYSTEM RULE YOUR THINKING

Your computer can make your work look great, but don't be fooled into thinking that fancy graphics and a slick presentation replace intelligent thinking. Your paper must be well organized and your data clearly presented; laying it out neatly and adding graphics are just finishing touches. The computer is an extremely useful tool, but first and foremost, your professor will want to see that you've been using your head!

cHApter 9

WRITING AN ESSAY OR EXAM

WRITING AN ESSAY

Whichever method you use to collect data for an essay, you will soon have a collection of research findings on your topic of interest. Your task is then to put these into meaningful order. You should be looking for

- findings that are repeated so often as to seem unassailable;
- findings that are disputed or opposed; and
- theories that seek to explain these findings.

Your goal here is to use the literature review to sharpen your own thinking about your research problem to the point where you can state hypotheses—predictions that can be tested with the data you will collect.

To return to our earlier example of teenage suicide, the literature may show that suicides by teenagers are most common around exam time; that suicide notes reflect a concern among teens with academic and other kinds of personal failure; and that suicide is more common among career-conscious middle-class teens than among job-conscious working-class teens. These findings would suggest the following hypotheses:

A. Teenage suicide will rise in periods when adults are expressing the greatest concern about the job market and their children's career prospects, and will decline in periods of economic prosperity; and
B. Teenage suicide will be greatest in countries where educational "streaming" is most severe—that is, where a child's life chances will be largely determined by a set of exams taken in adolescence.

Hypothesis A predicts that North American suicide rates for teenagers will be higher in the periods 1975–85 and 1929–39 (i.e., periods of high unemployment), while hypothesis B predicts that suicide rates for teenagers will be higher in Japan, France, and England (where educational streaming prevails) than in Canada and the United States (where it does not). Your research goal is now to test these hypotheses.

CREATING AN OUTLINE

Individual writers differ in their need for a formal plan. Some say they never have an outline, while others maintain they can't write without one; most fall somewhere in between. Since organization is such a common problem, though, it's a good idea to know how to draw up an effective plan. The exact form it takes will depend on the pattern you are using to develop your ideas—whether you are defining, classifying, or comparing, for example (see page 164–6).

If you have special problems with organizing material, your outline should be formal, written in complete sentences. On the other hand, if your mind is naturally logical, you may find it's enough just to jot down a few words on a scrap of paper. For most students, an informal but well-organized outline in point form is the most useful model:

I. Introduction
THESIS: When Prime Minister Pierre Elliott Trudeau first came to power in Canada, his style was seen as an enormous asset, but by the 80s the same style was increasingly seen as a liability.

II. Trudeau's early style perceived in a positive light
   A. Charismatic
      1. Public adulation; "Trudeaumania"
      2. Media awe
   B. Intellectual
   C. Tough
      1. Handling of journalists
      2. Handling of Quebec
   D. Anti-establishment
      1. Swinging lifestyle
      2. Disregard for government traditions

III. Later reversal: Trudeau's image becomes negative
   A. Irritating
      1. Public opinion polls
      2. Media disenchantment
   B. Out of touch with economic reality
   C. Confrontational
      1. With individual dissenters
      2. With premiers
      3. With Opposition leaders
   D. Arrogant
      1. Extravagant lifestyle in time of recession
      2. Autocratic approach to governing

IV. Conclusion

The guidelines for this kind of outline are simple:

- **Code your categories.** Use different sets of markings to establish the relative importance of your entries.
- **Categorize according to importance.** Make sure that only items of equal value are put in equivalent categories. Give major points more weight than minor ones.
- **Check lines of connection.** Make sure that each of the main categories is directly linked to the central thesis. Then see that each subcategory is directly linked to the larger category that contains it. Checking these lines of connection is the best way of preventing essay muddle.
- **Be consistent.** In arranging your points, be consistent. You may choose to move from the most important point to the least important, or vice versa, as long as you follow the same order every time.
- **Use parallel wording.** Phrasing each entry in a similar way will make it easier to be consistent in your presentation.
- **Be logical.** In addition to checking for lines of connection and organizational consistency, ensure that the overall development of your work is logical. Does each heading/idea/set of data/discussion flow into the next, leading the reader through your material in the most logical manner?

A FINAL WORD

Be prepared to change your outline at any time in the writing process. Your initial outline is not meant to put an iron clamp on your thinking but to relieve anxiety about where you're heading. A careful outline prevents frustration and dead ends—that "I'm stuck, where can I go from here?" feeling. But since the very act of writing will usually generate new ideas, you should be ready to modify your original plan. Just remember that any new outline must have the consistency and clear connections required for a unified essay.

THE WRITING STAGE

WRITING THE FIRST DRAFT

Rather than strive for perfection from the moment they begin to write, most writers find it easier to compose the first draft as quickly as possible and do extensive revisions later. However you begin, you cannot expect the first draft to be the final copy. Skilled writers know that revising is a necessary part of the writing process, and that care taken with revisions makes the difference between a mediocre essay and a good one.

You don't need to write all parts of the essay in the same order in which they are to appear in the final copy. In fact, many students find the introduction the hardest part to write. If you face the first blank page with a growing sense of paralysis, try leaving the introduction until later and start with the first idea in your outline. If you feel so intimidated that you haven't even been able to draw up an outline, you might try the approach suggested by John Trimble (1975:11) and charge right ahead with any kind of beginning—even a simple "My first thoughts on this subject are . . ." Instead of sharpening pencils or running out for a snack, try to get going. Don't worry about grammar or wording: at this stage, the object is just to get your writing juices flowing.

You can't expect this kind of exploratory writing to resemble the first draft that follows an outline. You will probably need to do a great deal more changing and reorganizing, but at least you will have the relief of seeing words on a page to work with. Many experienced writers—and not only those with writer's block—find this the most productive way to proceed.

DEVELOPING YOUR IDEAS: SOME COMMON PATTERNS

The way you develop your ideas will depend on your essay topic, and essay topics can vary enormously. Even so, most essays follow one or another of a handful of basic organizational patterns. Here are some of the patterns and ways to use them effectively:

DEFINING

Sometimes a whole essay is an extended definition, explaining the meaning of a term that is complicated, controversial, or simply important to your field of study: for example, *nationalism* in political science, *monetarism* in economics, or *culture* in anthropology. Perhaps you may want to begin a detailed discussion of a topic by defining a key term, and then shift to a different organizational pattern. In either case, make your definition exact: it should be broad enough to include all the things that belong in the category but narrow enough to exclude things that don't belong. A good definition builds a kind of verbal fence around a word, herding together all the members of the class and cutting off all outsiders.

For any discussion of a term that goes beyond a bare definition, you should give concrete illustrations or examples. Depending on the nature of your essay, these could vary in length from one or two sentences to several paragraphs or even pages. If you are defining monetarism, for instance, you would probably want to discuss at some length theories of leading monetarists.

In an extended definition, it's also useful to point out the differences between the term in question and any others that are connected or often confused with it. For instance, if you are defining *deviance* you might want to distinguish it from *criminality*; if you are defining *common law* you might want to distinguish it from *statute law*.

CLASSIFYING

Classifying means dividing something into its separate parts according to a given principle of selection. The principle or criterion may vary. You could classify kinship, for example, according to whether it is traced through the mother's line or the father's, or both; whether it is by blood or marriage; and whether it includes only immediate parent-child (nuclear) relationships or more distant (extended) relations. Members of a given population might be classified according to age group, occupation, income, and so on. If you are organizing your essay by a system of classification, remember the following:

- All members of a class must be accounted for. If any are left over, you need to alter some categories or add more.
- Categories can be divided into subcategories. You should consider using subcategories if there are significant differences within a category. If, for instance, you are classifying the work force according to occupation, you might want to create subcategories according to income level.
- Any subcategory should contain at least two items.

EXPLAINING A PROCESS

This kind of organization shows how something works or has worked, whether it be the process of urbanization, the process of justice, or the stages in a political or military campaign. The important guideline to remember is to take a systematic approach to break down the process into a series of steps or stages. Although at times it may vary, most often your order will be chronological, in which case you should see that the sequence is accurate and easy to follow. Whatever the arrangement, you can make the process easier to follow if you start a new paragraph for each new stage.

TRACING CAUSES OR EFFECTS

Showing how certain events have led to or resulted from other events is a complex process, and you must be careful not to oversimplify a relationship between cause and effect. For a detailed discussion of causal analysis, see Chapter 2.

COMPARING

Students sometimes forget that comparing things means showing differences as well as similarities—even if the instructions do not say "compare and contrast." The easiest way of comparing two things—though not always the best—is to discuss the first subject in the comparison thoroughly and then move on to the second:

Subject X:	Point 1
	Point 2
	Point 3
Subject Y:	Point 1
	Point 2
	Point 3

The problem with this kind of comparison is that it often sounds like two separate essays slapped together.

This kind of analysis is often more effective when you integrate the two subjects, first in your introduction (by putting them both in a single context) and again in your conclusion, where you should bring together the important points you have made about each. When discussing the second subject, try to refer repeatedly to your findings about the first subject (e.g., "Unlike *X*, *Y* does such and such . . .") This method may be the wisest choice if the subjects you are comparing seem so unalike that it is hard to create similar categories by which to discuss them—if the points you are making about *X* are of a different type than the points you are making about *Y*.

If you can find similar criteria or categories for discussing both subjects, however, the comparison will be more effective if you organize it like this:

Category 1:	Subject *X*
	Subject *Y*
Category 2:	Subject *X*
	Subject *Y*
Category 3:	Subject *X*
	Subject *Y*

Because this kind of comparison is more tightly integrated, it is easier for the reader to see the similarities and differences between the subjects. As a result, the essay is likely to be more forceful.

INTRODUCTIONS

The beginning of an essay has a dual purpose: to indicate your topic and the way you intend to approach it, and to whet your reader's interest in what you have to say. One effective way of introducing a topic is to place it in a context— to supply a kind of backdrop that will put it in perspective. The idea is to step back a pace and discuss the area into which your topic fits, and then gradually lead into your specific field of discussion. Sheridan Baker (1981:24–5) calls this the *funnel approach* (see page 169). For example, suppose that your topic is the industrial development of a particular Third-World country. You might begin with a more general discussion of industrialization in the West and then move on to industrialization in the most advanced Asian and African countries before focusing on your specific topic. A funnel opening is applicable to almost any kind of essay.

It's a good idea to try to grab your reader's interest right from the start. You know from your own reading how a dull beginning can put you off a book or an article. The fact that your instructor has to read on anyway makes no difference. If a reader has to get through thirty or forty similar essays, it's all the more important for yours to stand out. A funnel opening isn't the only way to catch the reader's attention. Here are three of the most common leads:

- **The quotation.** This approach works especially well when the quotation is taken from the person or work that you will be discussing. You can also use a quotation from an unrelated source, as long as it is relevant to your topic and not so well known that it will appear trite. A dictionary of quotations can be helpful here by letting you find quotes by author, key words, or, in some cases, topic.

- **The question.** A rhetorical question will only annoy the reader if it's commonplace or if the answer is obvious, but a thought-provoking question can make a strong opening. Just be sure that somewhere in your essay you answer the question.

- **The anecdote or telling fact.** This is the kind of concrete lead that journalists often use to grab their readers' attention. Save it for your least formal essays—and remember that the incident must really highlight the ideas you are going to discuss.

Whatever your lead, it must relate to your topic: never sacrifice relevance for originality. Finally, whether your introduction is one paragraph or several, make sure that by the end of it your reader knows exactly what the purpose of your essay is and how you intend to accomplish it.

CONCLUSIONS

Endings can be painful—sometimes for the reader as much as for the writer. Too often, the feeling that one ought to say something profound and memorable produces the kind of prose that suggests violins throbbing in the background. You know the sort of thing:

> Clearly, Milton Friedman's insight into the operation of Western economies is both intellectually and emotionally stimulating. He has opened broad vistas and forced us to reassess the moral and political underpinnings of economic decision making in the modern world.

Why is this embarrassing? Because it's nothing more than a collection of phoney clichés.

Experienced editors often say that many articles and essays would be better without their final paragraphs: in other words, when you have finished saying what you have to say, the only thing to do is stop. This advice may work for short essays, where you need to keep the central point firmly in the foreground and don't need to remind the reader of it at the end. However, for longer pieces, where you have developed a number of ideas or a complex line of argument, you should provide a sense of closure. Readers welcome an ending that helps tie the ideas together; they don't like to feel they've been left dangling. And since the final impression is often the most lasting, it's in your interest to finish strongly. Simply restating your thesis or summarizing what you have already said may not be forceful enough. What are the other options?

- **The inverse funnel.** The simplest and most basic conclusion is one that restates the thesis in different words and then discusses its implications. Baker (1981) calls this the inverse funnel approach, as opposed to the funnel approach of the opening paragraph. One danger in moving to a wider perspective is that you may try to embrace too much. When a conclusion expands too far it tends to lose focus and turn into an empty cliché, like the conclusion in the preceding example. It's always better to discuss specific implications than to leap into the thin air of vague generalities.
- **The new angle.** A variation of the basic inverse-funnel approach is to reintroduce your argument with a new twist. Suggesting some fresh angle can add excitement to your ending. Beware of introducing an entirely new idea, though, or one that's only loosely connected to your original argument: the result could be jarring or even off-topic.
- **The full circle.** If your introduction is based on an anecdote, a question, or a startling fact, you can complete the circle by referring to it again in relation to some of the insights revealed in the main body of your essay.
- **The stylistic flourish.** Some of the most successful conclusions end on a strong stylistic note. Try varying the sentence structure: if most

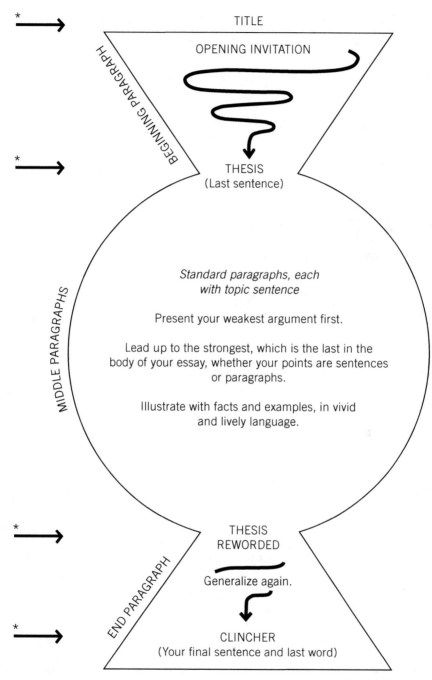

* → TITLE
OPENING INVITATION

BEGINNING PARAGRAPH

* → THESIS
(Last sentence)

MIDDLE PARAGRAPHS

Standard paragraphs, each with topic sentence

Present your weakest argument first.

Lead up to the strongest, which is the last in the body of your essay, whether your points are sentences or paragraphs.

Illustrate with facts and examples, in vivid and lively language.

* → THESIS REWORDED

END PARAGRAPH

Generalize again.

* → CLINCHER
(Your final sentence and last word)

*Focal points

SOURCE: Sheridan Baker and Laurence B. Gamache, *The Canadian Practical Stylist*, 4th ed. (Don Mills, ON: Addison-Wesley, 1998), p. 65. Reprinted by permission of Pearson Education Canada Inc.

of your sentences are long and complex, make the last one short and punchy, or vice versa. Sometimes you can dramatize your idea with a striking phrase or colourful image. When you are writing your essay, keep your eyes open and your ears tuned for fresh ways of putting things, and save the best for the end.

None of these approaches to endings is exclusive, of course. You may even find that several of them can be combined in a single essay. Whichever approach you take, just remember that a conclusion should never refer to facts that have not been mentioned in the main body of your essay.

THE EDITING STAGE

Often the best writer in a class is not the one who can dash off a fluent first draft, but the one who is the best editor. To edit well, you need to see your work as the reader will: you have to distinguish between what you meant to say and what is actually on the page. For this reason, it's a good idea to leave some time between drafts so that when you begin to edit, you will be looking at the writing afresh rather than reviewing it from memory. Now is the time to go to a movie or play some squash—do anything that will take your mind off your work. Without this distancing period, you can become so involved that it's hard to see your paper objectively.

Editing doesn't mean simply checking your work for errors in grammar or spelling. It means looking at the piece as a whole to see if the ideas are

- well organized,
- well documented, and
- well expressed.

It may mean making changes to the structure of your essay by adding paragraphs or sentences, deleting others, and moving others around. Experienced writers may be able to check several aspects of their work at the same time, but if you are inexperienced or in doubt about your writing, it's best to look at the organization of the ideas before you tackle sentence structure, diction, style, and documentation.

What follows is a checklist of questions to ask yourself as you begin editing. Far from all-inclusive, it focuses on the first step: examining the organization. You probably won't want to check through your work separately for each question: you can group some together and overlook others, depending on your own strengths and weaknesses as a writer.

PRELIMINARY EDITING CHECKLIST

- Are the purpose and approach of this essay evident from the beginning?
- Are all sections of the paper relevant to the topic?
- Is the organization logical?
- Are the ideas sufficiently developed? Is there enough evidence, explanation, and illustration?
- Would an educated person who hasn't read the primary material understand everything I'm saying? Should I clarify some parts or add any explanatory material?
- In presenting my argument, do I take into account opposing arguments or evidence?
- Do my paragraph divisions give coherence to my ideas? Do I use them to cluster similar ideas and signal changes of idea?
- Do any parts of the essay seem disjointed? Should I add more transitional words or logical indicators to make the sequence of ideas easier to follow?

Another approach would be to devise your own checklist based on comments you have received on previous assignments. This is particularly useful when you move from the overview to the close focus on sentence structure, diction, punctuation, spelling, and style. If you have a particularly weak area—for example, irrelevant evidence, faulty logic, or run-on sentences—you should give it special attention. Keeping a personal checklist will save you from repeating the same old mistakes.

A WARNING ABOUT PLAGIARISM

Plagiarism is a form of stealing. Within universities, penalties range from a zero grade for the work to outright expulsion. The way to avoid it is to give credit where credit is due. If you are using someone else's idea, acknowledge it, even if you have changed the wording or just summarized the main points. Don't be afraid that your work will seem weaker if you acknowledge the ideas of others. On the contrary, it will be all the more convincing: serious academic treatises are almost always built on the work of preceding scholars, with credit duly given to the earlier work.

Where should you draw the line on acknowledgements? As a rule, you don't need to give credit for anything that's common knowledge. You wouldn't footnote lines from "O Canada," or the date of Confederation, but you should acknowledge any clever turn of phrase that is neither well known nor your own.

And always document any unfamiliar fact or claim—statistical or otherwise—or one that's open to question.

Consider the following passage from John Mack Faragher's book *A Great and Noble Scheme*[1] :

> The removal of the Acadians . . . was executed methodically by officers of the government in accordance with a carefully conceived plan many years in the making. It utilized all the available resources of the state. It included the seizure and destruction of Acadian records and registers, the arrest and isolation of community leaders, the separation of men from women and children. In the nineteenth century, operations of that kind would be directed at Indian peoples such as the Cherokees, but before 1755, nothing like it had been seen in North America. Today, the universal condemnation of ethnic cleansing by world opinion makes it difficult to defend what was done. In 2003, Queen Elizabeth II issued a Royal Proclamation acknowledging British responsibility for the decision to deport the Acadian people and regretting its "tragic consequences."

Now imagine that a class has been assigned an essay on the expulsion of the French Acadians from Nova Scotia in 1755. One student's essay includes the following passage. It is plagiarized because exact phrasing is taken from the original and no acknowledgement is given:

✗   The expulsion of the Acadians in 1755 **included the seizure and destruction of Acadian records and registers, the arrest and isolation of community leaders, the separation of men from women and children**. It was in fact the first instance of **ethnic cleansing** in North America. **In 2003, Queen Elizabeth II issued a Royal Proclamation acknowledging British responsibility for the decision to deport the Acadian people and regretting its "tragic consequences."**

To avoid a charge of plagiarism and its unpleasant and sometimes disastrous consequences, all you need to do is acknowledge your source, either directly in the text ("As Faragher writes . . . ," with an appropriate identification of the source) or in a parenthetical reference. In the correctly documented passage below, words and phrases taken directly from the original are in quotation

---

[1] Faragher, John Mack. 2005. *A Great and Noble Scheme: The Tragic Story of the Expulsion of the French Acadians from Their American Homeland.* New York: W.W. Norton & Company.

marks, and a parenthetical text citation is included at the end of the passage. (See Chapter 10 for alternative citation styles.) A bibliography at the end of the essay gives complete publication information for the source.

> ✓ The expulsion of the Acadians in 1755 "included the seizure and destruction of Acadian records and registers, the arrest and isolation of community leaders, the separation of men from women and children". It was in fact the first instance of "ethnic cleansing" in North America. "In 2003, Queen Elizabeth II issued a Royal Proclamation acknowledging British responsibility for the decision to deport the Acadian people and regretting its 'tragic consequences' " (Faragher xix).

The following passage is also plagiarized. This student has made the common mistake of assuming that putting the information in his own words is good enough. It's not. The concept of ethnic cleansing is still "borrowed":

> ✗ In 1755 the first instance of ethnic cleansing in North America occurred when officers of the government removed the Acadians from Nova Scotia using all the state resources at their disposal.

Remember that plagiarism involves not just the use of someone else's *words* but also the use of someone else's *ideas* when it is not clear that they have been taken from another source.

In the correctly documented passage below, proper acknowledgment takes the form of a reference to the author in text with the page number cited at the end of the relevant material:

> ✓ As historian John Mack Faragher argues in his book *A Great and Noble Scheme*, the first instance of ethnic cleansing in North America occurred in 1755 when officers of the government removed the Acadians from Nova Scotia using all the state resources at their disposal (xix).

For more information on documenting sources, please see Chapter 12.

Remember that, as with other offences against the law, ignorance is no excuse, and "accidental" plagiarism is still plagiarism. When copying material from a book and especially when copying and pasting electronic text from a website, be sure to place the material within quotation marks and record the source. This will help you avoid inadvertently plagiarizing comments you thought were your own.

WRITING EXAMS

Exams typically call for quick answers to (often) difficult questions. In effect, writing an exam is likely writing a turbo-charged essay—the entire process is sped up. The same principles of good thinking and good writing apply to exams as apply to essays. To do well on an examination, you need to have really mastered the material and—equally important—mastered the thinking and writing skills we have discussed so far. Exams also demand memory work and clear, rapid thinking, and these call for a calm state of mind.

Most students feel nervous before tests and exams. Writing an essay exam—even the open-book or take-home kind—imposes special pressure because both the time and the questions are restricted: you can't write and rewrite the way you can in a regular essay, and you must often write on topics you would otherwise choose to avoid. On the surface, objective tests may look easier because you don't have to compose the answers. However, objective tests force you to be more decisive about your answers than essay exams do. To do your best you need to feel calm—but how? These general guidelines will help you approach any test or exam with confidence.

BEFORE THE EXAM
REVIEW REGULARLY
A weekly review of lecture notes and texts will help you to remember important material and relate new information to old. If you don't review regularly, at the end of the year you'll be faced with relearning rather than remembering.

SET MEMORY TRIGGERS
As you review, condense and focus the material by writing down in the margin key words or phrases that will trigger whole sets of details in your mind. The trigger might be a word that names or points to an important theory or definition, or a quantitative phrase such as "three causes of the decline in manufacturing" or "five reasons for inflation."

Sometimes you can create an acronym or a nonsense sentence that will trigger an otherwise hard-to-remember set of facts—something like the acronym HOMES (Huron, Ontario, Michigan, Erie, Superior) for the Great Lakes. Since the difficulty of memorizing increases with the number of individual items you are trying to remember, any method that will reduce that number will increase your effectiveness.

ASK QUESTIONS: TRY THE THREE-C APPROACH
Think of questions that will get to the heart of the material and force you to

examine the relations between various subjects or issues; then think about how you would answer them. The three-C approach, discussed in Chapter 8, may be a help. For example, reviewing the *components* of the subject could mean focusing on the main parts of an issue or on the definitions of major terms or theories. When reviewing *change* in the subject, you should ask yourself what changes have taken place in the subject, and what the causes or results of these changes are. To review *context* you might consider how certain aspects of the subject—issues, theories, actions, results—compare with others in the course. Essentially, the three-C approach forces you to look at the material from different perspectives.

Old exams can help you see what kinds of questions you might be asked and how well prepared you are. If old exams aren't available, you might get together with friends who are taking the same course and ask each other questions. Just remember that the most useful review questions are not the ones that require you to recall facts but those that force you to analyze, integrate, or evaluate information.

ALLOW EXTRA TIME
Give yourself lots of time to get to the exam. Nothing is more nerve-wracking than thinking you're going to be late. If you have to travel by car or public transit, don't forget that traffic can jam, and so can alarm clocks—remember Murphy's Law: whatever can go wrong, will. Anticipate any unusual difficulties and allow yourself a good margin.

WRITING AN ESSAY EXAM
READ THE EXAM
An exam is not a hundred-metre dash; instead of starting to write immediately, take time at the beginning to read through each question and create a plan. A few minutes spent on thinking and organizing will bring better results than the same time spent on writing a few more lines.

APPORTION YOUR TIME
Reread the instructions carefully to find out how many questions you must answer and to see if you have any choice. Subtract five minutes or so for the initial planning, then divide the time you have left by the number of questions you have to answer. If possible, allow for a little extra time at the end to reread and edit your work. Remember that the "rule of equal thirds" can be as useful a tool in writing an exam as in writing an essay. If you feel you have the time, it might be a good idea to spend as much as one-third of your time planning your answers and a third revising. If the instructions on the exam indicate that not all questions are of equal value, apportion your time accordingly.

CHOOSE YOUR QUESTIONS

Decide on the questions that you will do and the order in which you will do them. Your answers don't have to be in the same order as the questions. If you think you have lots of time, it's a good idea to place your strongest answer first, your weakest answers in the middle, and your second-best answer at the end in order to leave the reader on a high note. If you think you will be rushed, though, it's wiser to work from best to worst. That way you will be sure to get all the marks you can on your good answers, and you won't have to cut a good answer short at the end.

KEEP CALM

If your first reaction to reading the exam is "I can't do any of it!" force yourself to keep calm; take ten slow, deep breaths to help yourself relax. Decide which is the question that you can answer best. Even if the exam seems disastrous at first, you can probably find one question that looks manageable: that's the one to begin with. It will help you get rolling and increase your confidence. By the time you've finished your first answer, you're likely to find that your mind has worked through to the answer for another question.

READ EACH QUESTION CAREFULLY

As you turn to each question, read it again carefully and underline the key words. The wording will probably suggest the number of parts your answer should have; be sure you don't overlook anything (this is a common mistake when people are nervous). Just as when you are analyzing a prescribed essay topic (see Chapter 8), it is especially important that you interpret the verb used in an exam question correctly, since it's usually a guide for the approach to take in your answer. For this reason, it's a good idea to review the following definitions:

outline	state simply, without much development of each point (unless specifically asked).
trace	review by looking back—on stages or steps in a process, or on causes of an occurrence.
explain	show how or why something happens.
discuss	examine or analyze in an orderly way. This instruction allows you considerable freedom, as long as you take into account contrary evidence or ideas.
compare	examine differences as well as similarities—even if the question doesn't say "compare and contrast."
evaluate	analyze strengths and weaknesses to arrive at an overall assessment of worth.

MAKE NOTES

Before you even begin to organize your answer, jot down key ideas and information related to the topic on rough paper or the unlined pages of your answer booklet. These notes will save you the worry of forgetting something by the time you begin writing. Next, arrange those parts you want to use into a brief plan, using numbers to indicate their order; that way, if you change your mind, it will be easy to reorder them. At the close of the exam, be sure to cross out these notes so that the evaluator won't think they are your actual answers. You will have to submit any notes with the rest of your paper.

BE DIRECT

Get to the points quickly and use plenty of examples to illustrate them. In an exam, as opposed to a term paper, it's best to use a direct approach. Don't worry about composing a graceful introduction: simply state the main points you are going to discuss, then get on with developing them. Remember that your paper will likely be one of many read and marked by someone who has to work quickly—the clearer your answers are, the better they will be received. For each main point give the kind of specific details that will prove you really know the material. General statements will show you are able to assimilate information, but they need examples to back them up.

WRITE LEGIBLY

Poor handwriting makes readers cranky. When the marker has to struggle to decipher your ideas, you may get poorer results than you deserve. If for some special reason (such as a physical handicap) your writing is hard to read, see if you can make special arrangements to use a typewriter. If your writing is just plain bad, it's probably better to print.

WRITE ON ALTERNATE LINES

Writing on every other line will not only make your writing easier to read but will leave you space for changes and additions.

KEEP TO YOUR TIME PLAN

Keep to your plan and don't skip any questions. Try to write something on each topic. Remember that it's easier to score half marks for a question you don't know much about than it is to score full marks for one you could write pages on. If you find yourself running out of time on an answer and still haven't finished, summarize the remaining points and go on to the next question. Leave a large space between questions so that you can go back and add more if you have time. If you write a new ending, remember to cross out the old one—neatly.

REREAD YOUR ANSWERS

No matter how tired or fed up you are, reread your answers at the end, if there's time. Check especially for clarity of expression; try to get rid of confusing sentences and improve your transitions so that the logical connection between your ideas is clear. Revisions that make answers easier to read are always worth the effort.

WRITING AN OPEN-BOOK EXAM

If you think that permission to take your books into the exam room is an "open sesame" to success, be forewarned: do not fall into the trap of relying too heavily on them. You may spend so much time rifling through pages and looking things up that you won't have time to write good answers. The result may be worse than if you had been allowed no books at all.

If you want to do well, use your books only to check information and look up specific, hard-to-remember details for a topic you already know a good deal about. For instance, if your subject is history, you can look up exact dates or quotations; for a political subject, you can look up voting statistics; for an exam in social theory, you can check some classical references and find the authors' exact definitions of key concepts—if you know where to find them quickly. In other words, use the books to make sure your answers are precise and well illustrated. Never use them to replace studying and careful preparation.

WRITING A TAKE-HOME EXAM

The benefit of a take-home exam is that you have time to plan your answers and consult your texts and other sources. The catch is that the time you have to do this is usually less than you would have for an ordinary essay. Don't work yourself into a frenzy trying to respond with a polished research essay for each question; rather, use the extra time to create a well-written exam answer. Keep in mind that you were given this assignment to test your overall command of the course: your reader is likely to be less concerned with your specialized research than with evidence that you have understood and assimilated the material.

The guidelines for a take-home exam are therefore similar to those for a regular exam; the only difference is that you don't need to keep such a close eye on the clock:

- Keep your introduction short and get to the point quickly.
- Organize your answer in a straightforward and obvious way so that the reader can easily see your main ideas.
- Use plenty of concrete examples to back up your points.

- Where possible, show the range of your knowledge of course material by referring to a variety of sources rather than constantly using the same ones.
- Try to show that you can analyze and evaluate material: that you can do more than simply repeat information.
- If you are asked to acknowledge the sources of any quotations or data you use, be sure to jot them down as you go; you may not have time to do so at the end.

WRITING AN OBJECTIVE TEST

Objective tests are common in the social sciences. Although sometimes the questions are the true/false kind, most often they are multiple-choice. The main difficulty with these tests is that their questions are designed to confuse the student who is not certain of the correct answers. If you tend to second-guess yourself, or if you are the sort of person who readily sees two sides to every question, you may find objective tests particularly hard at first. Fortunately, practice almost always improves performance.

Preparation for objective tests is the same as for other kinds. Here, though, it's especially important to pay attention to definitions and unexpected or confusing pieces of information, since these kinds of things are often adapted to make objective-test questions. Although there is no sure recipe for doing well on an objective test—other than knowing the course material completely and confidently—these suggestions may help you to do better:

FIND OUT THE MARKING SCHEME

If marks are based solely on the number of right answers, you should pick an answer for every question even if you aren't sure it's the right one. For true/false questions you have a 50-per-cent chance of being right; and even for a multiple-choice question with four possible answers, you would get an average of 25 per cent right if you picked the answers blindfolded.

On the other hand, if there is a penalty for wrong answers—if marks are deducted for errors—you should guess only when you are sure you are right, or when you are able to rule out most of the possibilities. Don't make wild guesses.

DO THE EASY QUESTIONS FIRST

Go through the test at least twice. On the first round, don't waste time on troublesome questions. Since the questions are usually of equal value, it's best to get all the marks you can on the ones you find easy. You can tackle the more difficult questions on the next round. This approach has two advantages:

1. You won't be forced, because you have run out of time, to leave out any questions that you could easily have answered correctly.
2. When you come back to a difficult question on the second round, you may find that in the meantime you have figured out the answer.

MAKE YOUR GUESSES EDUCATED ONES

If you have decided to guess, at least increase your chance of getting the answers right. Forget about intuition, hunches, and lucky numbers. More important, forget about so-called patterns of correct answers—the idea that if there have been two "A" answers in a row, the next one can't possibly be "A," or that if there hasn't been a "true" for a while, "true" must be a good guess. Unfortunately, many test-setters either don't worry about patterns at all or else deliberately elude pattern-hunters by giving the right answer the same letter or number several times in a row.

Remember that constructing good objective tests is a special skill that not all instructors have mastered. Often the questions they pose, though sound enough as questions, do not produce enough realistic alternatives for answers. In such cases the test-setter may resort to some less realistic options, and if you keep your eyes open you can spot them. James F. Shepherd (1979, 1981) has suggested a number of tips that will help you increase your chances of making the right guess:

- Start by weeding out all the answers you know are wrong, rather than looking for the right one.
- Avoid any terms you don't recognize. Some students are taken in by anything that looks like sophisticated terminology and may assume that such answers must be correct. They are usually wrong: the unfamiliar term may well be a red herring, especially if it is close in sound to the correct one.
- Avoid extremes. Most often the right answer lies in between. For example, suppose that the options are the numbers 800,000; 350,000; 275,000; and 15: the highest and lowest numbers are likely to be wrong.
- Avoid absolutes, especially on questions dealing with people. Few aspects of human life are as certain as is implied by such words as *everyone*, *all*, or *no one*; *always*, *invariably*, or *never*. Statements containing these words are usually false.

- Avoid jokes or humorous statements.
- Avoid demeaning or insulting statements. Like jokes, these are usually inserted simply to provide a full complement of options.
- Choose the best available answer, even if it is not indisputably true.
- Choose the long answer over the short (it's more likely to contain the detail needed to make it right) and the particular statement over the general (generalizations are usually too sweeping to be true).
- Choose "all of the above" over individual answers. Test-setters know that students with a patchy knowledge of the course material will often fasten on the one fact they know. Only those with a thorough knowledge will recognize that all the answers listed are correct.

TWO FINAL TIPS

If you have time at the end of the exam, go back and reread the questions. One or two wrong answers caused by misreading can make a significant difference to your score. On the other hand, don't start second-guessing yourself and changing a lot of answers at the last minute. Studies have shown that when students make changes, they are often wrong. Stick to your decisions unless you know for certain you have made a mistake.

chApter 10

DOCUMENTATION

Documenting your sources accurately and completely is essential in academic writing. The purpose of documentation is not only to avoid charges of plagiarism, but also to show the body of knowledge that your work is building on. Academia is based on the premise that researchers are not working in a vacuum but are indebted to those that came before them. By documenting your sources, you are showing that you understand this concept and are ready to make your own contribution to the body of knowledge in your field.

QUOTATIONS

The most direct form of reference, the quotation, is used in every kind of academic writing. Judicious use of quotations can add authority to your writing, but you must use them with care. Never quote a passage just because it sounds impressive; be sure that it really adds to your discussion, either by expressing an idea with special force or cogency, or by giving substance to a debatable point. Here are some guidelines for incorporating quotations:

1. Integrate the quotation so that it makes sense in the context of your discussion and fits in grammatically:

   ✗ Whether Bill Gates is a visionary is debatable. "640K ought to be enough for anybody" is now very ironic.

   ✓ Whether Bill Gates is a visionary is debatable. His 1981 prediction that "640K ought to be enough for anybody" is now considered laughably ironic.

2. If the quotation is no more than four lines long, include it as part of your text, enclosed in quotation marks. If you are quoting four lines or fewer of poetry, these can also be included as part of your text. Use a slash (/) to indicate the end of a line:

   > In "Newfoundland" Pratt describes the winds as "Resonant with the hopes of spring, / Pungent with the airs of harvest."

For verse quotations of more than four lines, you should write the words line for line as originally written.

3. A long quotation is usually single-spaced and introduced by a colon, without quotation marks. If the first line of the quotation is the beginning of a paragraph, indent it an extra three spaces:

> In a recent column, a well-known journalist and historian remembered the late prime minister this way:
>
> > In his prime, Trudeau was exciting, charismatic, sexy. He drove sports cars, wore capes, ascots and floppy hats, and always the signature red rose in his lapel. He slid down banisters, canoed in white-water rapids, did pirouettes behind the Queen's back at Buckingham Palace. He made politics fashionable for the upbeat Sixties generation that emerged from the sleepy 1950s.

4. For a quotation within a quotation, use single quotation marks:

> One newspaper reports that NDP leader Jack Layton "dismisses Prime Minister Paul Martin as 'a CEO' and derides the 'corporate drift' in Canada."

5. Be accurate. Reproduce the exact wording, punctuation, and spelling of the original, including any errors. You can acknowledge a typo or mistake by the author by inserting the Latin word *sic* in brackets after it (see page 205). If you want to italicize any part of the quotation for emphasis, add "my emphasis" or "emphasis added" in brackets at the end:

> Rand and Gustaffson concluded that "flawed data was *not* the reason for the unexpected results" [my emphasis].

6. If you want to insert an explanatory comment into a quotation, enclose it in brackets:

> "He [Mr. Nebbeling] said he has yet to hear from the entire Liberal caucus, but is ready for negative and positive responses."

7. If you want to omit something from the original, use ellipsis marks:

> "The uprising was the result of indifference on the part of national leaders . . . and mismanagement on the part of civil servants."

Ellipsis marks are discussed further in Chapter 12.

REFERENCING YOUR WORK

There is a huge amount of variation in accepted formats for referencing your sources. Although different referencing styles have certain general guidelines in common, the specific details surrounding the use of commas, colons, parentheses, quotation marks, and italicization (or underlining) vary widely. In addition, methods of citing electronic sources of information are evolving rapidly as the digital age revolutionizes academic research. Some generally accepted practices are outlined below, but always be sure to check with your instructor on which format is acceptable.

A NOTE ON FOOTNOTES

The use of footnotes and endnotes is generally discouraged in social science writing, where the parenthetical-reference style is most often used to identify sources. You may have learned to use footnotes or endnotes to expand on or digress from the main argument of your work, and some academic departments and journals still recommend referencing styles that use a combination of parenthetical references and endnotes or footnotes; however, this practice is falling out of favour in the social sciences. As a rule, if your comments are important, they should be included in the main text of your essay or report; if the information is not immediately relevant, leave it out. You want the reader to be able to focus on the body of your work.

PARENTHETICAL REFERENCES, OR "CITATIONS"

The parenthetical-reference (or "scientific") style, used by most disciplines of social science, has two main features:

1. Brief references (called *citations*) are included in parentheses within the text wherever reference to another person's work is made.

2. At the end of a work, a section entitled *Reference List* or *Works Cited* includes the full publication information for those works *directly referred to* in the text; other works that you may have consulted but have not referred to directly in the text are not listed.

A leading form of this style is known as the Harvard method and is followed, with variations, by the American Psychological Association (APA) and the Modern Language Association of America (MLA). A third variation, the Social Science Style (SSS), is our own system—used throughout this book—which is based on widely accepted conventions followed in a number of social science journals and books.

These are three models you should consider using. Be aware of the fact that these three models differ widely in places, and, in addition, that each model is constantly undergoing revisions to keep up with new ways of doing research. You may wish to consult the APA and MLA websites to review the latest guidelines on citing electronic sources (http://www.apastyle.org/elecref.html for the APA; http://www.mla.org for the MLA).

You should also be aware that professors and journals vary widely in their requirements: you may be asked to use one of these methods, or a variation that combines elements of each, or a different style altogether. Make sure you are aware of the preferences and expectations of your department or professor. If your instructor does not refer you to a particular journal, or perhaps to a departmental website or booklet on style, you will have to make a choice based on the guidelines below. Whatever you do, remember the one "golden rule" for documentation: always be consistent. No matter what style you choose, use it consistently throughout any piece of work; never change in midstream.

GUIDELINES FOR USING CITATIONS

1. The citation is inserted in the text at the appropriate point, with the author's surname and, in most cases, the year of publication in parentheses. Note that the MLA style omits the year:

   SSS, APA   Additional research failed to confirm the findings (Kenobe, 2002).

   MLA   Additional research failed to confirm the findings (Kenobe).

2. If reference to the author has already been made within the text, it can be omitted from the citation:

   SSS, APA   Kenobe (2002) tested the findings.

   (or)   In 2002, Kenobe tested the findings.

   MLA   Kenobe tested the findings.

   If the reference is to a work as a whole, it is preferable to include the author's name in the text, rather than in a parenthetical reference.

3. If the page reference is not important, all you need to include is the year:

   SSS, APA   Thaler and Plowright (2004) support this hypothesis.

   If, however, the citation is to something specific within the source and not just to the work in general, then you must include the specific reference. When referring to a specific page or table, include the number. Note that the

APA style uses an ampersand (&) to separate authors, whereas the SSS and MLA use "and." Note also that APA includes the abbreviations "p." and "pp." before the page number or numbers:

SSS   (Smyth, 1999: 121–3)
(Craig, 2002: Table 3)
(Zakrewski, 1996: Fig. 5.3)
(Chumak and Chun, 1989: Chap. 3)

APA   (Smyth, 1999, pp. 121–3)
(Craig, 2002, Table 3)
(Zakrewski, 1996, fig. 5.3)
(Chumak & Chun, 1989, chap. 3)

MLA   (Smyth 121–3)
(Craig Table 3)
(Zakrewski fig. 5.3)
(Chumak and Chun ch. 3)

4. When referring to a work with two authors, always use the names of both authors in each citation of the work:

SSS   Analysis of the data (Chumak and Chun, 1989) revealed . . .
In their analysis, Chumak and Chun (1989) revealed . . .

APA   Analysis of the data (Chumak & Chun, 1989) revealed . . .
In their analysis, Chumak and Chun (1989) revealed . . .

MLA   Analysis of the data (Chumak and Chun) revealed . . .
In their analysis of the data, Chumak and Chun revealed . . .

In the SSS and APA styles, when there are more than two authors but fewer than six, list all of the authors in the first citation and only the first author followed by "et al." for subsequent citations:

SSS   . . . (Cameron, Jrang, Park, and Allaby, 2003).
. . . (Cameron et al., 2003)

APA   . . . (Cameron, Jrang, Park, & Allaby, 2003)
. . . (Cameron et al., 2003).

Remember that if you refer to the authors in the text, their names should be omitted from the citation:

As the study by Cameron et al. (2003) shows . . .

If the work has six or more authors, cite only the name of the first author followed by "et al." for the first and subsequent references. (In the reference list, however, provide the names of the first six authors, and shorten the remaining authors to "et al.")

5. When citing multiple works by different authors in one set of parentheses, use a semicolon to separate the items. In the APA and MLA styles, items are listed in alphabetical order (example *a*), but in the SSS style they may also be ranked by order of importance (example *b*):

   (a)   (Hsuing et al., 1999; Miller & Streicher, 1996; Roget, 2000)

   (b)   (Roget, 2000; Miller and Streicher, 1996; Hsuing et al., 1999)

6. If authors have the same last names, use initials to distinguish them:

   SSS, APA   (Chavez, H., 2002; Chavez, P., 2004)

   MLA   (Best, A.; Best, C.)

7. When using APA or SSS to cite multiple works by the same author, list the surname once, with the dates following in chronological order:

   SSS, APA   (Berberi, 1996, 1998)

When citing two or more works published within the same year, distinguish them with lower-case letters following the date:

   SSS, APA   (Thompson, 1995a, 1995b)

This letter is assigned in the reference list, and these kinds of references are ordered alphabetically by title.

   When citing one of multiple works by the same author(s) in MLA, include the title, shortened or in full, after the names of the author(s):

   MLA These findings are disproven in *Trial and Error: A Study of Legal Malpractice* (Sallese and McDougall 50).

   These findings have been disproven (Sallese and McDougall, *Trial* 50).

8. When a work has no known or declared author, list the first few words of the reference list entry (usually the title):

SSS, APA   ("Drug dependency a problem," 1999)

MLA   ("Drug Dependency a Problem")

9. If you know that the material you are using will be published soon, use "forthcoming" (SSS) or "in press" (APA) in place of the publication date. If the work has no listed publication date, use the abbreviation "n.d.":

SSS   (Levinson, 2001; Norton, forthcoming; Pieter, n.d.)

APA   (Levinson, 2001; Norton, in press; Pieter, n.d.)

10. When citing material that you have not read yourself but have seen cited by others, your citation must show this:

SSS   According to Verschreagen (1995, cited in Kabila, 1998: 62) . . . , (Verschreagen, 1955, cited in Kabila, 1998: 62)

APA   According to Verschreagen (1995, as cited in Kabila, 1998, p. 95) . . . ,

MLA   According to Verschreagen (qtd. in Kabila 62) . . . ,

In the reference list, give only the secondary source.

THE REFERENCE SECTION

In the reference section (often entitled *Reference List* or *Works Cited*) at the end of your work, you will list the complete source information for all of the citations in your text. Be sure to double-check that each citation in your paper has an accompanying reference in this section. Here are some general guidelines:

1. List your references alphabetically by author, surname first, followed by given names or initials; do not number them.

2. When referencing a work with multiple authors there are marked stylistic differences: the SSS lists all authors and reverses only the first; the APA provides the names of the first six authors, shortens the remaining authors to "et al.," and reverses all names; the MLA gives either all names in full or only the first followed by "et al.," and reverses only the first author's name.

3. When using SSS or APA to cite more than one work by a particular author, list entries in chronological order (the date should usually follow the author's name); for works published in the same year, add a letter marker to each date (2001a, 2001b, etc.). When using MLA, list entries alphabetically by title. After the first entry, omit the author's name and insert three hyphens followed by a period, then the rest of the entry.

4. Almost every style of referencing includes the following information:

   - surname of the author(s) (if no author is given, begin with the first significant word in the title);
   - first name of the author or authors (APA uses only initials);
   - date of publication;
   - full name of the work being cited.

5. For books, include

   - the location of the publisher;
   - "ed." or "trans." to indicate an editor or translator respectively;
   - the volume number(s), if any;
   - the name of the publisher. In most cases, the name of the publisher can be condensed. For example, *Macmillan of Canada Ltd.* can be listed as simply *Macmillan*. Note also that, generally, words like *Press* or *Publisher* are omitted, except for the names of university presses, e.g. *Oxford University Press* (written out in SSS and APA, and shortened to *Oxford UP* in MLA).

6. For journals, include

   - the name of the article and the name of the journal;
   - the volume number;
   - the issue number if, and only if, issues are paginated separately;
   - inclusive page references.

7. For websites, include

   - the name of the site and/or the organization that maintains the site;
   - the complete URL of the document being referenced;
   - the date the material was retrieved from the site.

Since references to web-based material vary significantly between styles, consult the examples at the end of this chapter for specifics.

8. For online databases, include

- the name of the database;
- the date the information was retrieved;
- the complete URL of the document being referenced.

9. For online journal, magazine, and newspaper articles based on a print source, include

- the documentation information of the print counterparts, modified as appropriate to the electronic source;
- the date of retrieval;
- the complete URL of the document being referenced.

SOME REFERENCE EXAMPLES

There is even more variation in reference style than there is in citation style. You will notice significant differences among styles regarding the use of commas, periods, colons, parentheses, quotation marks, capitalization, and italics. Once again, check with your instructor to see what style is preferred for your course or department. Once you have settled on a style, be sure to use it consistently.

BOOK BY ONE AUTHOR

SSS Manning, Erin. 2003. *Ephemeral Territories: Representing Nation, Home, and Identity in Canada*. Minneapolis: University of Minnesota Press.

APA Manning, E. (2003). *Ephemeral territories: Representing nation, home, and identity in Canada*. Minneapolis: University of Minnesota Press.

MLA Manning, Erin. *Ephemeral Territories: Representing Nation, Home, and Identity in Canada*. Minneapolis: U of Minnesota P, 2003.

Note that in titles and subtitles, the MLA capitalizes the first word and all remaining words except for articles (*a, an, the*), prepositions (*through, from, of,* etc.), coordinate conjunctions (*and, or,* etc.), and *to* in infinitives. The APA follows this convention for titles of periodicals only; otherwise, the APA capitalizes only proper nouns and the first letter of the title and subtitle. The SSS follows the MLA convention for capitalizing titles and subtitles of books and journals, but follows the APA convention for capitalizing shorter works, such as articles or chapters of books.

BOOK BY TWO AUTHORS

SSS   Brown, Jeffrey R. and Ramsay Cook. 1996. *Canada, 1896–1921: A Nation Transformed.* Toronto: McClelland & Stewart.

APA   Brown, J.R., & Cook, R. (1996). *Canada, 1896–1921: A nation transformed.* Toronto: McClelland & Stewart.

MLA   Brown, Jeffrey R., and Ramsay Cook. *Canada, 1896–1921: A Nation Transformed.* Toronto: McClelland & Stewart, 1996.

BOOK WITH EDITION NUMBER

SSS   Mankiw, Gregory N. 2004. *Principles of Economics*, 3rd Ed. Mason, OH: South-Western.

APA   Mankiw, G.N. (2004). *Principles of economics* (3rd ed.). Mason, OH: South-Western.

MLA   Mankiw, Gregory N. *Principles of Economics.* 3rd ed. Mason, OH: South-Western, 2004.

BOOK WITH ONE EDITOR

SSS   Osberg, Lars, ed. 2003. *The Economic Implications of Social Cohesion.* Toronto: University of Toronto Press.

APA   Osberg, L. (Ed.). (2003). *The economic implications of social cohesion.* Toronto: University of Toronto Press.

MLA   Osberg, Lars, ed. *The Economic Implications of Social Cohesion.* Toronto: U of Toronto P, 2003.

BOOK WITH TWO EDITORS

SSS   Donald, Moira and Linda Hurcombe, eds. 2000. *Representations of Gender from Prehistory to the Present.* New York: St. Martin's.

APA   Donald, M., & Hurcombe, L. (Eds.). (2000). *Representations of gender from prehistory to the present.* New York: St. Martin's.

MLA   Donald, Moira, and Linda Hurcombe, eds. *Representations of Gender from Prehistory to the Present*. New York: St. Martin's, 2000.

BOOK PUBLISHED IN TWO LOCATIONS BY DIFFERENT PRESSES

SSS   Daniels, Simeon. 2001. *A Misuse of Constants*. Toronto: Commercial; London: McChesney.

MLA   Daniels, Simeon. *A Misuse of Constants*. Toronto: Commercial; London: McChesney, 2001.

APA does not address co-publication.

CHAPTER IN AN EDITED BOOK

SSS   Hornyansky, Michael. 1995. "Is your English destroying your image?" *In the Name of Language*. Joseph Gold (ed.). Toronto: Macmillan. 44–78.

APA   Hornyansky, M. (1995). Is your English destroying your image? In J. Gold (Ed.), *In the name of language* (pp. 44–78). Toronto: Macmillan.

MLA   Hornyansky, Michael. "Is Your English Destroying Your Image?" *In the Name of Language*. Ed. Joseph Gold. Toronto: Macmillan, 1995. 44–78.

ARTICLE BY ONE AUTHOR IN A JOURNAL

SSS   Dodson, Kevin E. 2003. "Kant's socialism: A philosophical reconstruction," *Social Theory and Practice* v 29, 525–38.

APA   Dodson, K.E. (2003). Kant's socialism: A philosophical reconstruction. *Social Theory and Practice, 29*, 525–538.

MLA   Dodson, Kevin E. "Kant's Socialism: A Philosophical Reconstruction." *Social Theory and Practice* 29 (2003): 525–38.

ARTICLE BY TWO OR MORE AUTHORS IN A JOURNAL

SSS   Heath, Deborah, Erin Koch, Barbara Ley, and Michael Montoya. 1999. "Nodes and queries: Linking locations in networked fields of inquiry," *The American Behavioral Scientist* v 43, 450–63.

APA   Heath, D., Koch, E., Ley, B., & Montoya, M. (1999). Nodes and queries: Linking locations in networked fields of inquiry. *The American Behavioral Scientist, 43*, 450–463.

MLA   Heath, Deborah, Erin Koch, Barbara Ley, and Michael Montoya. "Nodes and Queries: Linking Locations in Networked Fields of Inquiry." *The American Behavioral Scientist* 43 (1999): 450–63.

SIGNED NEWSPAPER ARTICLE

SSS   Reinhart, Anthony. "Fallen soldier lives again in haunting new portrait," *Globe and Mail* 11 Nov. 2003, A7.

APA   Reinhart, A. (2003, November 11). Fallen soldier lives again in haunting new portrait. *The Globe and Mail*, p. A7.

MLA   Reinhart, Anthony. "Fallen Soldier Lives Again in Haunting New Portrait." *Globe and Mail* 11 Nov. 2003: A7.

UNSIGNED NEWSPAPER ARTICLE

SSS   "Freedom-of-information law holds no sway over Ontario universities," *Globe and Mail* 23 Apr. 2003, A10.

APA   Freedom-of-information law holds no sway over Ontario universities. (2003, April 23). *The Globe and Mail*, p. A10.

MLA   "Freedom-of-Information Law Holds No Sway over Ontario Universities." *Globe and Mail* 23 Apr. 2003: A10.

GOVERNMENT DOCUMENT

SSS   Human Resources Development Canada. 1998. *Changing Patterns in Women's Employment.* Ottawa: Queen's Printer.

APA   Human Resources Development Canada. (1998). *Changing patterns in women's employment.* Ottawa: Queen's Printer.

MLA   Human Resources Development Canada. *Changing Patterns in Women's Employment.* Ottawa: Queen's Printer, 1988.

WEBSITE

SSS   "Best practices in mental health reform: Discussion paper," Health Canada, 15 Jan. 2003. Retrieved on 7 Feb. 2004 http://www.hc-sc.gc.ca/hppb/mentalhealth/pubs/disc_paper/ e.disc8.html

APA   Health Canada. (2003, January 15). *Best practices in mental health reform: Discussion paper.* Retrieved February 7, 2004, from http://www.hc-sc.gc.ca/hppb/mentalhealth/pubs/disc_paper/ e.disc8.html

MLA   "Best Practices in Mental Health Reform: Discussion Paper." *Health Canada Online.* 15 Jan. 2003. Health Canada. 7 Feb. 2004 <http://www.hc-sc.gc.ca/hppb/mentalhealth/pubs/disc_paper/ e.disc8.html>.

ENTRY IN AN ONLINE REFERENCE DATABASE

SSS   "Social realism," *Encyclopaedia Britannica.* 2004. Retrieved on 7 Feb. 2004 http://www.britannica.com/eb/article?ev=70229

APA   *Encyclopaedia Britannica.* (2004). *Social realism.* Retrieved February 7, 2004, from http://www.britannica.com/eb/article?ev=70229

MLA   "Social Realism." *Encyclopaedia Britannica.* 2004. 7 Feb. 2004 <http://www.britannica.com/eb/article?ev=70229>.

ARTICLE IN AN ONLINE JOURNAL

SSS   Orleans, Myron. 2000. "Introducing low politics: For character, courage and charisma in everyday life," *Journal of Mundane Behavior* v 1 no 3. Retrieved on 14 Dec. 2000 http://www.mundanebehavior.org/ index.htm

APA   Orleans, M. (2000). Introducing low politics: For character, courage and charisma in everyday life. *Journal of Mundane Behavior, 1*(3). Retrieved December 14, 2000, from http://www.mundanebehavior .org/index.htm

MLA   Orleans, Myron. "Introducing Low Politics: For Character,
        Courage and Charisma in Everyday Life." *Journal of Mundane
        Behavior* 1.3 (2000). 14 Dec. 2000 <http://www.mundanebehavior
        .org/index.htm>.

ONLINE NEWSPAPER ARTICLE BASED ON A PRINT SOURCE

SSS   Scrivner, Leslie. "City of cultures, city of faith," 24 Jan. 2004. Retrieved
        on 7 Feb. 2004 http://www.thestar.com

APA   Scrivner, L. (2004, January 24). City of cultures, city of faith. *Toronto
        Star*. Retrieved February 7, 2004, from http://www.thestar.com

MLA   Scrivner, Leslie. "City of Cultures, City of Faith." *Toronto Star* 24 Jan.
        2004. 7 Feb. 2004 <http://www.thestar.com>.

CLOSING COMMENTS

As the examples in this chapter show, there is considerable variance in how to document sources, both in the text of an essay or report and in the *References* section. The three referencing methods highlighted here (and remember that these are just three of a number of methods) vary widely in places, and to complicate matters further, they are constantly changing, as new ways of conducting research demand updated guidelines for documenting.

How can you stay on top of the changes? Fortunately, many organizations and journals that recommend a particular referencing style have websites with up-to-date information on new or revised guidelines. In addition, your college or university department may have a website with information on how to document sources. It's always a good idea to check here first in case there are particular conventions or a particular style preferred by your department.

chapter 11

Common Errors in Grammar and Usage

This chapter is not a comprehensive grammar lesson: it's simply a survey of those areas where students most often make mistakes. It will help you keep a lookout for weaknesses as you are editing your work. Once you get into the habit of checking your work, it won't be long before you are correcting potential problems as you write.

The grammatical terms used here are the most basic and familiar ones; if you need to review some of them, see Chapter 12 or Glossary II. For a thorough treatment of grammar or usage, pick up one of the many excellent books currently available—your university bookstore will have several to choose from.

TROUBLES WITH SENTENCE UNITY

SENTENCE FRAGMENTS

To be complete, a sentence must have both a subject and a verb in an independent clause; if it doesn't, it's a fragment. Occasionally a sentence fragment is acceptable, as in

✓ Will the government try to abolish the Senate? <u>Not likely</u>.

Here the sentence fragment *Not likely* is intended to be understood as a short form of *It is not likely that it will try*. Unintentional sentence fragments, on the other hand, usually seem incomplete rather than shortened:

✗ Marx had little respect for capitalism. <u>Being a thinker who opposed exploitation</u>.

The last "sentence" is incomplete: where are the subject and verb? (Remember that a participle such as *being* is not a verb; *-ing* words by themselves are only verbals or part-verbs.) The fragment can be made into a complete sentence by adding a subject and a verb:

✓ Marx was a thinker who opposed exploitation.

Alternatively, you could join the fragment to the preceding sentence:

✓ Being a thinker who opposed exploitation, Marx had little respect for capitalism.

✓ Marx had little respect for capitalism, since he was a thinker who opposed exploitation.

RUN-ON SENTENCES

A run-on sentence is one that continues beyond the point where it should have stopped:

Capitalism is exploitative, but this doesn't stop workers from voting for "establishment" political parties, and such is the case in England.

This run-on sentence could be fixed by removing the *and* and adding a period or semicolon after *parties*.

Another kind of run-on sentence is one in which two independent clauses (phrases that could stand by themselves as sentences) are wrongly joined by a comma:

✗ C.B. Macpherson won international acclaim as a political theorist, he was a political science professor at the University of Toronto.

This error is known as a *comma splice*. There are three ways of correcting it:

1. by putting a period after *theorist* and starting a new sentence:

✓ . . . as a political theorist. He . . .

2. by replacing the comma with a semicolon:

✓ . . . as a political theorist; he . . .

3. by making one of the independent clauses subordinate to the other:

✓ C.B. Macpherson, who won international acclaim as a political theorist, was a political science professor at the University of Toronto.

The one exception to the rule that independent clauses cannot be joined by a comma arises when the clauses are short and arranged in a tight sequence:

✓ I examined the data, I saw my mistake, I changed my topic.

Such instances are not common.

Contrary to what many people think, words such as *however, therefore,* and *thus* cannot be used to join independent clauses:

> ✗ Two of my friends started out in Commerce, however they quickly decided they didn't like accounting.

This mistake can be corrected either by beginning a new sentence after *Commerce* or (preferably) by putting a semicolon in the same place:

> ✓ Two of my friends started out in Commerce; however, they quickly decided they didn't like accounting.

The only words that can be used to join independent clauses are the coordinating conjunctions—*and, or, nor, but, for, yet,* and *so*—and subordinating conjunctions such as *if, because, since, while, when, where, after, before,* and *until.*

FAULTY PREDICATION

When the subject of a sentence is not grammatically connected to what follows (the predicate), the result is *faulty predication*:

> ✗ The reason for his downfall was because he couldn't handle people.

The problem here is that *because* essentially means the same thing as *the reason for.* The subject needs a noun clause to complete it:

> ✓ The reason for his downfall was that he couldn't handle people.

Another solution would be to rephrase the sentence:

> ✓ He was defeated because he couldn't handle people.

Faulty predication also occurs with *is when* or *is where* constructions:

> ✗ The critical moment is when the researcher discovers the original source of the information.

You can correct this error in one of two ways:

1. Follow the *is* with a noun phrase to complete the sentence:

> ✓ The critical moment is the discovery of the original source by the researcher.

(or)

✓ The critical moment is <u>the researcher's discovery</u> of the original source.

2. Change the verb:

✓ The critical moment <u>occurs</u> when the researcher discovers the original source.

TROUBLES WITH SUBJECT-VERB AGREEMENT

IDENTIFYING THE SUBJECT

A verb should always agree in number with its subject. Sometimes, however, when the subject does not come at the beginning of the sentence, or when it is separated from the verb by other information, you may be tempted to use a verb form that does not agree:

✗ The <u>increase</u> in the rate for freight and passengers <u>were condemned</u> by the farmers.

The subject here is *increase*, not *freight and passengers*; therefore the verb should be the singular *was condemned*:

✓ The <u>increase</u> in the rate for freight and passengers <u>was condemned</u> by the farmers.

EITHER, NEITHER, EACH

The indefinite pronouns *either*, *neither*, and *each* always take singular verbs:

✗ <u>Neither</u> of the changing rooms <u>have</u> a sauna.

✓ <u>Each</u> of them <u>has</u> a shower.

COMPOUND SUBJECTS

When *or, either . . . or*, or *neither . . . nor* is used to create a compound subject, the verb should usually agree with the last item in the subject:

✓ <u>Neither</u> she nor her associates <u>are</u> attending the conference.

✓ <u>Either</u> the developers or the contractor <u>was</u> misinformed.

You may find, however, that in some cases it sounds awkward to use a singular verb when a singular item follows a plural item:

> (✓) Either my history books or my sociology <u>text is going</u> to gather dust this weekend.

In such instances, it's better to rephrase the sentence:

> ✓ This weekend, I will be reading either my history books or my sociology text.

Unlike the word *and*, which creates a compound subject and therefore takes a plural verb, the phrases *as well as* and *in addition to* do not create compound subjects; therefore the verb remains singular:

> ✓ Low pay <u>and</u> a dangerous working environment <u>are</u> causes of employee dissatisfaction.

> ✓ Low pay <u>as well as</u> a dangerous working environment <u>is</u> a cause of employee dissatisfaction.

COLLECTIVE NOUNS

A collective noun is a singular noun that includes a number of members, such as *family*, *army*, or *team*. If the noun refers to the members as a unit, it takes a singular verb:

> ✓ The <u>team</u> <u>is</u> playing an exhibition game tonight.

If, in the context of the sentence, the noun refers to the members as individuals, the verb becomes plural:

> ✓ The <u>team</u> <u>are receiving</u> their sweaters before the game.

> ✓ The <u>majority</u> of immigrants to Canada <u>settle</u> in cities.

TITLES

The title of a book or a movie is always considered singular, even if it contains plural words; therefore it takes a singular verb:

> *Modern Social Theories* <u>was</u> a best-seller.

TENSE TROUBLES

Native speakers of English usually know without thinking which verb tense to use in a given context; however, a few tenses can still be confusing.

THE PAST PERFECT

If the main verb is in the past tense and you want to refer to something that happened before that time, use the past perfect (*had* followed by the past participle). The time sequence will not be clear if you use the simple past in both clauses:

✗ He hoped that she <u>fixed</u> the printer.

✓ He hoped that she <u>had fixed</u> the printer.

Similarly, when you are reporting what someone said in the past—that is, when you are using past indirect discourse—you should use the past perfect tense in the clause describing what was said:

✗ He told the TA that he <u>wrote</u> the essay that week.

✓ He told the TA that he <u>had written</u> the essay that week.

USING "IF"

When you are describing a possibility in the future, use the present tense in the condition (*if*) clause and the future tense in the consequence clause:

✓ If she tests us on price theory, <u>I will fail</u>.

When the possibility is unlikely, it is conventional—especially in formal writing—to use the subjunctive in the *if* clause, and *would* followed by the base verb in the consequence clause:

✓ If she <u>were to cancel</u> the test, I <u>would cheer</u>.

When you are describing a hypothetical instance in the past, use the past subjunctive (it has the same form as the past perfect) in the *if* clause and *would have* followed by the past participle for the consequence. A common error is to use *would have* in both clauses:

✗ If he <u>would have been</u> clearer, I <u>would have understood</u> him better

✓ If he <u>had been</u> clearer, I <u>would have understood</u> him better.

WRITING ABOUT BOOKS

To describe a book in its historical context, use the past tense:

✓ John Porter wrote *The Vertical Mosaic* at a time when most people believed all Canadians had a good chance at upward mobility.

To discuss what goes on *within* the work, however, you should use the present tense:

✓ Porter sees educational opportunity as important to ordinary Canadians, but not to elites.

When you are discussing an episode or incident in the work and want to refer to a prior or future incident, use past or future tenses accordingly:

✓ The author reminds us that, historically, immigrants were admitted into Canada to do particular kinds of jobs; today, their descendents will often be prevented from moving into better jobs.

Be sure to return to the present tense when you have finished referring to events in the past or future.

PRONOUN TROUBLES

PRONOUN REFERENCE

The link between a pronoun and the noun it refers to must be clear. If the noun doesn't appear in the same sentence as the pronoun, it should appear in the preceding sentence:

✗ The <u>textbook supply</u> in the bookstore had run out, and so we borrowed <u>them</u> from the library.

Since *textbook* is used as an adjective rather than a noun, it cannot serve as referent or antecedent for the pronoun *them*. You must either replace *them* or change the phrase *textbook supply*.

✓ The <u>textbook supply</u> in the bookstore had run out, and so we borrowed the <u>texts</u> from the library.

✓ The bookstore had run out of <u>textbooks</u>, and so we borrowed <u>them</u> from the library.

When a sentence contains more than one noun, make sure there is no ambiguity about which noun the pronoun refers to:

✗ The public wants increased social <u>services</u> as well as lower <u>taxes</u>, but the government does not advocate <u>them</u>.

What does the pronoun *them* refer to? The taxes, the social services, or both?

✓ The public wants <u>increased</u> social <u>services</u> as well as lower taxes, but the government does not advocate such <u>increases</u>.

USING "IT" AND "THIS"

Using *it* and *this* without a clear referent can lead to confusion:

✗ Although the directors wanted to meet in January, <u>it</u> (<u>this</u>) didn't take place until May.

✓ Although the directors wanted to schedule <u>a meeting</u> for January, <u>it</u> (<u>this</u>) didn't take place until May.

✓ Although the directors wanted to meet in January, <u>the conference</u> didn't take place until May.

Make sure that *it* or *this* clearly refers to a specific noun or pronoun.

PRONOUN AGREEMENT AND GENDER

A pronoun should agree in number and person with the noun that it refers to. However, an increasing awareness of sexist or biased language has changed what is considered acceptable over the last few decades. In the past, the following sentence would have been considered incorrect:

When a Canadian civil <u>servant</u> retires, <u>their</u> pension is indexed.

It would have been "corrected" to read:

When a Canadian civil <u>servant</u> retires, <u>his</u> pension is indexed.

This is because, traditionally, the word *his* has been used to indicate both male and female. Although some language experts still maintain that *he* and *his* have dual meanings—one for an individual male and one for any human being—today this usage is widely regarded as sexist. Some have addressed this issue by using *he or she* (or *he/she*) and *his or her* (or *his/her*), but these phrases are awkward and cumbersome. For this reason, using *their* or *they* to indicate a single person of either gender is becoming increasingly common, and this trend appears to be gaining acceptance. As a result, the first sentence above would now be considered correct by many, though there are those who would still consider it incorrect. To be on the safe side, you may prefer to rephrase the sentence—in this case, by switching from the singular to the plural so that the phrase reads:

✓ When Canadian civil <u>servants</u> retire, <u>their</u> pensions are indexed.

Whichever form you choose, check for agreement between subjects and verbs. Use neutral nouns whenever possible, and, where appropriate, at least try to make clear in your examples and illustrations that you are referring to females as well as males—unless there is clear need to differentiate.

USING "ONE"

People often use the word *one* to avoid overusing *I* in their writing. Although in Britain this is common, in Canada and the United States frequent use of *one* may seem too formal and even a bit pompous:

> If <u>one</u> were to apply for the grant, <u>one</u> would find <u>oneself</u> engulfed in so many bureaucratic forms that <u>one's</u> patience would be stretched thin.

In the past, a common way around this problem was to use the third-person *his* or (less often) *her* as the adjectival form of *one*. Today, this usage is regarded with less acceptance. As we saw in the preceding section, you may also be able to substitute the plural *their*; just remember that some people still object to this usage as well. The best solution, again, may be to rephrase the sentence with a plural subject:

✓ If <u>researchers</u> were to apply for a grants, <u>they</u> would find <u>themselves</u> engulfed in so many bureaucratic forms that <u>their</u> patience would be stretched thin.

In any case, try to use *one* sparingly, and don't be afraid of the occasional *I*. The one serious error to avoid is mixing the third person *one* with the second person *you*.

✗ When <u>one</u> studies official statistics, <u>you</u> are surprised by their untrustworthiness.

In formal academic writing generally, *you* is not an appropriate substitution for *one*.

USING "ME" AND OTHER OBJECTIVE PRONOUNS

Remembering that it's wrong to say "Daria and me were invited to present our findings to the delegates," rather than "Daria and I were invited," many people use the subjective form of the pronoun even when it should be objective:

✗ The delegates invited Daria and I to present our findings.

✓ The delegates invited Daria and me to present our findings.

The verb *invited* requires an object; *me* is the objective case. Here is a simple hint: read the sentence with only the problem pronoun. You will know by ear which is correct.

✗ The delegates invited I to present the findings.

✓ The delegates invited me to present the findings.

Prepositions should also be followed by the objective case:

✗ Between you and I, Stan Wojcik is a bore.

✓ Between you and me, Stan Wojcik is a bore.

✗ Eating well is a problem for we students.

✓ Eating well is a problem for us students.

There are times, however, when the correct case can sound stiff or awkward:

(✓) To whom was the award given?

Rather than keeping to a correct but awkward form, try to reword the sentence:

✓ Who received the award?

EXCEPTIONS FOR PRONOUNS FOLLOWING PREPOSITIONS

The rule that a pronoun following a preposition takes the objective case has exceptions. When the preposition is followed by a clause, the pronoun should take the case required by its position in the clause:

✗ The students showed some concern <u>over whom would be selected</u> as Dean.

Although the pronoun follows the preposition *over*, it is also the subject of the verb *would be selected* and therefore requires the subjective case:

✓ The students showed some concern <u>over who would be selected</u> as Dean.

Similarly, when a gerund (a word that acts partly as a noun and partly as a verb) is the subject of a clause, the pronoun that modifies it takes the possessive case:

✗ Pella was elated <u>by him winning</u> the presidency.

✓ Pella was elated <u>by his winning</u> the presidency.

TROUBLES WITH MODIFYING

Adjectives modify nouns; adverbs modify verbs, adjectives, and other adverbs. Do not use an adjective to modify a verb:

✗ He played <u>good</u>. (adjective with verb)

✓ He played <u>well</u>. (adverb modifying verb)

✓ He played <u>really well</u>. (adverb modifying adverb)

✓ He had a <u>good style</u>. (adjective modifying noun)

✓ He had a <u>really good</u> style. (adverb modifying adjective)

SQUINTING MODIFERS

Remember that clarity largely depends on word order: to avoid confusion, the relations between the different parts of a sentence must be clear. Modifiers should therefore be as close as possible to the words they modify. A *squinting* modifier is one that, because of its position, seems to look in two directions at once:

✗ She expected <u>in the spring</u> a decline in the stock market.

Is *spring* the time of expectation or the time of the market decline? Try changing the order of the sentence to make the logical relation clearest:

✓ In the spring she <u>expected</u> a decline in the stock market.

✓ She expected a <u>spring decline</u> in the stock market.

Other squinting modifiers can be corrected in the same way:

✗ Our professor gave a lecture on Marx's <u>Capital</u>, which was well illustrated.

✓ Our professor gave a well-illustrated lecture on Marx's <u>Capital</u>.

DANGLING MODIFERS

Modifiers that have no grammatical connection with anything else in the sentence are said to be *dangling*:

✗ <u>Walking</u> around the campus in June, the river and trees made a picturesque scene.

Who is doing the walking? Here's another example:

✗ <u>Reflecting</u> on the results of the referendum, it was decided not to press for independence for a while.

Who is doing the reflecting? Clarify the meaning by connecting the dangling modifier to a new subject:

✓ <u>Walking</u> around the campus in June, she thought the river and trees made a picturesque scene.

✓ <u>Reflecting</u> on the results of the referendum, <u>the government</u> decided not to press for independence for a while.

TROUBLES WITH PAIRS (AND MORE)

COMPARISONS

Make sure that your comparisons are complete. The second element in a comparison should be equivalent to the first, whether the equivalence is stated or merely implied.

✗ Today's students have a greater understanding of new technology than their parents.

This sentence suggests that the two things being compared are *technology* and *parents*. Adding a second verb (*have*) that is equivalent to the first one shows that the two things being compared are *parents' understanding* and *students' understanding*:

> ✓ Today's students <u>have</u> a greater understanding of new technology than their parents <u>have</u>.

A similar problem arises in the following comparison:

> ✗ That cabinet minister is <u>a tiresome man</u> and so are his press conferences.

Press conferences may be tiresome, but they are not *a tiresome man*; to make sense, the two parts of the comparison must be parallel:

> ✓ That cabinet minister is <u>tiresome</u>, and so are his press conferences.

CORRELATIVES (COORDINATE CONSTRUCTIONS)

Constructions such as *both . . . and, not only . . . but,* and *neither . . . nor* are especially tricky. The coordinating term must not come too early or else one of the parts that come after will not connect with the common element. For the implied comparison to work, the two parts that come after the coordinating term must be grammatically equivalent:

> ✗ He <u>not only</u> understands mainframes <u>but</u> microcomputers too.

> ✓ He understands <u>not only</u> mainframes <u>but</u> microcomputers too.

PARALLEL PHRASING

A series of items in a sentence should be phrased in parallel wording. Make sure that all the parts of a parallel construction are in fact equal:

> ✗ Mackenzie King loved <u>his</u> job, <u>his</u> dogs, and mother.

> ✓ Mackenzie King loved <u>his</u> job, <u>his</u> dogs, and <u>his</u> mother.

Once you have decided to include the pronoun *his* in the first two elements, the third element must have it too.

For clarity as well as stylistic grace, keep similar ideas in similar form:

> ✗ He <u>failed</u> Economics and <u>barely passed</u> Statistics, but Political Science <u>was</u> a subject he did well in.

> ✓ He <u>failed</u> Economics and <u>barely passed</u> Statistics, but <u>did well</u> in Political Science.

cHApter 12

PUNCTUATION

Punctuation causes students so many problems that it deserves a chapter of its own. If your punctuation is faulty, your readers will be confused and may have to backtrack; worse still, they may be tempted to skip over the rough spots. Punctuation marks are the traffic signals of writing: use them with precision to keep readers moving smoothly through your work. Items in this chapter are arranged alphabetically: *apostrophe, brackets, colon, comma, dash, ellipsis, exclamation mark, hyphen, parentheses, period, quotation marks,* and *semicolon.*

APOSTROPHE [']

The apostrophe forms the possessive case for nouns and some pronouns.

1. **Add an apostrophe followed by *s* to**

   - all singular and plural nouns *not* ending in *s*:

     cat's meow; women's studies.

   - singular *proper* nouns ending in *s*:

     Keats's poetry; Carlos's ball.

     (Note, however, that the final *s* can be omitted if the word has a number of them already and would sound awkward, as in *Jesus'*, or in certain classical names.)

   - indefinite pronouns:

     someone's; anybody's.

2. **Add an apostrophe to plural nouns ending in *s*:**

   our families' pets; the lawyers' arguments.

3. **Use an apostrophe to show contractions of words:**

> isn't; can't; winter of '07.

Caution: don't confuse *it's* (the contraction of *it is*) with the possessive of "it" (*its*), which has no apostrophe.

BRACKETS [ ]

Brackets are square enclosures, not to be confused with parentheses (which are curved).

Use brackets to set off a remark of your own within a quotation:

> Fox maintains, "Obstacles to Western unification [in this decade] are as numerous as they are serious."

Brackets are sometimes used to enclose *sic*, which is used after an error, such as a misspelling, to show that the mistake was in the original. *Sic* may be italicized or underlined:

> The politician, in his letter to constituents, wrote about "these parlouse [*sic*] times of economic difficulty."

COLON [:]

A colon indicates that something is to follow.

1. **Use a colon before a formal statement or series:**

> ✓   The winners are the following: Dieter, Sonia, George, and Hugh.

Do not use a colon if the words preceding it do not form a complete sentence:

> ✗   The winners are: Dieter, Sonia, George, and Hugh.

> ✓   The winners are Dieter, Sonia, George, and Hugh.

Occasionally, however, a colon is used if the list is arranged vertically:

> ✓   The winners are: Dieter
>   Sonia
>   George
>   Hugh

2. **Use a colon for formality before a direct quotation:**

✓ The leaders of the anti-nuclear group repeated their message: "The world needs bread before bombs."

COMMA [,]

Commas are the trickiest of all punctuation marks; even the experts differ on when to use them. Most agree, however, that too many commas are as bad as too few, since they make writing choppy and awkward to read. Certainly recent writers use fewer commas than earlier stylists did. Whenever you are in doubt, let clarity be your guide. The most widely accepted conventions are these:

1. **Use a comma to separate two independent clauses joined by a coordinating conjunction (and, but, for, or, nor, yet, so).** By signalling that there are two clauses, the comma will prevent the reader from confusing the beginning of the second clause with the end of the first:

✗ He went out for dinner with his sister and his roommate joined them later.

✓ He went out for dinner with his sister, and his roommate joined them later.

When the second clause has the same subject as the first, you have the option of omitting both the second subject and the comma:

✓ He can make a convincing argument, but he can't write a report.

✓ He can make a convincing argument but can't write a report.

If you mistakenly punctuate two sentences as if they were one, the result will be a *run-on sentence*; if you use a comma but forget the coordinating conjunction, the result will be a *comma splice*:

✗ She went to the library, it was closed.

✓ She went to the library, but it was closed.

Remember that words such as *however*, *therefore*, and *thus* are conjunctive adverbs, not conjunctions: if you use one of them the way you would use a conjunction, the result will again be a *comma splice*:

✗ She was accepted into graduate school, however, she took a year off to earn her tuition.

✓ She was accepted into graduate school; however, she took a year off to earn her tuition.

Conjunctive adverbs are often confused with conjunctions. You can distinguish between the two if you remember that a conjunctive adverb's position in a sentence can be changed:

✓ She was accepted into graduate school; she took a year off, however, to earn her tuition.

The position of a conjunction, on the other hand, is invariable: it must be placed between the two clauses:

✓ She was accepted into graduate school, but she took a year off to earn her tuition.

When, in rare cases, the independent clauses are short and closely related, they may be joined by a comma alone:

✓ I came, I saw, I conquered.

A *fused sentence* is a run-on sentence in which independent clauses are slapped together with no punctuation at all:

✗ He watched the hockey game all afternoon the only exercise he got was going to the kitchen between periods.

A fused sentence sounds like breathless babbling—and it's a serious error.

2. **Use a comma between items in a series.** (Place a coordinating conjunction before the last item):

✓ She finally found an apartment that was large, bright, and clean.

✓ Then she had to scrounge around for dishes, pots, cutlery, and a kettle.

The comma before the conjunction is optional:

✓ She kept a cat, a dog and a budgie.

Sometimes, however, the final comma can help to prevent confusion:

✗   When we set off on our trip, we were warned about passport thieves, attacks on single women and baggage loss.

In this case, a comma can prevent the reader from thinking that *attacks* are made on *baggage* as well as on *single women*:

✓   When we set off on our trip, we were warned about passport thieves, attacks on single women, and baggage loss.

3. **Use a comma to separate adjectives preceding a noun when they modify the same element:**

✓   It was a rainy, windy night.

When the adjectives *do not* modify the same element, however, you should not use a comma:

✗   It was a pleasant, winter outing.

Here *winter* modifies *outing*, but *pleasant* modifies the whole phrase *winter outing*. A good way of checking whether or not you need a comma is to see if you can reverse the order of the adjectives. If you can reverse it (*rainy, windy night* or *windy, rainy night*), use a comma; if you can't (*winter pleasant outing*), omit the comma:

✓   It was a pleasant winter outing.

4. **Use commas to set off an interruption (or "parenthetical element"):**

✓   The film, I hear, isn't nearly as good as the book.

✓   My tutor, however, couldn't answer the question.

Remember to put commas on *both sides* of the interruption:

✗   The film I hear, isn't nearly as good as the book.

✗   The music, they say was adapted from a piece by Mozart.

✓   The music, they say, was adapted from a piece by Mozart.

5. **Use commas to set off words or phrases that provide additional but non-essential information:**

✓   Our president, Sue Stephens, does her job well.

✓ The golden retriever, his closest companion, went with him everywhere.

In these examples, *Sue Stephens* and *his closest companion* are "appositives": they give additional information about the nouns they refer to (*president* and *golden retriever*), but the sentences would still make sense without them. Here's another example:

✓ My oldest friend, who lives in Halifax, was married last week.

The phrase *who lives in Halifax* is called a *non-restrictive* modifier, because it does not limit the meaning of the word it modifies (*friend*). Without that modifying clause the sentence would still specify who was married. Since the information the clause provides is not necessary to the meaning of the sentence, you must use commas on both sides to set it off.

In contrast, a *restrictive* modifier is one that provides essential information; therefore it must not be set apart from the element it modifies, and commas should not be used:

✓ The man who came to dinner was my uncle.

Without the clause *who came to dinner*, the reader would not know which man was the uncle. To avoid confusion, be sure to distinguish carefully between essential and additional information. The difference can be important:

Students, who are not willing to work, should not receive grants.

Students who are not willing to work should not receive grants.

6. **Use a comma after an introductory phrase when omitting it would cause confusion:**

✗ On the balcony above the singers entertained the diners.

✓ On the balcony above, the singers entertained the diners.

✗ When he turned away the prisoner disappeared.

✓ When he turned away, the prisoner disappeared.

7. **Use a comma to separate elements in dates and addresses:**

February 2, 2007. (Commas are often omitted if the day comes first: 2 February 2007.)

117 Hudson Drive, Edmonton, Alberta.

They lived in Dartmouth, Nova Scotia.

8. **Use a comma before a quotation in a sentence:**

   ✓ He said, "Life is too short to worry."

   ✓ "The children's safety," he warned, "is in your hands."

For more formality, you may instead use a colon (see above).

9. **Use a comma with a name followed by a title:**

   D. Gunn, Ph.D.

   Patrice Lareau, M.D.

DASH [—]

A dash creates an abrupt pause, emphasizing the words that follow. (Never use dashes as casual substitutes for other punctuation: overuse can detract from the calm, well-reasoned effect you want.)

1. **Use a dash to stress a word or phrase:**

   The British—as a matter of honour—vowed to retake the islands.

   Ramirez was well received in the legislature—at first.

2. **Use a dash in interrupted or unfinished dialogue:**

   "It's a matter—to put it delicately—of personal hygiene."

   "I just thought—" Donald began before Mario cut him off: "Well, you were wrong."

In typing, use two hyphens together, with no spaces on either side, to show a dash. Your word processor may automatically convert this to a dash for you as you continue typing.

ELLIPSIS [. . .]

1. **Use an ellipsis (three spaced dots) to show an omission from a quotation:**

> He reported that "the drought in the thirties, to many farming families in the West . . . , resembled a biblical plague, even to the locusts."

If the omission comes at the beginning of the opening sentence, an ellipsis is not necessarily used:

> He reported that the drought "resembled a biblical plague, even to the locusts."

If the omission comes at the end of a sentence, indicate this by using four dots, with no space between the final word and the first dot:

> He reported that the drought "resembled a biblical plague. . . ."

2. **Use an ellipsis to show that a series of numbers continues indefinitely:**

> 1, 3, 5, 7, 9 . . .

EXCLAMATION MARK [!]

An exclamation mark helps to show emotion or feeling. It is usually found in dialogue:

> "Woe is me!" she mourned.

In academic writing, you should only use an exclamation mark in those rare instances when you want to give a point an emotional emphasis:

> He predicted that the dollar would rise in 2001. Some forecast!

HYPHEN [-]

1. **Use a hyphen if you must divide a word at the end of a line.** When a word is too long to fit at the end of a line, it's best to start a new line rather than break it. If you must divide, however, remember these rules:

- Divide between syllables.
- Never divide a one-syllable word.
- Never leave one letter by itself.
- Divide double consonants except when they come before a suffix, in which case divide before the suffix:

ar-rangement; embar-rassment; fall-ing; pass-able.

When a consonant has been doubled to form the suffix, keep the second consonant with the suffix:

refer-ral; begin-ning.

2. **Use a hyphen to separate the parts of certain compound words:**

- compound nouns:

  sister-in-law; vice-consul.

- compound verbs:

  test-drive; water-ski.

- compound nouns and adjectives used as modifiers preceding nouns:

  a well-considered plan; twentieth-century attitudes.

  Note that when these compounds do not modify a noun they precede, they are not hyphenated:

  The plan was well considered.

  These are attitudes of the twentieth century.

Most hyphenated nouns and verbs lose the hyphen over time. When in doubt, check a dictionary.

3. **Use a hyphen with certain prefixes (*all-*, *self-*, *ex-*, and those prefixes preceding a proper name):**

  all-party; self-imposed; ex-jockey; anti-nuclear; pro-Canadian.

4. **Use a hyphen to emphasize contrasting prefixes:**

  The coach agreed to give both pre- and post-game interviews.

5. **Use a hyphen for written-out compound numbers from one to ninety-nine and compound fractions:**

eighty-one years ago; two-thirds of a cup.

6. **Use a hyphen to separate parts of inclusive numbers or dates:**

the years 1890-1914; pages 22-40.

PARENTHESES [( )]

1. **Use parentheses to enclose an explanation, example, or qualification.** Parentheses show that the enclosed material is of incidental importance to the main idea. They mark an interruption that is more subtle than one marked off by dashes but more pronounced than one set off by commas:

My brother (who is older than I) is a superb cook and carpenter.

His latest plan (according to neighbours) is to dam the creek.

Remember that punctuation should not precede parentheses, but it may follow them if required by the sense of the sentence:

I like coffee in the morning (if it's not instant), but she prefers tea.

If the parenthetical statement comes between two complete sentences, it should be punctuated as a sentence, with the period, question mark, or exclamation point inside the parentheses:

I finished my last essay on Tuesday. (It was on Freud's theory of repression.) Fortunately, I had three weeks left to study for the exam.

They're out playing baseball. (Who plays baseball in February?) They should be back soon.

2. **Use parentheses to enclose references:** see Chapter 10 for details.

PERIOD [.]

1. **Use a period at the end of a sentence.** A period indicates a full stop, not just a pause.

2. **Use a period with abbreviations.** British style omits the period in certain cases, but North American style usually requires it for abbreviated titles (Mrs.,

Dr., Rev., Ph.D., etc.) as well as for place names (B.C., N.W.T., etc.). Although the abbreviations and acronyms for some organizations include periods, the most common ones generally do not (CARE, CIDA, CBC, RCMP, etc.).

3. **Use a period at the end of an indirect question.** Do *not* use a question mark:

 ✗ He asked if I wanted a substitute?

 ✓ He asked if I wanted a substitute.

QUOTATION MARKS [" "OR ' ']

Quotation marks are usually double in American style and single in British practice. In Canada either style is accepted as long as you are consistent.

1. **Use quotation marks to signify direct discourse (the actual words of a speaker):**

> I asked: "What is the matter?"
>
> "I have a pain in my big toe," he replied.

2. **Use quotation marks to show that words themselves are the issue:**

> The term "love" in tennis comes from the French word for "egg."

Alternatively, you may italicize or underline the terms in question.

 Sometimes quotation marks are used to mark a slang word or an inappropriate usage, to show that the writer is aware of the difficulty:

> Hitler's "final solution" was the most barbaric act of this century.

Use this device only when necessary. In general, it's better to let the context show your attitude, or to choose another term.

3. **Use quotation marks to enclose the titles of poems, short stories, paintings, songs, films, and articles in books or journals.** In contrast, titles of books, paintings, or longer musical works are italicized or underlined:

> The story I like best in Robert Weaver's Canadian Short Stories is "Bernadette," by Mavis Gallant.

4. Use quotation marks to enclose quotations within quotations (single or double, depending on your primary style):

> He said, "Hitler's 'final solution' was the most barbaric act of this century."

When the material being quoted is four lines or longer, it should be indented and single-spaced. No quotation marks should be used. If the block quotation is from the beginning of a paragraph, the normal indentation of the first word should be included.

PLACEMENT OF PUNCTUATION WITH QUOTATION MARKS

British and American methods of punctuating quotations differ. Again, both practices are accepted in Canada as long as you are consistent. British style usually places the punctuation outside the quotation marks, unless it is actually part of the quotation. The American practice, which is followed in this book, is increasingly common in Canada:

- A comma or period always goes inside the quotation marks:

  > He said, "Give me another chance," but I replied, "You've had enough chances."

- A semicolon or colon always goes outside the quotation marks:

  > George wants to watch "The Journal"; I'd rather watch the hockey game.

- A question mark, dash, or exclamation mark goes inside quotation marks if it is part of the quotation, but outside if it is not:

  > He asked, "What's for dinner?"

  > Did he really call the boss a "lily-livered hypocrite"?

  > His speech was hardly an appeal for "blood, sweat, and tears"!

  > I was just whispering to Louisa, "That instructor is a—" when suddenly he glanced at me.

- When a reference is given parenthetically (in round brackets) at the end of a quotation, the quotation marks precede the parentheses and the sentence punctuation follows them:

Lamarche suggests that we should "abandon the Foreign Investment Review Agency" (*Globe Weekly*, 12 April 2007).

SEMICOLON [;]

A semicolon indicates a degree of separation intermediate between a comma and a period.

1. Use a semicolon to join independent clauses (complete sentences) that are closely related:

> For five days he worked non-stop; by Saturday he was exhausted.

> His lecture was confusing; no one could understand the terminology.

A semicolon is especially useful when the second independent clause begins with a conjunctive adverb such as *however, moreover, consequently, nevertheless, in addition,* or *therefore* (usually followed by a comma):

> He brought in a box of doughnuts; however, no one was hungry.

Some grammarians may disagree, but it's usually acceptable to follow a semicolon with a coordinating conjunction if the second clause is complicated by other commas:

> Zoltan, my cousin, is a keen jogger in all weather; but sometimes, especially in winter, I think it does him more harm than good.

2. Use a semicolon to mark the divisions in a complicated series when individual items themselves need commas. Using a comma to mark the subdivisions and a semicolon to mark the main divisions will help to prevent mix-ups:

> ✗ He invited Maria DaSilva, the vice-principal, Marvin Goldman, and Christine Lai.

Is the vice-principal a separate person?

> ✓ He invited Maria DaSilva, the vice-principal; Marvin Goldman; and Christine Lai.

In a case such as this, the elements separated by the semicolon do not need to be independent clauses.

chapter 13

CATCHLIST OF MISUSED WORDS AND PHRASES

This chapter offers a catchlist of words and phrases that are often misused. A periodic read-through will refresh your memory and help you avoid needless mistakes.

accept, except. Accept is a verb meaning to *receive affirmatively;* **except**, when used as a verb, means to *exclude:*

> I <u>accept</u> your offer.

> The teacher <u>excepted</u> him from the general punishment.

accompanied by, accompanied with. Use **accompanied by** for people; use **accompanied with** for objects:

> He was <u>accompanied</u> by his wife.

> The brochure arrived, <u>accompanied with</u> a discount coupon.

advice, advise. Advice is a noun, **advise** a verb:

> He was <u>advised</u> to ignore the others' <u>advice</u>.

affect, effect. Affect is a verb meaning to *influence;* **effect** can be either a noun meaning *result* or a verb meaning to *bring about.*

> The eye drops <u>affect</u> his vision.

> The <u>effect</u> of higher government spending is higher inflation.

> People lack confidence in their ability to <u>effect</u> change in society.

all ready, already. To be **all ready** is simply to be ready for something; **already** means *beforehand* or *earlier:*

> The students were <u>all ready</u> for the lecture to begin.

> The professor had <u>already</u> left her office by the time Blair arrived.

all right. Write as two separate words: *all right.* This can mean *safe and sound, in good condition, okay; correct; satisfactory;* or *I agree.*

> Are you all right?

> The student's answers were all right.

(Note the ambiguity of the second example: does it mean that the answers were all correct or simply satisfactory? In this case, it might be better to use a clearer word.)

all together, altogether. All together means *in a group;* **altogether** is an adverb meaning *entirely:*

> He was altogether certain that the children were all together.

allusion, illusion. An **allusion** is an indirect reference to something; an **illusion** is a false perception:

> The rock image is an allusion to the myth of Sisyphus.

> He thought he saw a sea monster, but it was an illusion.

a lot. Write as two separate words: *a lot.*

alternate, alternative. Alternate means *every other* or *every second* thing in a series; **alternative** refers to a *choice* between options:

> The two sections of the class attended discussion groups on alternate weeks.

> The students could do an extra paper as an alternative to writing the exam.

among, between. Use **among** for three or more persons or objects, **between** for two:

> Between you and me, there's trouble among the team members.

amount, number. Amount indicates quantity when units are not discrete and not absolute; **number** indicates quantity when units are discrete and absolute:

> A large amount of timber.

> A large number of students.

See also **less, fewer.**

analysis. The plural is **analyses.**

anyone, any one. Anyone is written as two words to give numerical emphasis; otherwise it is written as one word:

Any one of us could do that.

Anyone could do that.

anyways. Non-standard English: use *anyway*.

as, because. As is a weaker conjunction than **because** and may be confused with *when*:

✗   As I was working, I ate at my desk.

✓   Because I was working, I ate at my desk.

✗   He arrived as I was leaving.

✓   He arrived when I was leaving.

as to. A common feature of bureaucratese. Replace it with a single-word preposition such as *about* or *on*:

✗   They were concerned as to the range of disagreement.

✓   They were concerned about the range of disagreement.

✗   They recorded his comments as to the treaty.

✓   They recorded his comments on the treaty.

bad, badly. Bad is an adjective meaning *not good*:

The meat tastes bad.

He felt bad about forgetting the dinner party.

Badly is an adverb meaning *not well*; when used with the verbs **want** or **need**, it means *very much*:

She thought he played the villain's part badly.

I badly need a new suit.

beside, besides. Beside is a preposition meaning *next to*:

She worked beside her assistant.

Besides has two uses: as a preposition it means *in addition to*; as a conjunctive adverb it means *moreover*:

Besides recommending the changes, the consultants are implementing them.

Besides, it was hot and we wanted to rest.

between. See **among**.

bring, take. One **brings** something to a closer place and **takes** it to a farther one:

> Take it with you when you go.

> Next time you come to visit, bring your friend along.

can, may. **Can** means to *be able;* **may** means to *have permission:*

> Can you fix the lock?

> May I have another piece of cake?

In speech, **can** is used to cover both meanings: in formal writing, however, you should observe the distinction.

can't hardly. A faulty combination of the phrases **can't** and **can hardly**. Use one or the other of them instead:

> He can't swim.

> He can hardly swim.

cite, sight, site. To **cite** something is to *quote* or *mention* it as an example or authority; **sight** can be used in many ways, all of which relate to the ability to *see;* **site** refers to a specific *location,* a particular place at which something is located.

complement, compliment. The verb to **complement** means to *complete;* to **compliment** means *to praise*.

> Her ability to analyze data complements her excellent research skills.

> I complimented her on her outstanding report.

compose, comprise. Both words mean *to constitute* or *make up,* but **compose** is preferred. **Comprise** is correctly used to mean *consist of,* or *be composed of.* Using **comprise** in the passive ("is comprised of")—as you might be tempted to do in the second example below—is usually frowned on in formal writing:

> These students compose the group which will go overseas.

> Each paragraph comprises an introduction, an argument, and a conclusion.

continual, continuous. **Continual** means *repeated over a period of time;* **continuous** means *constant* or *without interruption:*

> The strikes caused continual delays in building the road.

Five days of <u>continuous</u> rain ruined our holiday.

could of. Incorrect, as are **might of**, **should of**, and **would of**. Replace *of* with **have**:

✗   He <u>could of</u> done it.

✓   He <u>could have</u> done it.

✓   They <u>might have</u> been there.

✓   I <u>should have</u> known.

✓   We <u>would have</u> left earlier.

council, counsel. **Council** is a noun meaning an *advisory* or *deliberative assembly*. **Counsel** as a noun means *advice* or *lawyer*; as a verb it means to *give advice*.

The college <u>council</u> meets on Tuesday.

We respect her <u>counsel</u>, since she's seldom wrong.

As a camp <u>counsellor</u>, you may need to <u>counsel</u> parents as well as children.

criterion, criteria. A **criterion** is a standard for judging something. **Criteria** is the plural of **criterion** and thus requires a plural verb:

<u>These</u> are my <u>criteria</u> for grading the reports.

data. The plural of **datum**. The set of information, usually in numerical form, that is used for analysis as the basis for a study. Informally, **data** is often used as a singular noun, but in formal contexts it should be treated as a plural:

<u>These</u> data <u>were</u> gathered in an unsystematic fashion. Therefore <u>they</u> <u>are</u> inconclusive.

John reported that his data <u>are</u> exactly what he needs.

deduce, deduct. To **deduce** something is to *work it out by reasoning*; to **deduct** means to *subtract* or *take away* from something. The noun form of both words is **deduction**.

delusion, illusion. A **delusion** is a belief or perception that is distorted; an **illusion** is a false belief:

Hitler had <u>delusions</u> of grandeur.

> The desert pool he thought he saw was an <u>illusion</u>.

dependent, dependant. **Dependent** is an adjective meaning *contingent on* or *subject to*; **dependant** is a noun.

> Chedley's graduation is <u>dependent</u> upon his passing algebra.

> Chedley is a <u>dependant</u> of his father.

device, devise. The word ending in **-ice** is the noun; that ending in **-ise** is the verb.

different than. Incorrect. Use either **different from** (North American usage) or **different to** (British).

diminish, minimize. To **diminish** means to *make* or *become smaller*; to **minimize** is to *reduce* something to the smallest possible amount or size.

disinterested, uninterested. **Disinterested** implies impartiality or neutrality; **uninterested** implies a lack of interest:

> As a <u>disinterested</u> observer, he was in a good position to judge the issue fairly.

> <u>Uninterested</u> in the proceedings, he yawned repeatedly.

due to. Although increasingly used to mean *because of*, **due** is an adjective and therefore needs to modify something:

> ✗   <u>Due to</u> his impatience, we lost the contract. [<u>Due</u> is dangling.]

> ✓   The loss was <u>due to</u> his impatience.

e.g., i.e. **E.g.** means *for example*; **i.e.** means *that is*. The two are incorrectly used interchangeably.

entomology, etymology. **Entomology** is the study of insects; **etymology** is the study of the derivation and history of words.

exceptional, exceptionable. **Exceptional** means *unusual* or *outstanding*, whereas **exceptionable** means *open to objection* and is generally used in negative contexts.

> Her accomplishments are <u>exceptional</u>.

> There is nothing <u>exceptionable</u> in his behaviour.

farther, further. **Farther** refers to distance, **further** to extent:

> He paddled farther than his friends.

> She explained the plan further.

focus (noun). The plural may be either **focuses** (also spelled **focusses**) or **foci**.

good, well. **Good** is an adjective that modifies a noun; **well** is an adverb that modifies a verb.

> She is a good tennis player.

> The experiment went well.

hanged, hung. **Hanged** means *executed by hanging*. **Hung** means *suspended* or *clung to*:

> He was hanged at dawn for the murder.

> He hung the picture.

> She hung on to the boat when it capsized.

hereditary, heredity. **Heredity** is a noun; **hereditary** is an adjective. **Heredity** is the biological process whereby characteristics are passed from one generation to the next; **hereditary** describes those characteristics.

> Heredity has determined that you have brown hair.

> Your asthma may be hereditary.

hopefully. Use **hopefully** as an adverb meaning *full of hope*:

> She scanned the horizon hopefully, waiting for the lost boat to appear.

In formal writing, using **hopefully** to mean *I hope* is still frowned upon, although increasingly common; it's better to use *I hope*:

> ✗ Hopefully we'll make a bigger profit this year.

> ✓ I hope we'll make a bigger profit this year.

i.e. *Not* the same as **e.g.**! See **e.g.**

illusion. See **allusion, delusion**.

incite, insight. **Incite** is a verb meaning to *stir up*; **insight** is a noun meaning (often sudden) understanding.

infer, imply. To **infer** means to *deduce* or *conclude by reasoning*. It is often confused with **imply**, which means to *suggest* or *insinuate*.

> We can infer from the large population density that there is a large demand for services.

> The large population density implies that there is a high demand for services.

inflammable, flammable, non-flammable. Despite its **in-** prefix, **inflammable** is not the opposite of **flammable**: both words describe things that are *easily* set on fire. The opposite of **flammable** and **inflammable** is **non-flammable**. To prevent any possibility of confusion, it's best to avoid **inflammable** altogether.

irregardless. Redundant; use *regardless*.

its, it's. **Its** is a form of possessive pronoun; **it's** is a contraction of *it is*. Many people mistakenly put an apostrophe in **its** in order to show possession.

> ✗ The cub wanted it's mother.

> ✓ The cub wanted its mother.

> ✓ It's time to leave.

less, fewer. **Less** is used when units are *not* discrete and *not* absolute ("less information"). **Fewer** is used when the units *are* discrete and absolute ("fewer details").

lie, lay. To **lie** means to *assume a horizontal position;* to **lay** means to *put down*. The changes of tense often cause confusion:

Present	Past	Past participle
lie	lay	lain
lay	laid	laid

like, as. **Like** is a preposition, but it is often wrongly used as a conjunction. To join two independent clauses, use the conjunction **as**:

> ✗ I want to progress like you have this year.

> ✓ I want to progress as you have this year.

> ✓ Prof. Dodd is like my old school principal.

might of. See **could of**.

minimize. See **diminish**.

mitigate, militate. To **mitigate** means to *reduce the severity* of something; to **militate** against something means to *oppose* it.

myself, me. **Myself** is an intensifier of, not a substitute for, *I* or *me*:

- ✗ He gave it to Maria and myself.
- ✓ He gave it to Maria and me.
- ✗ Jane and myself are invited.
- ✓ Jane and I are invited.
- ✓ Myself, I would prefer a swivel chair.

nor, or. Use **nor** with **neither** and **or** by itself or with **either**:

> He is neither overworked nor underfed.

> The plant is either diseased or dried out.

off of. Remove the unnecessary **of**:

- ✗ The fence kept the children off of the premises.
- ✓ The fence kept the children off the premises.

phenomenon. A singular noun: the plural is **phenomena**.

plaintiff, plaintive. A **plaintiff** is a person who brings a case against someone else to court; **plaintive** is an adjective meaning *sorrowful*.

populace, populous. **Populace** is a noun meaning the *people* of a place; **populous** is an adjective meaning *thickly inhabited*:

> The populace of Hilltop village is not well educated.

> With so many people in such a small area, Hilltop village is a populous place.

practice, practise. **Practice** can be a noun or an adjective; **practise** is always a verb. Note, however, that in the U.S. and sometimes in Canada, the spelling of the verb is **practice**:

> The soccer players need practice. (noun)

> That was a practice game. (adjective)

> The players need to practise (or practice) their skills. (verb)

precede, proceed. To **precede** is to go *before* (earlier) or *in front of* others; to **proceed** is to *go on* or *ahead*:

> The faculty will <u>precede</u> the students into the hall.

> The medal winners will <u>proceed</u> to the front of the hall.

prescribe, proscribe. These words are sometimes confused, although they have quite different meanings. **Prescribe** means *to advise the use of* or *impose authoritatively*. **Proscribe** means to *reject, denounce,* or *ban*:

> The professor <u>prescribed</u> the conditions under which the equipment could be used.

> The student government <u>proscribed</u> the publication of unsigned editorials in the newspaper.

principle, principal. **Principle** is a noun meaning a *general truth* or *law*; **principal** can be used as either a noun or an adjective, meaning *chief*.

rational, rationale. **Rational** is an adjective meaning *logical* or *able to reason*. **Rationale** is a noun meaning *explanation*:

> That was not a <u>rational</u> decision.

> The president sent around a memo explaining the <u>rationale</u> for his decision.

real, really. **Real**, an adjective, means *true* or *genuine*; **really**, an adverb, means *actually, truly, very,* or *extremely*.

> The nugget was <u>real</u> gold.

> The nugget was <u>really</u> valuable.

seasonable, seasonal. **Seasonable** means *usual* or *suitable for the season*; **seasonal** means *of, depending on,* or *varying with the season*:

> The temperature is <u>seasonably</u> high.

> The clothes you pack must take into account <u>seasonal</u> changes in the weather.

should of. See **could of**.

their, there. **Their** is the possessive form of the third person plural pronoun. **There** is usually an adverb, meaning *at that place* or *at that point*:

> They parked <u>their</u> bikes <u>there</u>.

<u>There</u> is no point in arguing with you.

tortuous, torturous. The adjective **tortuous** means *full of twists and turns* or *circuitous*. **Torturous**, derived from *torture*, means *involving torture* or *excruciating*:

To avoid heavy traffic, they took a <u>tortuous</u> route home.

The concert was a <u>torturous</u> experience for the audience.

turbid, turgid. **Turbid**, with respect to a liquid or colour, means *muddy, not clear*, or (with respect to literary style) *confused*. **Turgid** means *swollen, inflated, or enlarged*, or (again with reference to literary style) *pompous* or *bombastic*.

unique. This word, which means *of which there is only one* or *unequalled,* is both overused and misused. Since there are no degrees of comparison—one thing cannot be "more unique" than another—expressions such as *very unique* are incorrect.

while. To avoid misreading, use **while** only when you mean *at the same time that*. Do not use *while* as a substitute for *although, whereas,* or *but*:

✗   While she's getting fair marks, she'd like to do better.

✗   I headed for home, <u>while</u> she decided to stay.

✓   He fell asleep <u>while</u> he was reading.

-wise. Never use **-wise** as a suffix to form new words when you mean *with regard to*:

✗   <u>Sales-wise</u>, the company did better last year.

✓   The company's sales increased last year.

your, you're. **Your** is a pronominal adjective used to show possession; **you're** is a contraction of *you are*:

<u>You're</u> likely to miss <u>your</u> train if you don't leave soon.

GLOSSARY I: SOCIAL SCIENCE

actual intervention. An action or program aimed at changing an existing social condition.

aggregate data. Statistics produced for large groups or categories of people, in which the characteristics of individual respondents are no longer identifiable.

anomaly. A finding that does not fit the thinking within a paradigm.

applied research. Research intended to provide decision makers with practical, action-oriented recommendations to solve a problem.

authority. A highly regarded scholar who is referenced to support a line of argument.

baseline. A measure of conditions or behaviour before experimental manipulation is carried out.

basic research. Research intended to make and test theories about some aspect of real life.

bias. See **researcher bias**.

conditioning variable. A characteristic that determines whether an independent variable will have a strong or weak effect on the dependent variable.

conditions, control. An absence of treatments (i.e., experimental conditions) that are predicted to change the attitudes or behaviours of experimental subjects.

conditions, experimental. Treatments that are predicted to change the attitudes or behaviour of experimental subjects.

constant. A characteristic or condition (of a person, group, or society) that does not change over time. (Compare **variable**.)

construct validity. A high degree of correlation among items believed to measure the same thing.

control (for). Examine the influence on the dependent variable of changes in one independent variable while holding constant (i.e., *controlling for*) other independent variables.

data. Facts or evidence, based on observation, experience, or experimentation, that can be checked or verified.

deduce. Infer by reasoning from known facts.

dependent variable. A characteristic or condition that results from change in another characteristic or condition; a variable assumed to be the effect of an independent variable.

disconfirmatory finding. An observed relationship that fails to prove a hypothesis.

distribution. The way in which a condition or characteristic is spread over members of a group or category of people.

experiment. A study of groups or individuals carried out in an environment controlled by the researcher, who manipulates some variables to see their effects on other variables.

face validity. The accuracy with which an indicator appears to measure the variable it is meant to represent.

folkways. Norms that are cause for only mild or informal punishment when violated. (Compare **mores**.)

hypothesis. An untested statement of an expected relationship between two or more variables.

imagined intervention. An action or program, imagined but not carried out, that would aim to change an existing social condition.

independent variable. A characteristic or condition that causes change in another characteristic or condition; a causal or explanatory variable presumed to be the cause of a dependent variable.

interval measure. The level or type of measurement that is based on categories that are an equal distance, or interval, from one another, with no absolute zero.

intervening variable. A characteristic or condition that explains the link between a cause and an effect; a variable through which the independent variable acts on the dependent variable.

intervention. An action or manipulation whose effect on a group of people is to be studied.

longitudinal study. A study that involves collecting data from the same sample at intervals over time.

model. A theoretical "picture" of the relations among causes and effects.

mores. Norms that carry moral significance, which are therefore cause for severe punishment when violated. (Compare **folkways**.)

negative relationship. A relationship between two variables, in which an increase in one produces a decrease in the other. (Compare **positive relationship**.)

nominal measure. The level or type of measurement that places people into named categories (e.g., male/female).

norms. Rules or expectations about proper behaviour in particular situations, which serve as guidelines for an individual's actions.

operationalize. Devise measures to accurately represent the concepts or variables in a theory.

ordinal measure. The level or type of measurement that places people in order from most to least in respect to some characteristic.

paradigm. A theoretical perspective or way of viewing the world.

policy instrument (or **policy tool**). An organizational resource (e.g., the right to legislate and enforce a policy) that can be used to influence social problems.

policy research. See **applied research**.

positive relationship. A relationship between two variables, in which an increase in one produces an increase in the other. (Compare **negative relationship**.)

proposition. See **hypothesis**.

pure research. See **basic research**.

qualitative data. Data that cannot be satisfactorily described by numbers and must be described in words.

quantitative data. Data that can be satisfactorily described by numbers.

quasi-experiment. A modified experiment, in which the experimenter cannot exercise complete control over sampling or the research environment.

ratio measure. The level or type of measurement used to measure phenomena where absolute zero exists (e.g., height or weight).

reactivity. A condition in which research subjects behave differently from usual because they are aware that they are being studied.

relationship. An association or connection between variables, such that a change in one produces a change in the other.

reliability. The extent to which a measuring procedure produces consistent results over time or with different investigators.

researcher bias. The way in which a researcher's beliefs or expectations affect or influence the findings of a study.

scale. A set of measured items combined to provide a single overall measure of some concept or variable.

significance (or **statistical significance**). The likelihood that an observed relationship has occurred by chance alone.

sociogram. A diagram of relationships among members of a group, which shows who interacts with whom, and who are the most popular, influential, or otherwise "central" people.

speculative study (or **thought experiment**). An attempt to predict the effects of an independent variable on a dependent variable, based on a combination of imagined and real data.

strong relationship. A relationship between two variables, in which a large change in one variable produces a large change in the other. (Compare **weak relationship**.)

test (or **verify**). Examine the correctness of a theory by matching predicted against observed findings.

theory. A set of interconnected statements or propositions that attempts to explain a causal relationship.

unobtrusive measure. Any method of data collection in which research subjects are not aware of being studied and therefore do not change their behaviour.

validity. The ability of an indicator or measure to accurately represent the variable it is meant to represent.

value neutrality. A way of conducting research that seeks to ensure a fair and objective hearing for what the data actually show.

variable. A characteristic or condition that can differ from one person, group, or situation to another. (Compare **constant**.)

verify (or **validate**). See **test**.

weak relationship. A relationship between two variables, in which a large change in one variable produces a small change in the other. (Compare **strong relationship**.)

GLOSSARY II: GRAMMAR

abstract. A summary accompanying a formal scientific report or paper, briefly outlining the contents.

abstract language. Language that deals with theoretical, intangible concepts or details: e.g., *justice*; *goodness*; *truth*. (Compare **concrete language**.)

acronym. A pronounceable word made up of the first letters of the words in a phrase or name: e.g., *NATO* (from *North Atlantic Treaty Organization*). A group of initial letters that are pronounced separately is an **initialism**: e.g., *CBC*; *NHL*.

active voice. See **voice**.

adjectival phrase (or **adjectival clause**). A group of words modifying a noun or pronoun: e.g., *the dog that belongs to my brother*.

adjective. A word that modifies or describes a noun or pronoun: e.g., *red*; *beautiful*; *solemn*.

adverb. A word that modifies or qualifies a verb, adjective, or adverb, often answering a question such as *how? why? when?* or *where?*: e.g., *slowly*; *fortunately*; *early*; *abroad*. (See also **conjunctive adverb**.)

adverbial phrase (or **adverbial clause**). A group of words modifying a verb, adjective, or adverb: e.g., *The dog ran with great speed*.

agreement. Consistency in tense, number, or person between related parts of a sentence: e.g., between subject and verb, or noun and related pronoun.

ambiguity. Vague or equivocal language; meaning that can be taken two ways.

antecedent (or **referent**). The noun for which a following pronoun stands: e.g., *cats* in *Cats are happiest when they are sleeping*.

appositive. A word or phrase that identifies a preceding noun or pronoun: e.g., *Mrs. Jones, my aunt, is sick*. The second phrase is said to be **in apposition to** the first.

article. See **definite article**, **indefinite article**.

assertion. A positive statement or claim: e.g., The data are inconclusive.

auxiliary verb. A verb used to form the tenses, moods, and voices of other verbs: e.g., *am* in *I am swimming*. The main auxiliary verbs in English are *be, do, have, can, could, may, might, must, shall, should,* and *will*.

bibliography. 1. A list of works used or referred to in writing an essay or report. 2. A reference book listing works available on a particular subject.

case. Any of the inflected forms of a pronoun (see **inflection**).

> **Subjective case**: *I, we, he, she, it, they.*
> **Objective case**: *me, us, him, her, it, them.*
> **Possessive case**: *my, our, his, her, its, their.*

circumlocution. A roundabout or circuitous expression, often used in a deliberate attempt to be vague or evasive: e.g., *in a family way* for *pregnant*; *at this point in time* for *now*.

clause. A group of words containing a subject and predicate. An **independent clause** can stand by itself as a complete sentence: e.g., *I bought a hamburger*. A **subordinate** (or **dependent**) **clause** cannot stand by itself but must be connected to another clause: e.g., *Since I was hungry, I bought a hamburger.*

cliché. A phrase or opinion that has lost its impact through overuse and betrays a lack of original thought: e.g., *slept like a log; gave 110 per cent.*

collective noun. A noun that is singular in form but refers to a group: e.g., *family; team; jury*. It may take either a singular or plural verb, depending on whether it refers to individual members or to the group as a whole.

comma splice. See **run-on sentence**.

complement. A completing word or phrase that usually follows a linking verb to form a **subjective complement**: e.g., (1) *He is my father*; (2) *That cigar smells terrible*. If the complement is an adjective it is sometimes called a **predicate adjective**. An **objective complement** completes the direct object rather than the subject: e.g., *We found him honest and trustworthy.*

complex sentence. A sentence containing a dependent clause as well as an independent one: e.g., *I bought the ring, although it was expensive.*

compound sentence. A sentence containing two or more independent clauses: e.g., *I saw the accident and I reported it.* A sentence is called **compound-complex**

if it contains a dependent clause as well as two independent ones: e.g., *When the fog lifted, I saw the accident and I reported it.*

conclusion. The part of an essay in which the findings are pulled together or the implications revealed so that the reader has a sense of closure or completion.

concrete language. Specific language that deals with particular details: e.g., *red corduroy dress; three long-stemmed roses.* (Compare **abstract language**.)

conjunction. An uninflected word used to link words, phrases, or clauses. A **coordinating conjunction** (e.g., *and, or, but, for, yet*) links two equal parts of a sentence. A **subordinating conjunction**, placed at the beginning of a subordinate clause, shows the logical dependence of that clause on another: e.g., (1) *Although I am poor, I am happy*; (2) *While others slept, he studied.* **Correlative conjunctions** are pairs of coordinating conjunctions (see **correlatives**).

conjunctive adverb. A type of adverb that shows the logical relation between the phrase or clause that it modifies and a preceding one: e.g., (1) *I sent the letter; it never arrived, however.* (2) *The battery died; therefore the car wouldn't start.*

connotation. The range of ideas or meanings suggested by a certain word in addition to its literal meaning. Apparent synonyms, such as *poor* and *underprivileged*, may have different connotations. (Compare **denotation**.)

context. The text surrounding a particular passage that helps to establish its meaning.

contraction. A word formed by combining and shortening two words: e.g., *isn't* from *is not; we're* from *we are.*

coordinate construction. A grammatical construction that uses correlatives.

coordinating conjunction. Each of a pair of correlatives.

copula verb. See **linking verb**.

correlatives (or **coordinates**). Pairs of coordinating conjunctions: e.g., *either/or; neither/nor; not only/but.*

dangling modifier. A modifying word or phrase (often including a participle) that is not grammatically connected to any part of the sentence: e.g., *Walking to school, the street was slippery.*

definite article. The word *the*, which precedes a noun and implies that it has already been mentioned or is common knowledge. (Compare **indefinite article**.)

demonstrative pronoun. A pronoun that points out something: e.g., (1) *This is his reason*; (2) *That looks like my lost earring*. When used to modify a noun or pronoun, a demonstrative pronoun becomes a kind of **pronominal adjective**: e.g., *this* hat, *those* people.

denotation. The literal or dictionary meaning of a word. (Compare **connotation**.)

dependent clause. See **clause**.

diction. The choice of words with regard to their tone, degree of formality, or register. Formal diction is the language of orations and serious essays. The informal diction of everyday speech or conversational writing can, at its extreme, become slang.

direct object. See **object**.

discourse. Talk, either oral or written. **Direct discourse** (or **direct speech**) gives the actual words spoken or written: e.g., *Donne said, "No man is an island."* In writing, direct discourse is put in quotation marks. **Indirect discourse** (or **indirect speech**) gives the meaning of the speech rather than the actual words. In writing, indirect discourse is not put in quotation marks: e.g., *He said that no one exists in an island of isolation.*

ellipsis marks. Three spaced periods indicating an omission from a quoted passage.

essay. A literary composition on any subject. Some essays are descriptive or narrative, but in an academic setting most are expository (explanatory) or argumentative.

euphemism. A word or phrase used to avoid some other word or phrase that might be considered offensive or too harsh: e.g., *pass away* for *die*.

expletive. 1. A word or phrase used to fill out a sentence without adding to the sense.
2. A swear word.

exploratory writing. The informal writing done to help generate ideas before formal planning begins.

fused sentence. See **run-on sentence**.

general language. Language that lacks specific details; abstract language.

gerund. A verbal (part-verb) that functions as a noun and is marked by an *-ing* ending: e.g., *Swimming can help you become fit.*

grammar. The study of the forms and relations of words, and of the rules governing their use in speech and writing.

hypothesis. A supposition or trial proposition made as a starting point for further investigation.

hypothetical instance. A supposed occurrence, often indicated by a clause beginning with *if.*

indefinite article. The word *a*, which introduces a noun and suggests that it is non-specific. (Compare **definite article.**)

independent clause. See **clause.**

indirect discourse (or **indirect speech**). See **discourse.**

indirect object. See **object.**

infinitive. A type of verbal not connected to any subject: e.g., *to ask.* The **base infinitive** omits the *to*: e.g., *ask.*

inflection. The change in the form of a word to indicate number, person, case, tense, or degree.

initialism. See **acronym.**

integrate. Combine or blend together.

intensifier (or **qualifier**). A word that modifies and adds emphasis to another word or phrase: e.g., *very* tired; *quite* happy; I *myself.*

interjection. An abrupt remark or exclamation, usually accompanied by an exclamation mark: e.g., *Oh dear! Alas!*

interrogative sentence. A sentence that asks a question: e.g., *What is the time?*

intransitive verb. A verb that does not take a direct object: e.g., *fall; sleep; talk.* (Compare **transitive verb.**)

introduction. A section at the start of an essay that tells the reader what is going to be discussed and why.

italics. Slanting type used for emphasis or to indicate the title of a book or journal.

jargon. Technical terms used unnecessarily or in inappropriate places: e.g., *peer-group interaction* for *friendship*.

linking verb (or **copula verb**). The verb *to be* used to join subject to complement: e.g., *The apples <u>were</u> ripe.*

literal meaning. The primary, or denotative, meaning of a word.

logical indicator. A word or phrase—usually a conjunction or conjunctive adverb—that shows the logical relation between sentences or clauses: e.g., *since*; *furthermore*; *therefore*.

misplaced modifier. A word or group of words that can cause confusion because it is not placed next to the element it should modify: e.g., *I <u>only</u> ate the pie.* [Revised: *I ate <u>only</u> the pie.*]

modifier. A word or group of words that describes or limits another element in the sentence.

mood. 1. As a grammatical term, the form that shows a verb's function.

> **Indicative mood:** *She is going.*
> **Imperative mood:** *Go!*
> **Interrogative mood:** *Is she going?*
> **Subjunctive mood:** *It is important that she go.*

2. When applied to literature generally, the atmosphere or tone created by the author.

non-restrictive modifier (or **non-restrictive element**). See **restrictive modifier**.

noun. An inflected part of speech marking a person, place, thing, idea, action, or feeling, and usually serving as subject, object, or complement. A **common noun** is a general term: e.g., *dog*; *paper*; *automobile*. A **proper noun** is a specific name: e.g., *Martin*; *Sudbury*; *Skidoo*.

object. 1. A noun or pronoun that completes the action of a verb is called a **direct object**: e.g., *He passed <u>the puck</u>.* An **indirect object** is the person or thing receiving the direct object: e.g., *He passed <u>the puck</u>* (direct object) *to <u>Markus</u>* (indirect object).

2. The noun or pronoun in a group of words beginning with a preposition: e.g., *at the house*; *about her*; *for me*.

objective complement. See **complement**.

objectivity. A position or stance taken without personal bias or prejudice. (Compare **subjectivity**.)

outline. With regard to an essay or report, a brief sketch of the main parts; a written plan.

paragraph. A unit of sentences arranged logically to explain or describe an idea, event, or object. The start of a paragraph is usually marked by indentation of the first line.

parallel wording. Wording in which a series of items has a similar grammatical form: e.g., *At her marriage my grandmother promised to love, to honour, and to obey her husband.*

paraphrase. Restate in different words.

parentheses. Curved lines enclosing and setting off a passage; not to be confused with square brackets.

parenthetical element. A word or phrase inserted as an explanation or afterthought into a passage that is grammatically complete without it: e.g., *My musical career, if it can be called that, consisted of playing the triangle in kindergarten.*

participle. A verbal (part-verb) that functions as an adjective. Participles can be either **present**—usually marked by an *-ing* ending—(e.g., *taking*), or **past** (e.g., *having taken*); they can also be **passive** (e.g., *being taken* or *having been taken*).

part of speech. Each of the major categories into which words are placed according to their grammatical function. Some grammarians include only function words (nouns, verbs, adjectives, and adverbs); others also include pronouns, prepositions, conjunctions, and interjections.

passive voice. See **voice**.

past participle. See **participle**.

periodic sentence. A sentence in which the normal order is inverted or in which an essential element is suspended until the very end: e.g., *Out of the house, past the grocery store, through the school yard, and down the railway tracks raced the frightened boy.*

person. In grammar, the three classes of personal pronouns referring to the person speaking (**first person**), the person spoken to (**second person**), and the person spoken about (**third person**). With verbs, only the third person singular has a distinctive inflected form.

personal pronoun. See **pronoun**.

phrase. A unit of words lacking a subject-predicate combination, typically forming part of a clause. The most common kind is the **prepositional phrase**—a unit consisting of a preposition and an object: e.g., *They are waiting at the house.*

plural. Indicating two or more in number. Nouns, pronouns, and verbs all have plural forms.

possessive case. See **case**.

prefix. An element placed in front of the root form of a word to make a new word: e.g., *pro-*; *in-*; *sub-*; *anti-*. (Compare **suffix**.)

preposition. A short word heading a unit of words containing an object, thus forming a **prepositional phrase**: e.g., *under the tree*, *before my time*.

pronoun. A word that stands in for a noun. A **personal pronoun** stands for the name of a person: *I; he; she; we; they;* etc.

punctuation. A conventional system of signs (e.g., comma, period, semicolon, etc.) used to indicate stops or divisions in a sentence and to make meaning clearer.

reference works. Sources consulted when preparing an essay or report.

referent. See **antecedent**.

reflexive verb. A verb that has the same person as both subject and object: e.g., *Isabel taught herself to skate.*

register. The degree of formality in word choice and sentence structure.

relative clause. A clause introduced by a relative pronoun: e.g., *The man who came to dinner is my uncle.*

relative pronoun. *Who, which, what, that,* or their compounds, used to introduce an adjective or noun clause: e.g., *the house that Jack built; whatever you say.*

restrictive modifier (or **restrictive element**). A phrase or clause that identifies or is essential to the meaning of a term: e.g., *The book that my aunt gave me* *is missing.* It should not be set off by commas. A **non-restrictive element** is not needed to identify the term and is usually set off by commas: e.g., *This book, which my aunt gave me, is one of my favourites.*

rhetorical question. A question posed and answered by a writer or speaker to draw attention to a point; no response is expected on the part of the audience: e.g., *How significant are these findings? In my opinion, they are extremely significant, for the following reasons . . . :*

run-on sentence. A sentence that goes on beyond the point where it should have stopped. The term covers both the **comma splice** (two sentences incorrectly joined by a comma) and the **fused sentence** (two sentences incorrectly joined without any punctuation).

sentence. A grammatical unit that includes both a subject and a predicate. The end of a sentence is marked by a period.

sentence fragment. A group of words lacking either a subject or a verb; an incomplete sentence.

simple sentence. A sentence made up of only one clause: e.g., *Joaquim climbed the tree.*

slang. Colloquial speech considered inappropriate for academic writing; it is often used in a special sense by a particular group: e.g., *stoked* for *excited*; *dis* for *show disrespect for.*

split infinitive. A construction in which a word is placed between *to* and the base verb: e.g., *to completely finish.* Many still object to this kind of construction, but splitting infinitives is sometimes necessary when the alternatives are awkward or ambiguous.

squinting modifier. A kind of misplaced modifier that could be connected to elements on either side, making meaning ambiguous: e.g., *When he wrote the letter finally his boss thanked him.*

standard English. The English currently spoken or written by literate people and widely accepted as the correct and standard form.

subject. In grammar, the noun or noun equivalent with which the verb agrees and about which the rest of the clause is predicated: e.g., *They swim every day when the pool is open.*

subjectivity. A stance that is based on personal feelings or opinions and is not impartial. (Compare **objectivity**.)

subjunctive. See **mood**.

subordinate clause. See **clause**.

subordinating conjunction. See **conjunction**.

subordination. Making one clause in a sentence dependent on another.

suffix. An element added to the end of a word to form a derivative: e.g., *prepare, preparation*; *sing, singing*. (Compare **prefix**.)

synonym. A word with the same dictionary meaning as another word: e.g., *begin* and *commence*.

syntax. Sentence construction; the grammatical arrangement of words and phrases.

tense. A set of inflected forms taken by a verb to indicate the time (i.e., past, present, future) of the action.

theme. A recurring or dominant idea.

thesis statement. A one-sentence assertion that gives the central argument of an essay.

topic sentence. The sentence in a paragraph that expresses the main or controlling idea.

transition word. A word that shows the logical relation between sentences or parts of a sentence and thus helps to signal the change from one idea to another: e.g., *therefore*; *also*; *however*.

transitive verb. A verb that takes an object: e.g., *hit*; *bring*; *cover*. (Compare **intransitive verb**.)

usage. The way in which a word or phrase is normally and correctly used; accepted practice.

verb. That part of a predicate expressing an action, state of being, or condition, which tells what a subject is or does. Verbs are inflected to show tense (time). The principal parts of a verb are the three basic forms from which all tenses are made: the base infinitive, the past tense, and the past participle.

verbal. A word that is similar in form to a verb but does not function as one: a participle, a gerund, or an infinitive.

voice. The form of a verb that shows whether the subject acted (**active voice**) or was acted upon (**passive voice**): e.g., *He stole the money* (active). *The money was stolen by him* (passive). Only transitive verbs (verbs taking objects) can be passive.

REFERENCES

Adler, Patricia A. and Peter Adler. 1999. "The ethnographers' ball revisited," *Journal of Contemporary Ethnography* v 28 no 5, 442–50.

Adorno, T.W., Else Frenkel-Brunswik, Daniel J. Levinson, and R. Nevitte Sanford. 1969. *The Authoritarian Personality*. New York: W.W. Norton.

American Sociological Association Code of Ethics. 1997. American Sociological Association. Retrieved on 5 Oct. 2000 http://www.asanet.org/members/ecoderev.

Amooti-Kaguna, B. and F. Nuwaha. 2000. "Factors influencing choice of delivery sites in Rakai district of Uganda," *Social Science and Medicine* v 50 no 2, 203–13.

Armstrong, David, Ann Gosling, and John Weinman. 1997. "The place of inter-rater reliability in qualitative research: An empirical study," *Sociology* v 31, 597–606.

Avins, Andrew L. 1990. "Can unequal be more fair? Ethics, subject allocation, and randomized clinical trials," *Journal of Medical Ethics* v 24 no 6, 401–8.

Bacon, Francis. 1620. *Novum Organum*.

Baker, Sheridan. 1981. *The Practical Stylist*, 5th Ed. New York: Harper and Row.

Bergmann, Reinhard, John Ludbrook, and Will P.J.M. Spooren. 2000. "Different outcomes of the Wilcoxon-Mann-Whitney test from different statistics packages," *The American Statistician* v 54 no 1, 72–7.

Berlin, Isaiah. 1953. *The Hedgehog and the Fox: An Essay on Tolstoy's View of History*. London: Weidenfeld & Nicolson.

Blane, D.B. 1996. "Collecting retrospective data: Development of a reliable method and a pilot study of its use," *Social Science and Medicine* v 42 no 5, 751–7.

Bluenthal, Daniel S. and Ralph J. DiClemente 2004. *Community-Based Health Research Issues and Methods*. New York: Springer Publishing Company, Inc.

Brace, Catherine. 1999. "Looking back: The Cotswolds and English national identity, c. 1890–1950," *Journal of Historical Geography* v 25 no 4, 502–16.

Brody, Janet L. and Holly B. Waldron. 2000. "Ethical issues in research on the treatment of adolescent substance abuse disorders," *Addictive Behaviors* v 25 no 2, 217–28.

Brunt, Lodewijk. 1999. "Thinking about ethnography," *Journal of Contemporary Ethnography* v 28 no 5, 500–9.

Calahan, Charles A. and Walter R. Schumm. 1995. "An exploratory analysis of family social science mail survey response rates," *Psychological Reports* v 76 pt 2, 1379–88.

Chojnacka, Helena. 2000. "Early marriage and polygyny: Feature characteristics of nuptiality in Africa," *Genus* v 56 no 3–4, 179–208.

"Citation guides for electronic documents," International Federation of Library Associations and Institutions. Retrieved on 30 Sept. 1999 http://www.ifla.org/I/training/citation/citing.htm.

Cluett, Robert, and Lee Ahlborn. 1965. *Effective English Prose*. New York: L.W. Singer.

Comte, Auguste. 1855. *The Positive Philosophy*. Harriet Martineau (trans.). 3 vols. New York: Calvin Blanchard.

Cooper, H.M. 1984. *The Integrative Research Review: A Systematic Approach*. Newbury Park, California: Sage.

Côté, Marguerite Michelle. 1992. "A painful situation still crying out for a solution: Montreal's street youth," *Revue internationale d'action communautaire* v 27 no 67, 145–52.

Couper, Mick and Linda L. Stinson. 1999. "Completion of self-administered questionnaires in a sex survey," *The Journal of Sex Research* v 36 no 4, 321–30.

Creswell, John W. 1992. *Qualitative and Quantitative Approaches*. Thousand Oaks, CA: Sage

Cunningham, John A., Donna Ansara, and T. Cameron Wild. 1999. "What is the price of perfection? The hidden costs of using detailed assessment instruments to measure alcohol consumption," *Journal of Studies on Alcohol* v 60 no 6, 756–8.

Curtis, Karen A. 1999. "'Bottom-up' poverty and welfare policy discourse: Ethnography to the rescue?" *Urban Anthropology and Studies of Cultural Systems and World Economic Development* v 28 no 2, 103–40.

Daily, Catherine M. and Janet P. Near. 2000. "CEO satisfaction and firm performance in family firms: Divergence between theory and practice," *Social Indicators Research* v 51, 125–70.

Dalton, Dan R., James C. Wimbush, and Catherine M. Daily. 1996. "Candor, privacy and 'legal immunity' in business ethics research: An empirical assessment of the randomized response technique (RRT)," *Business Ethics Quarterly* v 6, 87–99.

Denzin, Norman K. 1998. "The new ethnography: Review article," *Journal of Contemporary Ethnography* v 27 no 3, 405–15.

_____. 1999. "Interpretive ethnography for the next century," *Journal of Contemporary Ethnography* v 28 no 5, 510–19.

Dohan, Daniel and Martin Sanchez-Jankowski. 1998. "Using computers to analyze ethnographic field data: Theoretical and practical considerations: CAQDAS," *Annual Review of Sociology* v 24, 477–98.

Durkheim, Emile. 1951. *Suicide: A Study in Sociology.* John A. Spaulding and George Simpson (trans.). New York: Free Press of Glencoe.

Easton, Alyssa, James H. Price, and Susan K. Telljohann. 1997. "An informational versus monetary incentive in increasing physicians' response rates," *Psychological Reports* v 81 no 3 pt 1, 968–970.

Economist, The. 1998. "Deconsecrating Gandhi: Iconoclastic and critical works on India's history," *The Economist* v 348, 73–4

Eder, Donna and William Corsaro. 1999. "Ethnographic studies of children and youth: Theoretical and ethical issues," *Journal of Contemporary Ethnography* v 28 no 5, 520–31.

Evans, Geoffrey and Colin Mills. 1999. "Are there classes in post-communist societies? A new approach to identifying class structure," *Sociology* v 33 no 1, 23–46.

Fine, Gary Alan. 1999. "Field labor and ethnographic reality," *Journal of Contemporary Ethnography* v 28 no 5, 532–9.

Fisher, Celia B., Ann D'Alessandro-Higgins, and Jean Marie B. Rau. 1996. "Referring and reporting research participants at risk: Views from urban adolescents," *Child Development* v 67, 2086–2100.

Fontes, Lisa Aronson. 1998. "Ethics in family violence research: Cross-cultural issues," *Family Relations* v 47 no 1, 53–61.

Fraenkel, Jack R. and Norman E. Wallen. 1996. *How to Design and Evaluate Research in Education.* McGraw-Hill, Inc.

Freud, Sigmund. 1963. *Civilization and Its Discontents.* Joan Riviere (trans.). London: Hogarth Press.

Gaber, Ivor. 1996. "Hocus-pocus polling: The use of focus groups by political parties," *New Statesmen* v 125 Aug 16, 20–1.

Gans, Herbert J. 1999. "Participant observation in the era of 'ethnography'," *Journal of Contemporary Ethnography* v 28 no 5, 540–8.

Gibaldi, Joseph. 1999. *MLA Handbook for Writers of Research Papers*, 5th Ed. New York: The Modern Language Association of America.

Glaser, Barney G. 1978. *Theoretical Sensitivity: Advances in the Methodology of Grounded Theory.* California: The Sociology Press.

Gondolf, Edward and Ellen R. Fisher. 1988. *Battered Women as Survivors: An Alternative to Treating Learned Helplessness.* Lexington, Mass: Lexington Books.

Gubrium, Jaber F. and James A. Holstein. 1997. *The New Language of Qualitative Method.* New York: Oxford University Press.

_____. 1999. "At the border of narrative and ethnography," *Journal of Comparative Ethnography* v 28 no 5, 561–73.

Hammersley, Martyn. 1999. "Not bricolage but boatbuilding: Exploring two metaphors for thinking about ethnography," *Journal of Contemporary Ethnography* v 28 no 5, 574–85.

Hampton, Keith and Barry Wellman. 1999. "Netville online and offline: Observing and surveying a wired suburb," *The American Behavioral Scientist* v 43 no 3, 475–92.

Hare, Sheri, James H. Price, and Michael G. Flynn. 1998. "Increasing return rates of a mail survey to exercise professionals using a modest monetary incentive," *Perceptual and Motor Skills* v 86 no 1, 217–18.

Harshbarger, Thad R. 1971. *Introductory Statistics: A Decision Map.* New York: Macmillan.

Hays, Samuel. 1970. *An Outline of Statistics.* London: Longmans.

Heather, Rebecca Piirto. 1994. "Future focus groups," *American Demographics* v 16, 6.

Heckelman, Jac C. 1997. "Determining who voted in historical elections: An aggregated logic approach," *Social Science Research* v 26, 121–34.

Hesse-Biber, Sharlene Nagy, Patricia Leavy, and Michele L. Yaiser. 2004. "Feminist approaches to research as a process: Reconceptualizing epistemology, methodology, and method." In Hesse-Biber, Sharlene Nagy and Michelle L. Yaiser (Eds), *Feminist Perspectives on Social Research.* New York: Oxford University Press.

Karp, David A. 1999. "Social science, progress and the ethnographer's craft," *Journal of Contemporary Ethnography* v 28 no 6, 597–609.

Kasper, Anne. 1994. "A feminist, qualitative methodology: A study of women with breast cancer," *Qualitative Sociology* v 17 no 3, 263–81.

Kaye, Sanford. 1998. *Writing Under Pressure: The Quick Writing Process.* New York: Oxford University Press.

Kenyon, Gary M. 1996. "Ethical issues in ageing and biography," *Ageing and Society* v 16, 659–75.

Krause, Allison M., Linda D. Grant, and Bonita C. Long. 1999. "Sources of stress reported by daughters of nursing home residents," *Journal of Aging Studies* v 13 no 3, 349–64.

Kupek, Emil. 1999. "Estimation of the number of sexual partners for the non-respondents to a large national survey," *Archives of Sexual Behavior* v 28 no 3, 23–42.

Lal, Vinay. 1997. "Discipline and authority: Some notes on future histories and epistemologies of India," *Futures* (London, England) v 29 no 10, 985–1000.

Levy, C. Michael and Sarah Randsell. 1995. "Is writing as difficult as it seems?" *Memory and Cognition* v 23, 767–79.

Li, Peter. 1986. "Methods of sociology research," *The Social World: An introduction to sociology*. Lorne Tepperman and R. Jack Richardson (eds.). Toronto: McGraw-Hill Ryerson.

Liefooghe, R., N. Michiels, and S. Habib. 1995. "Perception and social consequences of tuberculosis: A focus group study of tuberculosis patients in Sialkot, Pakistan," *Social Science and Medicine* v 41 no 12, 1685–92.

Lipset, Seymour Martin. 1956. *Union democracy: The internal politics of the International Typographical Union [by] Seymour Martin Lipset, Martin A. Trow [and] James S. Coleman.* Glencoe, Ill.: Free Press.

McAuliffe, William E., Stephanie Geller, and Richard LaBrie. 1998. "Are telephone surveys suitable for studying substance abuse? Cost, administration, coverage and response rate issues," *Journal of Drug Issues* v 28 no 2, 455–81.

McCrady, Barbara S. and Donald A. Bux, Jr. 1999. "Ethical issues in informed consent with substance abusers," *Journal of Consulting and Clinical Psychology* v 67 no 2, 186–93.

McCullough, B.D. 1999. "Assessing the reliability of statistical software: Part I," *The American Statistician* v 52 no 4, 358–66.

————. 1999. "Assessing the reliability of statistical software: Part II," *The American Statistician* v 53 no 2, 149–59.

Mahoney, James. 1999. "Nominal, ordinal, and narrative appraisal in macro-causal analysis," *American Journal of Sociology* v 104 no 4, 1154–96.

Malthus, T.R. 1958. *An Essay on Population.* Toronto: Dent.

Mann, Susan A., Michael D. Grimes, and Alice Abel Kemp. 1997. "Paradigm shifts in family sociology? Evidence from three decades of family textbooks," *Journal of Family Issues* v 18, 315–49.

Marcus, George E. 1998. "The once and future ethnographic archive," *History of the Human Sciences* v 11 no 4, 49–63.

Marx, Karl. 1961. *Economic and Philosophical Manuscripts of 1844.* Moscow: Foreign Languages Publishing House.

Maynard, Michael L. 1996. "Effectiveness of 'begging' as a persuasive tactic for improving response rate on a client/agency mail survey," *Psychological Reports* v 78, 204–6.

Mein, Sinda and Marilyn Winkleby. 1998. "Concerns and misconceptions about cardiovascular disease risk factors: A focus group evaluation with low-income women," *Hispanic Journal of Behavioral Sciences* v 20 no 2, 192–211.

Merriam, Sharan B. 1988. *Case Study Research in Education: A qualitative Approach.* San Francisco, CA: Jossey-Bass Publishers.

Meter, Karl M. van. 1994. "Sociological methodology," *International Social Science Journal* v 46, 15–25.

Mill, John Stuart. 1859. *On Liberty.* n.p.

Milner, Stephen J. 1999. "Partial readings: Addressing a Renaissance archive," *History of the Human Sciences* v 12 no 2, 89–105.

Mintz, Sidney W. 2000. "Sows' ears and silver linings: A backward look at ethnography," *Current Anthropology* v 41 no 2, 169–77, 188–9.

Modern Language Association of America. 1998. *MLA Style Manual and Guide to Scholarly Publishing,* 2nd Ed. New York: Modern Language Association of America.

Morgan, David L. 1996. "Focus groups," *Annual Review of Sociology* v 22, 129–52.

Moshiri, Saeed. 1999. "Producing quality graphs with econometrics and statistics software," *The Economic Journal* v 109, F756–71.

Myers, G. and Phil Macnaghten. 1998. "Rhetorics of environmental sustainability: Commonplaces and places," *Environment and Planning A* v 30 no 2, 333–53.

Nelder, Mary and Susan J. Snelling. 2000. *Women Speak: Research on Women Abuse.* Canada: Ministry of Justice Canada.

Novick, Alvin. 1996. "One small ethical issue arising in ethnographic research," *AIDS and Public Policy Journal* v 11, 115–17.

Oakley, Ann. 1981. "Interviewing women: A contradiction in terms." In H. Roberts (Ed.), *Doing Feminist Research* (pp 30–61). London: Routledge & Kegan Paul.

Oden, Lorette and James H. Price. 1999. "Effects of a small monetary incentive and follow-up mailings on return rates of a survey to nurse practitioners," *Psychological Reports* v 85 no 3 pt 2, 1154–6.

Offiong, Daniel A. 1999. "Traditional healers in the Nigerian health care delivery system and the debate over integrating traditional and scientific medicine," *Anthropological Quarterly* v 72 no 3, 118–30.

Olesen, Virginia L. 2000. "Feminisms and qualitative research at and into the Millennium." In Denzin, Norman K. and Yvonna S. Lincoln (Eds), *Handbook of Qualitative Research: Second Edition*. California: Sage Publication Inc.

Oster, Robert A. 1998. "An examination of five statistical software packages for epidemiology," *The American Statistician* v 52 no 3, 267–80.

Paulos, John Allen. 1998. *Once Upon a Number: The Hidden Mathematical Logic of Stories*. New York: Perseus (Basic Books).

Pavlik, Volory N., David J. Hyman, and Carlos Vallbona. 1996. "Response rates to random digit dialing for recruiting participants to an onsite health study," *Public Health Reports* v 111, 444–50.

Pierre Trudeau. 2000. On-line biography. Canada History. Retrieved on 30 Oct. 2000 http://www.canadahistory.com/pierre.htm.

Plotnick, Robert D. and Saul D. Hoffman. 1999. "The effect of neighbourhood characteristics on young adult outcomes: Alternative estimates," *Social Science Quarterly* v 80 no 1, 1–18.

Pourjaili, Hamid and Janet Kimbrell. 1994. "Effects of four instrumental variables on survey response," *Psychological Reports* v 75, 895–8.

Pratt, E.J. 2001. "Newfoundland," *15 Canadian Poets × 3*. Gary Geddes (ed.). Toronto: Oxford.

Reichardt, Charles S. and Thomas D. Cook. 1979. "Beyond qualitative versus quantitative methods," *Qualitative and Quantitative Methods in Evaluation Research*. Charles S. Reichardt and Thomas D. Cook (eds.). Beverly Hills: Sage Publications.

Reinharz, Shulamit. 1992. *Feminist Methods in Social Research*. New York: Oxford University Press.

Rendall, Michael S., Lynda Clarke, and H. Elizabeth Peters. 1999. "Incomplete reporting of men's fertility in the United States and Britain: A research note," *Demography* v 36 no 1, 135–44.

Ristock, Janice L. and Joan Pennel. 1996. *Community Research As Empowerment: Feminist Links, Postmodern Interruptions*. Toronto: Oxford University Press

Scarce, Rik. 1994. "(No) trial (but) tribulations: When courts and ethnography conflict," *Journal of Contemporary Ethnography* v 23, 123–49.

Schuster, Elizabeth. 1996. "Ethical considerations when conducting ethnographic research in a nursing home setting," *Journal of Aging Studies* v 10, 57–67.

Shepherd, James F. 1979. *College Study Skills*. Boston: Houghton Mifflin.

————. 1981. *RSVP: The Houghton Mifflin Reading, Study, and Vocabulary Program*. Boston: Houghton Mifflin.

Smith, Tom W. 1995. "Some aspects of measuring education," *Social Science Research* v 24, 215–42.

"Statement of Ethical Practice." 1994. Canadian Sociology and Anthropology Association. Retrieved on 5 Oct. 2000 http://www.unb.ca/web/anthropology/csaa/csaa.html.

"Statement of Professional Ethics." 1999. British Sociological Association. Retrieved on 5 Oct. 2000 http://www.britsoc.org.uk.

Steinberg, Alan M., Robert S. Pynoos, and Armen K. Goenjian. 1999. "Are researchers bound by child abuse reporting laws?" *Child Abuse and Neglect* v 23 no 8, 771–7.

Stiffman, Arlene Rubin. 1989. "Physical and sexual abuse in runaway youths," *Child Abuse and Neglect* v 13 no 3, 417–26.

Stone, Emma and Mark Priestley. 1996. "Parasites, pawns and partners: Disability research and the role of non-disabled researchers," *The British Journal of Sociology* v 47, 699–716.

Stringer, Ernie. 1997. *Community-Based Ethnography: Breaking Tradtional Boundaries of Research, Teaching, and Learning.* New Jersey: Lawrence Erlbaum Associates, Inc.

Sullivan, Cris M., Maureen H. Rumptz, and Rebecca Campbell. 1996. "Retaining participants in longitudinal community research: A comprehensive protocol," *The Journal of Applied Behavioral Science* v 32, 262–76.

Summers, Jodi and James H. Price. 1997. "Increasing return rates to a mail survey among health educators," *Psychological Reports* v 81, 551–4.

Teare, John F., Karen Authier, and Roger Peterson. 1994. "Differential patterns of post-shelter placement as a function of problem type and severity," *Journal of Child and Family Studies* v 3 no 1, 7–22.

Thomas, Francis-Noel and Mark Turner. 1996. *Clear and Simple as the Truth: Writing Classic Prose.* Princeton: Princeton University Press.

Thompson, A.J. and A.V. Martinet. 1980. *A Practical English Grammar*, 3rd Ed. Oxford: Oxford University Press.

Tierney, Patrick. 1999. *Darkness in El Dorado: How Scientists and Journalists Devastated the Amazon.* Boston: Norton.

Trimble, John R. 1975. *Writing with Style: Conversations on the Art of Writing.* Englewood Cliffs, NJ: Prentice-Hall.

Trimmer, Joseph F. 1998. *Writing with a Purpose*, 12th Ed. Boston: Houghton Mifflin Co.

Trujillo, Nick. 1999. "Teaching ethnography in the twenty-first century using collaborative learning," *Journal of Contemporary Ethnography* v 28 no 6, 705–719.

Turabian, Kate. 1967. *A Manual for Writers of Term Papers, Theses, and Dissertations*, 3rd Ed. revised. Chicago: University of Chicago Press.

Unger, Rhoda K. 1999. "Comments on 'Focus Groups': Comment on S. Wilkinson," *Psychology of Women Quarterly* v 23 no 2, 245–6.

Visser, Penny S., Jon A. Krosnick, and Jesse Marquette. 1996. "Mail surveys for election forecasting? An evaluation of the Columbus dispatch poll," *The Public Opinion Quarterly* v 60 Summer, 181–227.

Waldram, James B. 1998. "Anthropology in prison: Negotiating consent and accountability with a 'captured' population," *Human Organization* v 57 no 2, 238–44.

Warriner, Keith, John Goyder, and Heidi Gjertsen. 1996. "Charities, no; lotteries, no; cash, yes: Main effects and interactions in a Canadian incentives experiment," *The Public Opinion Quarterly* v 60, 542–62.

Webb, Christine. 1984. "Feminist methodology in nursing research," *Journal of Advanced Nursing* v 9, 249–56.

Webb, Wilse B. 1998. "Writing history and accident reports: A metaphorical analysis," *Perceptual and Motor Skills* v 86 no 2, 631–41.

Weinberger, Morris, Jeffrey A. Ferguson, and Glenda Westmoreland. 1998. "Can raters consistently evaluate the content of focus groups?" *Social Science and Medicine* v 46 no 7, 929–33.

Wenger, Neil S., Stanley G. Korenman, and Richard Berk. 1999. "Reporting unethical research behavior," *Evaluation Review* v 23 no 5, 553–70.

Wiederman, Michael W., David L. Weis, and Elizabeth Rice Allegeier. 1994. "The effect of question preface on response rates to a telephone survey of sexual experience," *Archives of Sexual Behavior* v 23, 203–15.

Willmack, Diane K., Howard Schuman, and Beth Ellen Pennell. 1995. "Effects of a prepaid nonmonetary incentive on response rates and response quality in a face-to-face survey," *The Public Opinion Quarterly* v 59, 78–92.

Winkvist, Anna and Humaira Zareen Akhtar. 2000. "God should give daughters to rich families only: Attitudes toward childbearing among low-income women in Punjab, Pakistan," *Social Science and Medicine* v 51 no 1, 73–81.

Wishart, David J. 1997. "The selectivity of historical representation," *Journal of Historical Geography* v 23, 111–18.

Wrigley, E.A. 1969. *Population and History*. New York: World History Library.

INDEX

THE MAKING SENSE SERIES

Margot Northey with Joan McKibbin
MAKING SENSE
A Student's Guide to Research and Writing
Fifth Edition

Margot Northey and David B. Knight
MAKING SENSE IN GEOGRAPHY AND ENVIRONMENTAL SCIENCES
A Student's Guide to Research and Writing
Third Edition

Margot Northey and Judy Jewinski
MAKING SENSE IN ENGINEERING AND THE TECHNICAL SCIENCES
A Student's Guide to Research and Writing
Second Edition

Margot Northey and Lorne Tepperman
MAKING SENSE IN THE SOCIAL SCIENCES
A Student's Guide to Research and Writing
Third Edition

Margot Northey and Brian Timney
MAKING SENSE IN PSYCHOLOGY AND THE LIFE SCIENCES
A Student's Guide to Research and Writing
Fourth Edition